THE CATHOLIC UNIVERSITY OF AMERICA
CANON LAW STUDIES
No. 142

THE CANONICAL EPISCOPAL VISITATION OF THE DIOCESE

AN HISTORICAL SYNOPSIS AND COMMENTARY

A DISSERTATION

Submitted to the Faculty of Canon Law of the Catholic University of America in Partial Fulfillment of the Requirements for the Degree of
DOCTOR OF CANON LAW

BY

ANDREW LEONARD SLAFKOSKY, A. B., J. C. L.
Priest of the Archdiocese of Philadelphia

THE CATHOLIC UNIVERSITY OF AMERICA PRESS
WASHINGTON, D. C.
1941

Nihil obstat.
EDUARDUS G. ROELKER, S. T. D., J. C. D.,
Censor deputatus.
Washingtonii, die 30 maii, 1941.

Imprimatur.
✠ D. CARD. DOUGHERTY,
Archiepiscopus Philadelphiensis.
Philadelphia, die 3 iunii, 1941.

PRINTED IN THE UNITED STATES OF AMERICA
BY ST. ANTHONY GUILD PRESS, PATERSON, N. J.

TO

MY FATHER AND MOTHER

FOREWORD

The first part of the present study is an investigation into the history of the canonical visitation of the diocese. The method adopted is to divide the history into periods in which each pertinent element of the visitation receives particular treatment. The reason for this arrangement lies in the fact that the study is an investigation of the entire visitation and not of any individual item. Furthermore, in this way a composite picture of the visitation of the diocese is given in each separate period. However, a disadvantage of this method is a repetition of certain points. But wherever it was possible this repetition has been reduced to a minimum.

The climax in the development of the canonical visitation came in the legislation of the Council of Trent. Up to that point there was no universal law complete in every detail of the visitation. This the Council effected at a time when the utility of the visitation was recognized as a suitable means of reform. The Code practically renewed the entire Tridentine legislation.

The second part of this study is a commentary on the canons devoted to the general visitation of the diocese. The canons are 343-346 of the Code of Canon Law. The first paragraph of the first of these canons refers to the purpose of the visitation, the obligation of the bishop to perform it and the use of a substitute. The second paragraph treats of co-visitors. The third paragraph states the law requiring the metropolitan to visit the diocese, should the bishop neglect it. The second canon deals with the material object of the visitation which includes persons, places and things. This matter receives treatment in direct relation to the visit of the bishop. Obviously it is beyond the scope of this dissertation to treat all the objects completely from a liturgical as well as from a canonical standpoint. Whenever it is necessary to consider the liturgy this consideration is included. The third canon treats of the procedure in the course of the visitation and the effect of the visitor's decrees. Finally the procuration and traveling expenses receive consideration. In this section prescription is discussed in relation to procuration. Here, also, the old law is explained in an effort to throw light on what may be conceived as legitimate customs.

The author takes occasion to express his gratitude to His Eminence Dennis Cardinal Dougherty, Archbishop of Philadelphia, for the opportunity of advanced study, and all who helped in any way in the preparation of this dissertation.

TABLE OF CONTENTS

CHAPTER III

CHAPTER IV

PART II — CANONICAL COMMENTARY

CHAPTER V

CHAPTER VI

CHAPTER IX

PRELIMINARY NOTIONS

The Definition and Purpose of the Visitation

Among the duties of a bishop, enumerated in the Code of Canon Law, is the obligation of making a diocesan visitation. This visitation is called canonical because it is founded on jurisdiction and is prescribed by the Canon Law of the Church.[1] The legislator has not deemed it necessary to amplify the term "visitation." A general definition commonly given by authors, which is based more or less on the expression of the purpose of the visitation, as stated by the Council of Trent[2] and substantially repeated by the Code of Canon Law,[3] is as follows: "Visitation is the act of making an inquiry into existing excesses and defects, punishing what needs chastisement, and amending with suitable remedies what is in need of correction, preserving the observance of prevalent obligations according to the requirements of every person and place, and restoring matters to their former condition, wherever a relaxation has occurred."[4]

The Code of Canon Law states explicitly the object to which the visitation should be directed in the words: "To preserve sound and orthodox doctrine, to maintain good morals, to correct such as are evil,

1. Pejska, *Ius canonicum religiosorum* (3. ed., Friburgi Brisgoviae: Herder & Co., 1927), p. 240.

2. Conc. Trid., sess. XXIV, *de ref.*, c. 3 — Harduinus, *Acta conciliorum et epistolae decretales ac constitutiones summorum pontificum* (Parisiis, 1715), X, 155; Mansi, *Sacrorum conciliorum nova et amplissima collectio* (Paris, Arnhem, Leipzig, 1901-1927), XXXIII, 158; Hefele-Leclercq, *Histoire des conciles* (Paris, 1907-1938), X, 569. Hereafter these works will be referred to as Hardouin, Mansi, and Hefele-Leclercq.

3. C. 343, § 1.

4. Barbosa (*De officio et potestate episcopi* [Lugduni, 1656], pars III, alleg. 73, n. 1): — "Visitare enim nihil aliud est, quam excessus inquirere et inquisitos castigare, et emendare, atque observationem obligationum juxta cuiusque personae ac rei exigentiam, ubi adhuc viget, conservare et ubi deficit, in statum pristinum restituere." Cf. Bouix, *Tractatus de episcopo* (Parisiis, 1859), II, 21, n. 1; Ferraris, *Bibliotheca canonica, juridica, moralis, theologica, necnon ascetica, polemica, rubricistica, historica* (Romae, 1885-1892), v. "visitare, visitatio, visitator", n. 1; Maupied, *Juris canonici compendium* (Parisiis, 1863), I, 539; Bargilliat, *Praelectiones juris canonici* (Parisiis, 1907), I, 631 a; Taunton, *The law of the church* (London, 1906), p. 635.

to promote peace, innocence, piety, and discipline among the people as well as the clergy, and to establish other means for the good of religion, as the nature of the circumstances demands."[5]

Obligation of the Visitation

The obligation to make the visitation of the diocese is incumbent on the bishop as pastor of his flock. He must discharge it himself if he is in a position to do so.[6]

However, although the duty is primarily the bishop's, the obligation to provide for the visitation remains even though he himself cannot directly fulfill it. Therefore whenever a legitimate cause impedes him from doing so he is to delegate the vicar general or any other person to perform the visitation in his name.[7] As will be seen, this has been the practice throughout the history of the institution.

Furthermore the bishop has the right to select two clerics, even canons of a cathedral chapter, as co-visitors. According to the Code of Canon Law this right of choice respects no contrary privilege or custom.[8] The amount of time allotted for the visitation is extended to five years for the entire diocese, but a part of every year must be devoted to this work.[9]

The Material Object of the Visitation

The object of the visitation is the persons, places, and things which are within the confines of the bishop's territory,[10] and which are not exempt. Therefore since the visitation has to do with persons, places and things, it may be called personal, local and real. The personal visitation is the inquiry into the life and character of persons as well as their duties in order to see whether they perform them in the proper manner. The real visitation is an inquiry into the ad-

5. C. 343, § 1: — "Ad sanam et orthodoxam doctrinam conservandam, bonos mores tuendos, pravos corrigendos, pacem, innocentiam, pietatem, et disciplinam in populo et clero promovendam ceteraque pro ratione adiunctorum ad bonum religionis constituenda."

6. C. 343, § 1.

7. C. 343, § 1.

8. C. 343, § 2.

9. C. 343, § 1.

10. C. 344.

ministration, care and state of things, that is, of church appointments, church property, legacies and pious causes, while the local visitation is an inspection of churches, oratories, cemeteries, religious houses, and other pious places.

Manner of Proceeding

The Code of Canon Law also lays down the mode of procedure to be adopted by the bishop while he investigates the material or moral condition of the object of the visitation. There are two general procedures available, the paternal and the judicial. With respect to those things which concern the object and purpose of the visitation, the Code enjoins the bishop to proceed in a paternal manner. The law admits only recourse *in devolutivo* from the decrees or regulations the bishop may pass in the course of the visitation. In other matters the bishop is to act in accord with the prescriptions of the law.[11]

Procuration

While making the visitation, the bishop is advised not to prolong it unduly, and not to cause superfluous expenses or to become a burden to anyone. The law allows for the expenses of the journey and the procuration according to the prevalent local custom. Procuration is the contribution in food and lodging which the parish or place visited must provide for the visitor and his retinue. However, neither the bishop nor his companions are permitted to ask for or accept any gift or donation.[12]

11. C. 345.
12. C. 346.

PART I

HISTORICAL SYNOPSIS

CHAPTER I

THE EARLY PERIOD

Article 1. The Chorepiscopi and Periodeutai

Originally the Christian religion was preached in the cities. There churches were established and bishops set over them. The bishop then was naturally the pastor. He was assisted in his work by priests and clerics.

In the Orient toward the latter part of the 3rd century[1] as conversions extended into the country and villages at a distance from the mother church, rural bishops or chorepiscopi were constituted. According to the more common opinion these bishops originally enjoyed their jurisdiction independently of the city bishops.[2] In due time, however, they became subordinated to the city bishops and as a consequence acted in the capacity of vicars.[3]

Their main duty was to preside over the country laity and clergy. Hence, St. Basil (330-379) required his chorepiscopi to inquire into the manner of living of the clergy and to make a report of their find-

1. The Synodal letter of the Council of Antioch (269) directed against Paul of Samosota is the oldest document to mention "land bishops". Eusebius, *Historia ecclesiastica,* VII, 30 — Migne, *Patrologiae cursus completus — Series graeca* (Parisiis, 1857-1866), XX, 709; Kirch, *Enchiridion fontium historiae ecclesiae antiquae* (11. ed., Friburgi Brisgoviae, 1937), n. 325.

2. Gillmann, *Das institut der chorbischöfe im orient* (München, 1903), p. 122.

3. Maroto, *Institutiones iuris canonici* (2 vols., Madrid, Editorial del Corazón de Maria, 1919), II, 87. In the West the persecutions retarded the territorial expansion of the Church. Thus chorepiscopi are not mentioned till the end of the 4th century. In contrast to the chorepiscopi of the East, they were not subject to the city bishops. Nevertheless, the chorepiscopi failed to become firmly established in the West till the 8th century when they assumed the character of coadjutors. Cf. Maroto, *op. cit.,* p. 89.

ings.[4] Sozomen (†443) relates that a certain Prapidius performed the episcopal function in several villages.[5]

A blow was struck at the chorepiscopi at the Council of Laodicea (343-381),[6] for it ordained that bishops were not to be set up in villages or country districts. Their place was to be taken by the periodeutai, περιοδευταί, itinerant or visiting priests.[7] Thus priests instead of rural bishops were to act as visitors of the country churches and clergy. Theodoret (393-453) spoke of a certain Bassus who presided over the country priests and who visited many villages.[8] The periodeutai and chorepiscopi exist to this day among the Maronites.[9] From what has been said it is evident that the chorepiscopi and periodeutai performed the visitation in the name of the bishop. However, one cannot conclude that the bishop as a consequence did not perform this duty. Evidence is available to the contrary in the writings of the Fathers.

Article 2. The Practice of the Fathers

St. Gregory of Nyssa (331-395) in his life of St. Gregory Thaumaturgus (213-270) related how his namesake surveyed his territory when peace had been restored after the Decian persecution. In his last days, sensing his death to be nigh, he satisfied his desire of knowing how many were still in error by making a final visitation of his district.[10] When St. Athanasius (295-373) was accused of excesses during the course of his visits, he offered as his defense the testimony

4. Epistola LIV, *St. Basilii epist. II ad chorep.* "...ac vobis scribo, ut mittatis mihi catalogum ministrorum cujusque pagi et a quoquisque introductus sit et quae ejus sit vivendi ratio...." — *MPG*, XXXII, 399.

5. *Historia ecclesiastica*, lib. VII, cap. XIX — *MPG*, LXVII, 1475.

6. C. 57 — Hardouin, I, 791; Mansi, II, 582; Hefele-Leclercq, I, 1024.

7. Reference is made to both chorepiscopi and periodeutai in the Code of Justinian, but not in regard to the visitation. Cf. C. (1. 3) 38, 2; (1. 3) 41, 19, 23.

8. *Religio historica seu ascetica vivendi ratio*, cap. XXVI — *MPG*, LXXXII, 1470.

9. Cf. the Syrian Council (1736) held at Mount Libanus, pars III, cap. III, 3, II et III — *Collectio Lacensis, Acta et decreta sacrorum conciliorum recentiorum* (Friburgi Brisgoviae, 1870-1890), II, 283. (Hereafter cited as *Coll. Lac.*)

10. *De vita S. Gregorii Thaumaturgi* — *MPG*, XLVI, 954.

of his companions. The latter stated they were always with him when he made his visitation of the Mareotis and that he never went about alone.[11]

Socrates (†400) wrote that when St. Basil was made bishop of Caesarea in Cappadocia he hastened there and diligently instructed the people and confirmed the faith of those whose minds were wavering. This he did because he feared the Arians would also overrun the province of Pontus. He noted also that when St. Gregory Nazianzen (328-390) was constituted bishop of Nazianzen, a small city of Cappadocia over which his father had presided, he followed the example of St. Basil, for he went through the various cities and strengthened the weak in faith.[12]

In one of his homilies St. John Chrysostom (344-407) exhorted bishops to take care of their health. For he asks: "Upon what mission could an infirm bishop go, what visitation could he undertake?"[13] St. Jerome (342-420) claimed it was the custom for bishops to visit the villages and remote places to confer the Sacrament of Confirmation.[14] Sulpicius Severus (363-425) testified it was the ancient custom for bishops to visit their churches.[15] He likewise stated he accompanied St. Martin of Tours (317-397) when he visited the different parishes of his diocese.[16]

St. Augustine (354-430) in one of his epistles spoke of the necessity of visiting the churches committed to his care.[17] In another he stated that, realizing he could not give the necessary attention to a certain part of his diocese, he arranged for a bishop to be consecrated

11. *Apologia contra Arianos*, § 74 — *MPG*, XXV, 381; *Nicene and Post-Nicene Fathers*, Second Series (New York, 1904-1905), IV, 139.

12. *Historia ecclesiastica*, lib. IV, cap. 26, *De Basilio Caesarensi et Gregorio Nazianzeno* — *MPG*, LXVII, 531; *Nicene and Post-Nicene Fathers*, Second Series, II, 111.

13. *Opera omnia Joannis Chrysostomi* (Migne: Parisiis, 1838), *In ep. ad Titum*, homil. I, cap. 1, t. XI, 797 — *MPG*, LXII, 670.

14. *Dialogus contra luciferanos*, cap. 9 — Migne, *Patrologiae cursus completus — Series latina* (Parisiis, 1844-1855), XXIII, 164 (hereafter referred to as *MPL*).

15. *Ep. I ad Eusebium* — *MPL*, XX, 79.

16. *Dialogus* II, cap. 3 — *MPL*, XX, 203.

17. *Ep. LVI* — *MPL*, XXXIII, 223.

and appointed there.[18] Possidius in his life of St. Augustine alludes to the fact that St. Augustine made frequent visits among his people.[19] Theodoret (393-453) disclosed the work he accomplished among the heretics within his diocese and the trials he sustained in bringing them back to the fold. Moreover, he claimed he had done pastoral work in eight hundred churches.[20]

A thorough perusal of the acts of the councils of this period for a distinct trace of legislation on the episcopal visitation was of no avail. There is no evidence of a written law till the sixth century, when the visitation is acknowledged as a custom of long standing. On the other hand, the Council of Turin (397) made mention of the right and duty of the metropolitans of Arles and Vienne to visit the bishoprics of their provinces.[21] The Council of Hippo (393) also ordered the bishop of Carthage who was exarch or the patriarch of the African provinces[22] to visit all the provinces before the celebration of the plenary council.[23]

18. *Ep. CCIX — MPL,* XXXIII, 953.

19. *Cap. XIII — MPL,* XXXII, 43.

20. *Ep. CXIII — MPG,* LXXXIII, 1315. Cf. also *Ep. CXVI — MPG,* LXXXIII, 1323.

21. ". . . decretum est, ut si placet memoratarum urbium episcopis unaquaeque de his viciniores sibi intra provinciam vindicet civitates, atque eas ecclesias visitet quas oppidis suis vicinas magis esse constiterit." — c. 2, Bruns, *Canones apostolorum et conciliorum* (Berolini, 1839), II, 114. (Further references to this work will be made as Bruns.)

22. Thomassin, *Ancienne et nouvelle discipline de l'église* (Paris, 1725), part II, liv. 3, chap. 78, n. 2.

23. C. 52, De visitandis provinciis, *Canones ecclesiae africanae,* Bruns, I, 167; Mansi, III, 742; Hardouin, I, 887.

CHAPTER II

THE SIXTH CENTURY TO THE ELEVENTH CENTURY

ARTICLE 1. PURPOSE OF THE VISITATION

The establishment of this canonical institution, as of all other ecclesiastical institutions, owes its origin to the unique and specific organization of the Church. The diffusion and spread of the Gospel required the erection of churches throughout the countryside. Then the nature of the hierarchical order placed these same churches under the protection, care, and immediate supervision of the bishop. As a consequence, the bishop found himself unable to offer his priestly ministrations to his entire flock. On that account, first chorepiscopi and then priests were stationed in these rural parishes or districts charged with the care of souls. As they were placed there by the bishop, and received their jurisdiction from him, they were also subject to him, as the head of the diocese. However, owing to the weakness of human nature, situations inevitably arose which warranted authoritative inquiry and action. Not being under the observance of the watchful eye of their superior, the priests and people as well engaged at times in unlawful practices, and failed to comply with the full requirements of the Church. Hence the bishop made periodical visits to these churches to see whether everything was in due order.

Upon an examination of the acts of councils and synods, one finds that the first written law enjoining the bishop to make the diocesan visitation is the eighth canon passed by the Council of Tarragona, held in the year 516.[1]

1. Hardouin, II, 1042; Mansi, VIII, 542, 543; Hefele-Leclercq, II, 1028; Bruns, II, 17. Cf. also, Wernz-Vidal, *Ius canonicum,* II (2. ed., Romae: apud Aedes Universitatis Gregorianae, 1928), n. 608; Thomassin, *Ancienne et nouvelle discipline de l'église,* p. II, lib. x, cap. 78, n. 14; Bingham, *Antiquities of the Christian Church* (London, 1865), vol. I, bk. IX, cap. 6, sec. 22; Van Espen, *Ius ecclesiasticum universum* (Louvanii, 1753), I, pars I, tit. XVII, c. 1, n. 2; De Rosa, *De vera residentia episcoporum* (Neapoli, 1679), cap. IV, sec. 6, p. 223, n. 18; Kraus, *Realencyklopädie der christlichen alterhümer* (Freiburg, 1882-1886), v. "Visitationen"; Rampf, "Die bischöflichen visitationen — *Archiv für katholisches Kirchenrecht,* XXXI (1874), 386; Catalanus, *Pontificale romanum* (Parisiis, 1852), t. III, tit. *Ordo ad visitandas parochias,*

a) *Inquiry into the State of Repair of Churches and their Financial Condition*

With the initial appearance of a law on the diocesan visitation, various express purposes evoking it have been adduced usually in the law itself. Without a doubt where but a material investigation was called for the moral inquest was at least implied. Particular stress may have been placed on some point that needed immediate attention. This becomes patent from the words of the earliest legislation on visitation which expressly acknowledged the fact that experience had taught the Fathers of the council of the neglect of the churches throughout the dioceses. Hence to remedy this condition the council ordered the bishop to make an annual visit throughout the diocese to see whether any church was in need of repair.[2] The IV Council of Toledo (633) also asserted this purpose and added the examination of the financial condition of the churches.[3] It is worthy of note that during the remainder of this period no other council enjoined this specific objective upon the bishop or his delegate.

b) *Teaching and Preaching of the Gospel*

Among the bishop's obligations, teaching and preaching the Word of God hold an important place. The bishops in obedience to the command of Christ were active in this regard long before any human ecclesiastical law was enacted to urge them on in this duty. Their zeal was manifested in the number of conversions and the diffusion of the faith throughout the world. Once parishes were formed as units of the diocese, what better opportunity offered itself to the bishop to preach and teach than on the occasion of the visitation? The II Council of Braga in Portugal (572) set forth the obligation of the bishop

n. 1; Ayrinhac, *Constitution of the Church in the new code of canon law* (New York: Longmans, Green and Co., 1930), p. 173; Cappello, *De visitatione ss. liminum et dioeceseon* (Romae, 1912), I, 60.

2. Council of Tarragona (516), c. 8 — Hardouin, II, 1042; Mansi, VIII, 542, 543; Hefele-Leclercq, II, 1028; Bruns, II, 17; Bingham, *Antiquities of the Christian Church*, I, bk. IX, chap. 6, sec. 22, p. 378.

3. C. 36 — Hardouin, III, 587; Mansi, X, 629; Hefele-Leclercq, III, 272; Bruns, I, 233.

as to the proper instruction of his priests with regard to the celebration of Mass, the administration of Baptism and the instruction of the laity.[4]

The Council of Clovesho or Clyff in England (747) directed the bishop to assemble the laity of both sexes in every station of life and teach them plainly the Word of God, especially those who rarely heard it.[5] This canon is based directly on a canon contained in a letter of St. Boniface to Cuthbert, archbishop of Canterbury, written prior to the convocation of the council, which among other things admonished the bishops to instruct the people.[6] This injunction was renewed by the Council of Cealchythe (Chelsea or Chelsey) (787) under the presidency of George, cardinal archbishop of Ostia, and legate of Pope Hadrian, with the exhortation that the bishops fear no one while preaching the Word of God, even though it be offensive to the secular power.[7] Under Charlemagne, and later under Charles the Bald, the law found its way into the Capitularies.[8]

Moreover the VI Council of Paris (829), while discussing the bishop's income during the visitation, prefaced the law itself with a short discourse on the evil of preaching and performing divine services for temporal gain.[9] Whereas the Council of Tribur (895) in treating of the conflict of rights between the bishop and count (*graf*) at the time of the visitation, quoted from an epistle of St. Clement wherein he

4. C. 1 — Hardouin, III, 386; Mansi, IX, 838, 839; Hefele-Leclercq, III, 194; Bruns, II, 39.

5. Cap. 3 — Haddan and Stubbs, *Councils and ecclesiastical documents relating to Great Britain and Ireland* (Oxford, 1869-1873), III, 363; Wilkins, *Concilia Magnae Britanniae et Hiberniae* (Londini, 1737), I, 93; Hardouin, III, 1953; Mansi, XII, 396; Hefele-Leclercq, III, 906. Cf. Cutts, *Parish priests and their people in the Middle Ages in England* (London, 1898), 60; Hunt, *A history of the English Church* (London, 1901), I, 157.

6. Hardouin, III, 1947; Mansi, XII, 388.

7. Cap. 3 — Haddan and Stubbs, III, 449; Wilkins, I, 146; Hardouin, III, 2073; Mansi, XII, 940; Hefele-Leclercq, III, 396; Hunt, *A history of the English Church*, I, 238.

8. *Capitulare Caroli Magni* (813), c. 16 — Hardouin, IV, 1044; *Capitulare Generale* (769-771), c. 8 — *MPL*, XCVII, 123; *Monumenta Germaniae Historica* (*MGH*), *Leges*, 5 vols., I-IV, ed. Pertz: V, ed. Pertz-Waitz-Brunner, Hanoverae, 1835-1889, I, 33; *Capitulare Tolosanum* (844), cap. 4 — Hardouin, IV, 1458; Mansi, XVIII B, Baluzius II, 23; *MGH, Leges*, I, 379.

9. Lib. I, c. 31 — Hardouin, IV, 1317; Mansi, XIV, 559.

mentioned the duty of instructing the people.[10] Lastly Odo of Canterbury (943) in his constitutions called upon the bishops to preach the Word of God fearlessly lest anyone because of the carelessness of the pastor go astray in his ignorance.[11]

c) *Investigation into the Life of the Laity: to Combat Pagan Practices and Correct Abuses*

Naturally the direct aim of preaching and teaching was to preserve orthodoxy, eradicate pagan practices, and correct abuses. Consequently these aims were purposes of the visitation which were to be effected through preaching and teaching. The II Council of Braga (572) advised the bishop to instruct the people to flee the worship of idols and crimes, such as homicide, adultery, perjury, and false testimony.[12] The I National German Council (742) decreed that the bishop was to see that the people did not indulge in any pagan practice. To effect this he was to avail himself of the helpful services of a count (*graf*), who was considered to be the defender of his church.[13] Thus the Church used the strong arm of the state to stamp out any remnants of pagan belief and pagan practices or rites. This is an indication of the increased dependence of the Church upon the State during this period of history.

Prior to the Council of Clovesho (747), St. Boniface wrote a letter to Cuthbert, archbishop of Canterbury. In it he included the decrees passed by a synod over which he presided. Here are found enumerated some of the pagan practices which the bishop is to prohibit at the time

10. C. 9 — Hardouin, VI, 441.
11. Cap. 3 — Hardouin, VI, 590; Mansi, XVIII A, 396; Wilkins, I, 213.
12. C. 1 — Hardouin, III, 386; Mansi, IX, 838, 839; Hefele-Leclercq, III, 194; Bruns, II, 39.
13. C. 5 — Hardouin, III, 1920; Mansi, XII, 367; Hefele-Leclercq, III, 823; *MGH, Leges*, I, 17. During the Frankish epoch the count (*graf*) was the representative of the king in his district. His authority was extensive, for he was the instrument of royal government in judicial, fiscal, military and administrative matters. Thus he had supreme power in the administration of justice in his territory. In ecclesiastical affairs the count was to help the bishop. Moreover he was to be obedient to the latter.

of the visitation. They are divination, fortune-telling, augury, auspice, and incantations.[14] Cuthbert in turn included the same legislation in the canons of the Council of Clovesho (747).[15] Another English Council, that of Chelsea (787), practically renewed the same law.[16]

Whereas the English Councils were intent on eradicating pagan belief and pagan practices, in the Frankish Kingdom the emphasis was against, and the concern was about, other lapses in the moral law. The Capitulary of Charlemagne for the year 801 commanded the bishop on the occasion of the visitation to make a diligent inquiry as to the existence of incest, patricide, fratricide, adultery, *cenodoxia,* and other evils,[17] while the Capitulary of Toulouse, composed under Charles the Bald in 844, advised the bishops to make an inquiry into the things concerning which the people have erred, and then to correct them.[18]

d) *Care of the Poor*

The Council of Arles (813), which was convoked by Charlemagne, proposed an unusual purpose for the visitation. After indicating that the bishops are to make the visit once a year, it brings to their attention the fact that the care of the people, and especially of the poor, is their concern. On that account they are to defend them against unscrupulous judges, rulers, and officials. They are to admonish these

14. Hardouin, III, 1947; Mansi, XII, 388.

15. Cap. 3 — Hardouin, III, 1953; Mansi, XII, 396; Hefele-Leclercq, III, 906; Haddan and Stubbs, III, 363; Wilkins, I, 93.

16. Cap. 3 — Hardouin, III, 2073; Mansi, XII, 940; Hefele-Leclercq, III, 996; Haddan and Stubbs, III, 449; Wilkins, I, 146.

17. *Capitula Ecclesiastica* (801), cap. 32, "Ut episcopi . . . inquirendi studium habeant de incestu, de parricidiis, fratricidiis, adulteriis, Cendoxiis, et aliis malis quae contraria sunt Deo . . ." — Hardouin, IV, 956; Mansi, XIII, 1068; *Capitulare. Aquisgranense* (Aix-la-Chapelle — 813), cap. 1 — *MPL,* XCVII, 359. Du Cange is of the opinion that the word *cenodoxiis* in the text refers to any other delict or crime, "Cenodoxiae vocem pro quovis delicto videtur usurpare Capitulare 2 Caroli Magni (813), cap. 1" — Du Cange, *Glossarium ad scriptores mediae et infimae latinitatis* (Parisiis, 1733), ad verbum *"cenodoxiae".*

18. Cap. 4 — Hardouin, IV, 1458; Mansi, XVII B, Baluzius II, 23; *MGH, Leges,* I, 379.

men in a manner befitting their sacerdotal dignity. But if the warnings are of no avail, they should be denounced to the king.[19]

e) *Inquiry into the Life of the Clergy*

However, not only were the laity subject to an inquiry, to advice, and to correction, but also the clergy. In fact, an investigation into their mode of life is of vital importance to the well-being of the Church. For if the immediate pastors fail in their trust, the bishops cannot expect the faith to flourish within the diocese. Without their edification, through exemplary Christian living and faithfulness as well as exactness in the fulfillment of their duties, the people cannot be expected to lead holy lives. Hence the II Council of Braga (572) in Portugal charged the bishops to investigate the life of the clerics and to inquire into the manner in which the clergy administered the sacraments, especially Baptism, how they celebrated Mass, and how they performed all other church functions.[20]

The IV Council of Toledo (633) followed the example of the Council of Braga, and ordered an inquiry into the life of the sacred ministers.[21] The I National German Council (742) deemed it opportune to remind the bishops to take occasion during the course of the visitation to be witness to the chastity, upright life, faith, and knowledge or learning of the priests within their dioceses.[22] Because of the prevalence of illiteracy among the clergy, Charlemagne in his Capitulary of Aix-la-Chapelle (789) bid the bishops to examine the priests at the time of the visitation as to their faith, the administration of Baptism, the celebration of Mass, their knowledge and understanding of

19. Hardouin, IV, 1005; Mansi, XIV, 61; Hefele-Leclercq, III, 1136. This situation was the result of the lack of public assistance. The Church in the person of the bishop shouldered the burden of feeding, clothing and sheltering the poor. The *mensa episcopalis* was used to provide for the destitute and the sick. Hence the bishop offered protection to the weak and the orphans, as he was their guardian.

20. C. 1—Hardouin, III, 386; Mansi, IX, 838; Hefele-Leclercq, III, 194; Bruns, II, 39.

21. C. 36—Bruns, I, 233; Hardouin, III, 587; Mansi, X, 629; Hefele-Leclercq, III, 272.

22. C. 3—Hardouin, III, 1920; Mansi, XII, 366; Hefele-Leclercq, III, 822.

the prayers at Mass, especially the Lord's Prayer, and their ability to chant the Psalms in the proper manner.[23]

Undoubtedly intended as an aid for the discharge of the visitation, the first part of the third canon of the I National German Council required the priests of the diocese to render an account of their ministry, with regard to Baptism, their faith, the prayers and the ordinary of the Mass. It was to be presented personally to the bishop during the Lenten season.[24] Two years later the Council of Soissons (744) enacted similar legislation, with the exception that it specified Holy Thursday as the day when the report was to be given to the bishop.[25] Today this practice has its counterpart in the annual statement or general report on the *status animarum* made by the pastors of parishes.[26]

f) *Confirmation*

Another purpose for the visitation at times took on the aspect of being the principal or main purpose of the visitation. It was the administration of the Sacrament of Confirmation. At present, as under the Tridentine law, it does not form a necessary part of the visitation, although as a practical matter for the convenience of the bishop Confirmation and the visitation are associated with each other. It was the I National German Council (742) which was the first to specify Confirmation as a purpose for the visitation. By its use of the words *jure canonico,* it seems to indicate that it was the law at that time, and that the principal purpose of the visitation was the conferring of the sacrament.[27]

Most likely it was generally understood that the administration of this sacrament was to take place on the occasion of the visitation, and on that account mention of it as of something that was obligatory failed to find its way into the acts of the early councils. For already St. Jerome

23. Cap. 69 — *MGH, Leges,* I, 64.

24. Hardouin, III, 1920; Mansi, XII, 366; Hefele-Leclercq, III, 822.

25. C. 4 — Hardouin, III, 1933; Hefele-Leclercq, III, 857.

26. Cf. e. g., *Statuta Synodi Philadelphiensis* (*1934*), n. 85; *Statuta Synodi Trentoniensis* (*1931*), n. 90.

27. C. 3: "... Et quandocumque *jure canonico* episcopus circumierit parochiam ad confirmandos populos, presbyter semper paratus sit ad suscipiendum episcopum, cum collectione et adjutorio populi qui ibi confirmari debet ..." — Hardouin, III, 1920; Mansi, XII, 366; Hefele-Leclercq, III, 822.

(†419 or 420) tells us that it was the custom of the Church that the bishop would visit the country districts to confirm those who had been baptized by the priests.[28] From St. Jerome's testimony it is not clear whether it was just a partial or the principal purpose of the visitation, or, on the other hand, whether the administration of Confirmation was the occasion for another visit to the rural parishes. However, the view taken by Thomassin, namely, that this canon of the German Council implies that the visitation was primarily instituted for the administration of the Sacrament of Confirmation certainly cannot be established by the intrinsic content of the text of the canon. For, although the law required the bishop to visit his diocese to confirm the people, this in itself does not establish the purpose for which the diocesan visitation was instituted.[29]

Bingham is of the same opinion, for he claims that the visitation of the diocese was instituted to prevent baptized persons from dying without the Sacrament of Confirmation. He cites the words of St. Jerome, and adds that, to prevent such occurrences, the obligation was made an annual one. Furthermore, he adduces the partition of the larger dioceses, as ordered by the Council of Lugo (569), as a plan which was conceived to enable bishops to make their visitations of the various churches within a year's time.[30]

The Council of Soissons (744), held two years after the National German Council,[31] St. Boniface's letter written to Cuthbert before the English Council of Clovesho (747),[32] the Council of Cealchythe (Chelsea) (787),[33] the Capitulary of Toulouse (844)[34] and the Coun-

28. *Dialogus contra luciferianos* (382), cap. 9—*MPL,* XXIII, 164; Rouet de Journel, *Enchiridion patristicum,* n. 102.

29. "Ce Canon fait voir manifestement le but et les principales utilitez de la visite, en nous insinuant qu'elle a été principalement institutée pour donner la Confirmation au habitans des Paroisses champêtres."—*Ancienne et nouvelle discipline de l'église,* part II, liv. 3, chap. 78, n. 1.

30. Bingham, *Antiquities of the Christian Church,* vol. I, bk. XII, chap. 1, sec. 1, p. 543.

31. C. 4—Hardouin, III, 1933; Hefele-Leclercq, III, 857.

32. Hardouin, III, 1947; Mansi, XII, 388.

33. Cap. 3—Hardouin, III, 2073; Mansi, XII, 940; Hefele-Leclercq, III, 996; Haddan and Stubbs, III, 449; Wilkins, I, 146.

34. Cap. 4—Hardouin, IV, 1458; *MGH, Leges,* I, 379.

cil of Pavia (855)[35] all include the administration of the Sacrament of Confirmation in the purpose of the visitation.

Article 2. The Obligation of the Bishop

It has been indicated above that the first written law on the diocesan visitation was enacted by the Council of Tarragona (516). Here the visitation was acknowledged as a custom of long standing. Hence, what had been a general rule and custom now became a canonical institution; for with the erection of rural parishes it became necessary for the bishop to visit them, to see that everything was in proper ecclesiastical working order. Evidently it was also the practice in some places to visit ordinarily once a year, as the canon in question lays this injunction on the bishop.[36]

The bishops were commanded to make this visitation because it was found by experience that many churches were neglected throughout the dioceses.[37] Furthermore, if a diocese was so large that a bishop could not fulfill this law, that reason alone was deemed sufficient for dividing the diocese. This is evident from the words addressed to the Fathers of the Council of Lugo (569), by Theodomir, King of the Suevi, who convoked it, and by the action of the bishops, who selected other sees for which bishops were to be consecrated.[38]

Within the next four centuries, the provincial and national councils continually brought the duty of the diocesan visitation to the attention of the bishops. During the seventh century in the year 633, the IV

35. Mansi, XV, 19.

36. Cf. Bingham, *Antiquities of the Christian Church,* vol. I, bk. IX, cap. 6, sec. 22, p. 398.

37. Cf. Van Espen, *Ius ecclesiasticum universum,* I, pars I, tit. XVII, cap. 1, n. 2; Bingham, *Antiquities of the Christian Church,* vol. I, bk. IX, cap. 6, sec. 22, p. 398.

38. Hardouin, III, 373; Mansi, IX, 815; Hefele-Leclercq, III, p. 193; Van Espen, *Ius ecclesias. univ.,* I, pars I, tit. XVII, c. 1, n. 2; Bingham, *Antiquities of the Christian Church,* vol. I, bk. IX, chap. 6, sec. 16, p. 392 and sec. 22, p. 398. The editor of *España Sagrada,* Florez, in the fourth volume of this work denied the existence of this council, and the one who continued the work, Augustine Manuel Risco, in the fortieth volume supports his predecessor's position. "Disertacion sobre los documentos de la Santa Iglesia de Lugo que se dicen Concilios Lucenses celebrados en el Regnado de los Suevos", *España Sagrada,* XL, 229-289.

Council of Toledo in Spain passed a law obliging the bishop to make the diocesan visitation annually.[39] In the eighth century there was the II Council of Clovesho, England, held under Cuthbert, archbishop of Canterbury, in the year 747.[40] Then in the last year of the reign of Charlemagne (813), the VI Council of Arles, held at his instance, insisted on the same point.[41] Finally in the tenth century, Odo, the archbishop of Canterbury, in his constitutions of the year 943 reminded the bishops of this annual duty.[42]

The failure on the part of all the councils of this period except the IV Council of Toledo (633) to state any reason why the bishops

39. C. 36 — Hardouin, III, 587; Mansi, X, 629; Hefele-Leclercq, III, 272; Bruns, I, 233; Thomassin, *Ancienne et nouvelle discipline de l'église,* p. II, liv. III, chap. 78, n. 17; Catalanus, *Pontificale romanum,* t. III, tit. XXI, *Ordo ad visitandas parochias,* § 4, n. 2, p. 317.

40. C. 3 — Haddan and Stubbs, III, 363; Wilkins, I, 91; Hardouin, III, 1947; Mansi, XII, 388; Hefele-Leclercq, III, 905. Cf. also Hunt, *A history of the English Church,* I, 231; Flanagan, *History of the Church in England,* I, 157; Cutts, *Parish priests and their people in the Middle Ages in England,* pp. 60-61.

41. C. 17 — Hardouin, IV, 1005; Mansi, XIV, 61; Hefele-Leclercq, III, 1136; Thomassin, *Ancienne et nouvelle discipline de l'église,* part II, liv. 2, chap. 79, nn. 4 and 5.

42. Cap. 3 — Wilkins, I, 213; Hardouin, VI, 590; for other references to the visitation of the diocese confer the II Council of Braga (572), cc. 1, 2 — Hardouin, III, 386; Mansi, IX, 838; Hefele-Leclercq, III, 194; the VII Council of Toledo (646), c. 4 — Hardouin, III, 622; Mansi, X, 768, 769; Hefele-Leclercq, III, 286, 287; the Council of Chalons on the Saône (650), c. 11 — Hardouin, III, 948; Mansi, X, 1191; Hefele-Leclercq, III, 283; the Council of Rouen (650), c. 16 — Hardouin, VI, 208; Mansi, X, 1203; the I National German Council (742), c. 3 — Hardouin, III, 1920; Mansi, XII, 366, 367; Hefele-Leclercq, III, 822, 823; the Council of Soissons (744), c. 4 — Hardouin, III, 1933; Hefele-Leclercq, III, 857; the Council of Chelsea (Chelsey), England (787) — Hardouin, III, 2073; Mansi, XII, 740; Hefele-Leclercq, III, 396. The Capitularies of Charlemagne — *Capitulare Generale* (769-771), capp. 7 and 8 — *MGH, Leges,* I, 33; *Capitulare Aquisgranense* (Ecclesiasticum) (789), cap. 69 — *MGH, Leges,* I, 64; *Capitulare Aquisgranense* (813), c. 1 — *MGH, Leges,* I, 188; the VI Council of Paris (829), lib. 1, c. 31 — Hardouin, IV, 1317; Mansi, XIV, 559; *Capitulare Tolosanum* (844), capp. 2, 4, 5, 6 — Hardouin, IV, 1457-1459; the Council of Meaux (845), c. 29 — Hardouin, IV, 1488; Mansi, XIV, 1488; Mansi, XIV, 826; the Council of Valence (855), c. 17 — Hardouin, V, 94; Mansi, XV, 11; the Council of Tribur (895), c. 9 — Hardouin, VI, 441.

would be excused from this work is an indication and proof of the view of the councils as regards the true personal nature of the diocesan visitation. It is first and foremost the bishop's duty, and even the IV Council of Toledo, which allowed for sickness and the presence of other work as valid excuses exempting from personal performance, imposed the obligation on the bishop.

However, this concession was abused. Consequently, the frequent or exclusive use of substitutes, such as the archdeacon, caused the Council of Meaux (845) to style the failure of certain bishops to make the visitation personally a reprehensible, condemnable custom, not in accord with the evangelical, apostolical and ecclesiastical order.[43]

The above-mentioned Council of Toledo (633) was the first to legislate for the case in which the bishop was not in a position to make the visitation. It acknowledged besides sickness, as stated above, the urgency of other duties which prevented the visit. In such a case the bishop was to select priests or deacons of an upright character and delegate them to act in his name.[44]

From this time on the archdeacon became practically the exclusive substitute for the bishop.[45] St. Isidore of Seville (†636) in one of his letters declared that the archdeacon performed the visitation *cum jussione episcopi.*[46] Furthermore the archdeacon gradually acquired the right of making the visitation. As early as the latter part of the ninth century he is found making the visitation. Hincmar of Rheims, in his capitula of the year 877 which were addressed to the archdeacon priests, Guntarus and Odelhardus, speaks of them as visiting the rural parishes committed to their care either in his company or by themselves and advises them as to their conduct while on these visitations.[47]

43. C. 29: "Ut quorumdam episcoporum reprehensibilis, immo *damnabilis consuetudo* omnimodis corrigatur, qui plebes sibi creditas, aut raro, aut numquam per seipsos, juxta ordinem evangelicum et apostolicum atque ecclesiasticum, visitant . . ." — Hardouin, IV, 1488; Mansi, XIV, 826; Hefele-Leclercq, IV, 121.

44. C. 36 — Hardouin, III, 587; Mansi, X, 629.

45. Schröder, *Entwicklung des archidiakonats bis zum elften jahrhundert* (Augsburg, 1890), p. 79.

46. *Ep.* ad Ludifredum — *MPL*, LXXXIII, 896.

47. *Capitula Synodica Hincmari*, V. *Capitula archidiaconibus data*, capp. 1, 2, 4 — *MPL*, CXXV, 800, 801; Hardouin, V, 413; Mansi, XV, 497; Thomassin,

Co-Visitors

The present law allows the bishop to have two clerics as aides or assistants. During the period under consideration, with the exception of the VII Council of Toledo (646), which restricted the entourage to the number of fifty persons and horses,[48] no mention was made of the number or status of the persons who formed the retinue. However, it seems that the bishops, even as early as the middle of the seventh century, must have had public officials (*judices publici*) in their train, undoubtedly for the purpose of helping them to enforce certain regulations or decrees. This is evident from the eleventh canon of the Council of Chalons (650), which forbade them to make their rounds within the diocese without the express invitation of the priests or abbots. By so doing they naturally made demands on the parishes and monasteries. The council intended to remedy this state of affairs since it was contrary to the ancient custom, not in accord with religion and not permitted by the authority of the canons.[49]

The I National German Council reminded the bishop to manifest great concern about the resurgence of pagan practices. In stamping them out, he was to have the aid of a count (*graf*), who during the Carolingian period was an authoritative assistant to the bishop,[50] since he was considered a defender of the Church.[51]

Article 3. Objects Visited

Visitation implies to come in contact with something, to look in on something, to investigate something. Thus visitation can connote the

Ancienne et nouvelle discipline de l'église, part I, liv. 2, chap. 19, n. 4; Zaplotnik, *De vicariis foraneis* (The Catholic University of America, Canon Law Studies, n. 47, Washington, D. C., 1927), p. 25.

48. C. 4 — Hardouin, III, 622; Mansi, X, 768, 759; Bruns, I, 263.

49. Hardouin, III, 948; Mansi, XIV, 96; Hefele-Leclercq, III, 283; Bruns, II, 266.

50. *The Cambridge Medieval History* (New York: Macmillan Co., 1926), II, 679.

51. C. 5 — Hardouin, III, 1920, 1921; Mansi, XII, 367; Hefele-Leclercq, III, 823. Cf. also *Capitulare Generale* (769-771), cap. 6 — *MPL*, XCVII, 123. *MGH*, *Leges*, I, 33.

power of jurisdiction. Hence the bishop's canonical visitation becomes an investigation of the persons, places and things constituted under his jurisdiction. In this first period of conciliar legislation the councils give but very meager information concerning the objects subject to the episcopal visitation. They refer but to churches,[52] monasteries,[53] priests and people.[54]

However, Hincmar, archbishop of Rheims, in his *Capitula* (852), addressed to his auxiliaries or assistants designated as "magistri" and *decani* (rural deans),[55] and Regino of Prüm in his work (906)[56] on the canonical visitation, both[57] give a list of questions relating to the canonical visitation. These questions give an idea as to what were some of the objects subject to a visitation. Among those mentioned

52. Council of Tarragona (516), c. 8—Hardouin, II, 1042; Mansi, VIII, 542; Bruns, II, 15; Hefele-Leclercq, II, 1028.

53. Council of Chalons on the Saône (650), c. 11—Hardouin, III, 948; Mansi, X, 1191; Bruns, II, 266; Hefele-Leclercq, III, 283.

54. II Council of Braga (572), c. 1—Bruns, II, 39; Hardouin, III, 386; Mansi, IX, 838; Hefele-Leclercq, III, 194.

55. *Capitula Synodica,* II—*MPL,* CXXV, 777-780; Hardouin, V, 395-397; Mansi, XV, 479-480.

56. *Libellus de ecclesiasticis disciplinis et religione christiana collectus seu Libri duo de synodalibus causis et de disciplinis ecclesiasticis* (a collection of ecclesiastical laws and the Christian religion or Two books on synodal causes and ecclesiastical laws)—*MPL,* CXXXII, 185-455. The work is divided into two books, the first of which treats of ecclesiastical persons and things while the second has to do with laymen. The first book begins with Articles of Inquiry (a list of ninety-five questions) concerning the church, church furniture and the clergy, followed by canons or citations which refer to these questions. The second book begins with the mode of procedure at a synodal cause or the real investigation with a list of eighty-nine questions concerning the laity, followed by canons and citations. Cf. Van Hove, *Commentarium lovaniense in codicem juris canonici,* vol. I, t. I, *Prolegomena* (Mechlinae-Romae: Dessain, 1928), n. 170; Cicognani, *Canon law* (2. rev. ed. Philadelphia: Dolphin Press, 1935), p. 252.

57. It cannot be determined whether Regino used the short list of Hincmar that is now available or whether he used a larger set of questions issued by Hincmar which are not extant. Furthermore, it cannot be established whether Hincmar obtained his set from an older formula from which Regino of Prüm later may have also derived his list or whether he formulated the question himself. Fournier-Le Bras claim Regino took his list from Hincmar—*Histoire des collections canoniques en occident* (Paris, Recueil Sirey: 1931), I, 249.

are the altar, altar cloths, crosses, relics, chalices, patens, corporals, the *lavabo,* pyx, liturgical books (Missal, *Psalterium, Lectionarium, Antiphonarium*), vestments, candlesticks, candles, thurible, incense, the Martyrology, the Roman Penitential and the Baptismal Font. The cemetery and the house of the priest were also examined. Thus, even in this period persons, places and things were visited by the bishop.

Article 4. Manner of Proceeding

According to the II Council of Braga (572) the bishop was to spend two days[58] at a church. On the first day he was to examine the clerics as to their competence in their ministry and, if need be, to instruct them in that regard. On the second day the people were to assemble before the bishop.[59] At the I National German Council (742)[60] and at the Council of Soissons (744)[61] it was decreed that the priest and people were to be prepared to meet the bishop; and he was to take the occasion to preach to them and to instruct them in their faith.[62]

The sixteenth canon of the Council of Rouen (650) gives a further insight into the practice during the seventh century. The archdeacon or archpriest preceded the bishop by one or two days to the parish to be visited. He was to announce the bishop's coming and to require all the people, except the sick in the parish, to be present at the synod of the bishop[63] under pain of excommunication, and to make prepara-

58. The VII Council of Toledo (646) allowed one day. C. 4 — Bruns, I, 263; Hardouin, III, 622.

59. Cf. also the Council of Clovesho (747), c. 3 — Haddan and Stubbs, III, 363; Wilkins, I, 93; Hardouin, III, 1953; Mansi, XII, 396; Hefele-Leclercq, III, 906; the Council of Chelsea (787) — Haddan and Stubbs, III, 449; Wilkins, I, 146; Hardouin, III, 2073; Mansi, XII, 940; Hefele-Leclercq, III, 996.

60. C. 3 — Hardouin, III, 1920; Mansi, XII, 366; Hefele-Leclercq, III, 822.

61. C. 4 — Hardouin, III, 1933; Hefele-Leclercq, III, 857.

62. C. 1 — Hardouin, III, 386; Mansi, IX, 838; Bruns, II, 39; Hefele-Leclercq, III, 194.

63. When small churches were to be visited, a central point was to be selected whither the priests and people of four other small churches were to come. Cf. the Capitulary of Toulouse (844), c. 4 — Hardouin, IV, 1458; Mansi, XVIII B, Baluzius II, 21; Hefele-Leclercq, IV, 116.

tion for it. He was also to settle matters of lesser importance with the priests of the neighborhood who owed obedience to the bishop.[64]

By reason of the influence of the Frankish law the visitations took on a most important aspect during the Carolingian period. The investigation was carried out in a synodal court, that is, after the fashion of an assize or synod.[65] To insure the expeditious operation of these assemblies the head of the diocese adopted a standard form of procedure that was used by the Frankish administration.[66] This is outlined by Regino of Prüm at the beginning of the second book of his work, *"De Ecclesiasticis Disciplinis et Religione Christiana"*,[67] which offers great help for obtaining a complete picture and explanation of the practice in vogue.

On the appointed day when priests, people and bishop were assembled together in a synod, the bishop first gave a suitable address for the occasion. He then chose seven men, or more or less as he deemed expedient, who were among the more mature, upright and truthful persons in the parish.[68] They were then sworn in by the bishop to give information out of their past or present knowledge — or also out of such knowledge as they could acquire in the meantime if they were to be questioned in the future — of any abuses committed against the will of God and Christianity; and to permit neither any affection, fear, bribery, or relationship to deter them from disclosing anything to the bishop (of Treves) or to his representative (for example, the archdeacon). The oath was administered in the words: "So help you God and these relics of the saints."[69]

After they all had taken the oath, the bishop in addressing them reminded them that they swore to God and not to man and that they should not conceal anything lest, because of another's sin, they bring damnation upon themselves.[70] Following this talk on the part of the

64. Mansi, X, 1203; Bruns, II, 271.
65. These *"placita ecclesiastica"* are known in German as *"Sendgerichte"*.
66. Fournier-Le Bras, *Histoire des collections canoniques en occident,* I, 245.
67. Cap. 1 — *MPL,* CXXXII, 279-281.
68. Cap. 2 — *MPL,* CXXXII, 281.
69. Cap. 3 — *loc. cit.*
70. Cap. 4 — *loc. cit.*

bishop, they were then interrogated according to the order of questions contained in the formularies. These questions reveal the direct and primary aim of these public investigations which was to inquire into the existence of public crimes.[71]

In effecting the reforms and in correcting disorders the bishop naturally had to apply sanctions. In times of necessity, especially during the Carolingian period, he received the aid of a civil official, a count (*graf*) who accompanied him on his visitation.[72]

However, the bishops were reminded to be just in their actions toward the delinquents. Odo, archbishop of Canterbury, in his constitutions warned his bishops not to condemn or sentence any one unjustly.[73]

In general, however, the bishops were expected to treat all in a paternal manner, as is seen from the fourteenth canon of the II Council of Chalons on the Saône (813) which lamented the tyranny, the lack of charity and the invective manifested by the visitors toward their subjects especially with regard to procuration.[74] No mention was made in the then current legislation that any redress could be sought against the bishop's precepts and decrees as published in the course

71. As has been stated above, the text for this mode of action prefaced the second book's list of questions and canons referring to the lay people. Undoubtedly these synodal witnesses were also questioned concerning the clergy, for it is only from the seventy-fifth question onward (there are ninety-five) that the priest was directly questioned by the bishop or his representative. Cf. Stephani Baluzii "Notae ad libros Regiminis de ecclesiasticis disciplinis: Notae ad capitula inquisitionis," cap. 1—*MPL*, CXXXII, 407. The formulary directed to the clergy had to do with the condition of the church, its furnishings, the surrounding property, the life and conversation of the priest, his ancestry or parentage, ordination, assignment, civil status, physical integrity and matters concerning his ministry.—*MPL*, CXXXII, 187-191. The second list of questions was concerned with the serious breaches of the moral law that were committed by the lay people.—*MPL*, CXXXII, 282-287.

72. The I National German Council (742), c. 15—Hardouin, III, 1920; Mansi, XII, 367; Hefele-Leclercq, III, 823.

73. C. 3: "...neminem injuste damnare...."—Hardouin, III, 2073; Wilkins, I, 213; Mansi, XVIII A, 396.

74. Hardouin, IV, 1034; Mansi, XIV, 96; cf. also the VII Council of Toledo (646), cap. 4—Hardouin, III, 622.

of the visitation. Correspondingly it seems correct to assume that no possibility was provided by way of appeal to suspend the operative force of the visitor's demands.

Article 5. Procuration

This section will treat of the history of something intimately connected with the visitation — the matter of procuration — the abuse of which undoubtedly was the cause of the practice of the visitation falling into desuetude at different intervals. Time and again laws were passed which sought to restrain the bishops from burdening the persons and places visited by making excessive demands, by tarrying too long or by employing too large a retinue. Despite this common abuse it was not until the twelfth century that a general law was enacted to that effect.[75]

The first particular law on the right of the bishop in the matter of procuration was passed by the II Council of Braga (572).[76] It decreed that the bishops in the course of their visitations were not to receive anything from the churches except two *solidi* by way of honorary acknowledgment.[77] Besides, the bishops were not to be overbearing toward their priests by requiring any menial services of them.[78] Furthermore, while outlining the order of procedure during the visitation, the

75. The III General Lateran Council (1179), c. 4 — Hardouin, VII, 1675; Mansi, XXII, 219; Hefele-Leclercq, V, 1091; c. 6, X, *de censibus, exactionibus et procurationibus,* III, 39; Schroeder, *Disciplinary decrees of the general councils* (St. Louis: B. Herder Book Co., 1937), p. 218.

76. Cf. Couly, "Droit de visite ou procuration" — *Le canoniste contemporain,* XLIV (1921), 209.

77. This amount was the revenue procured by the bishop. It later assumed the name of *cathedraticum.* It was purported to be a sign, a proof and an acknowledgment of subjection and honor which the other churches owed the cathedral church as to their parent or mother. Soglia, *Institutiones iuris privati,* 9, p. 19; Thomassin, *Ancienne et nouvelle discipline de l'église,* part II, liv. 3, chap. 78, n. 18 (c. 1, C. X, q. 3). The canon in question offers no definite indication that at this time the right of procuration was distinct from the right to the *cathedraticum.*

78. C. 2 — Bruns, II, 39; Hardouin, III, 386; Mansi, IX, 839; Hefele-Leclercq, III, 194.

council in its first canon limits the stay at any one church to *two* days.[79] Thus, through this restriction the canon in the light of future developments gives an intimation of the right to hospitality.[80]

Through the complaints of priests the covetousness and excessive demands of some of the bishops in the province of Galicia, Spain, came to the knowledge of the National Council of Toledo (the VII of Toledo, 646), convoked by King Chindaswinthe. In certain instances the demands of the bishops had reached such proportions that the treasuries of the churches were practically exhausted. The Fathers of the council decided to remedy the situation by forbidding any bishop of the province to demand more than two *solidi* yearly in accord with the second canon of the Council of Braga. The convent churches, however, were not subject to this tax. Moreover, while visiting their dioceses the bishops were not to be a burden on anyone because of their large train. As a consequence it was not to exceed the number of fifty. And the time allotted for the stay was of a *day's* duration. The council further decreed a sort of sanction against any bishop's acting contrary to these prescriptions, in as much as the said bishop would be subject to reproof as a transgressor of the synodal constitutions and a corrupter of the injunctions or ordinances of the ancient Fathers.[81]

As Thomassin aptly observes, this rightful demand of the bishop upon each parish church in the sum of two *solidi* was different from his right of procuration. The canon affords evidence to that effect, for it mentions the annual payment (*annua illatio*) and thereupon admonishes the bishop not to be a burden through an excessive entourage. This without a doubt refers directly to the food and lodg-

79. C. 1 — Hardouin, III, 386; Mansi, IX, 838; Hefele-Leclercq, III, 194.

80. Sulpicius Severus in his account of a visitation of St. Martin of Tours made reference to the accommodations prepared for the saintly bishop: "Cum ad dioecesin quandam pro solemni consuetudine, sicut episcopis visitare ecclesias suas moris est, media fere hieme venisset, mansionem ei in secretario ecclesiae clerici paraverunt." *Ep. I ad Eusebium — MPL,* XX, 79; *Nicene and Post-Nicene Fathers of the Christian Church,* Second Series, XI, p. 19.

81. C. 4 — Hardouin, III, 622; Mansi, X, 768; Hefele-Leclercq, III, 286; Bruns, I, 263.

ing that would have to be given to all concerned, and on that account the retinue was restricted to fifty.[82]

It seems that the bishops of the province of Rouen were allotted a certain sum from each parish, or they themselves prescribed a certain amount for each stay or visit. For the Council of Rouen (650) exhorted the archpriest or archdeacon, who was dispatched one or two days ahead of the bishop, to take care of the matters of lesser importance, lest the bishop on his arrival be taken up with them and be delayed any longer than the time for which — so the canon puts it — "expensa sufficiat".[83]

Another mode of expression (*cum collectione et cum adjutorio populi*), contained in an injunction to priests and people and issued by the I German National Council (742),[84] appears at first sight rather vague. One would scarcely be inclined to suspect that the word

82. Thomassin, *Ancienne et nouvelle discipline de l'église,* part II, liv. 2, chap. 78, n. 18. With reference to the number of horses the bishop was allowed to have, it must be said that other readings have five instead of fifty, which is the common reading. Thomassin adheres to the former and claims that the latter, an exorbitant number, was adopted and authorized by Alexander III at the III General Lateran Council (1179) (c. 4 — Hardouin, VII, 1675; Mansi, XXII, 219; Hefele-Leclercq, V, 1091; c. 6, X, *de censibus, exactionibus et procurationibus,* III, 39), in as much as such a lavish entourage was much more readily tolerated in the twelfth century than in the seventh, when the Council of Toledo was so intent upon alleviating the burdens of the parishes and parish priests occasioned by the uncalled-for display in the retinues of certain prelates. *Ancienne et nouvelle discipline de l'église,* part II, liv. 3, chap. 78, n. 18.

83. C. 16 — Mansi, X, 1203; Bruns, II, 271; Hardouin, VI, 208. Bessin, in his edition of the councils of the Province of Rouen (*Concilia Provinciae Rothomagensis,* 1717) placed this council in the middle of the seventh century, and essayed to prove his contention that it belonged to that time. Mansi likewise included it in this period in his edition, and endeavored also to prove his stand. — Mansi, X, 1199. Hardouin, on the other hand, dates the council for the year 878. Hefele is inclined to think that only three canons of this council refer to this later time, and that canon 16 is among them. He seems to believe that the canon in question should be relegated to the Carolingian period, the time of the itinerant episcopal tribunals. Cf. Hefele-Leclercq, III, 289. As is evident the author has adopted the view of Bessin and Mansi.

84. C. 3: "Et quandocumque *jure canonico* episcopus circumierit parochiam ad confirmandos populos, presbyter semper paratus sit ad suscipiendum episcopum, *cum collectione et adjutorio populi* qui ibi confirmari debet. . . ." — Hardouin, III, 1920; Mansi, XII, 366; Hefele-Leclercq, III, 822.

adjutorium makes reference to procuration or the expenses for the visitation. However, upon closer examination, especially when one notes that only two years later at the Council of Soissons (744)[85] the same term was used in unmistakable designation of a duty on the part of the clergy to supply the needs of the bishop at the time of his visitation, it becomes evident that canon 3 of the German National Council does touch upon the question of procuration. Thus, by the regulations of these two councils, the priests and also the people to be confirmed were under obligation of defraying the expenses of the bishop and his travelling companions during their stay.[86]

As is seen in the canons referred to, both of these councils use the term "jure canonico". Hence, if any doubt had been entertained concerning the right of the bishop to procuration, it seems that these canons resolved and dispelled it. For it is apparent that the use of this term at these councils with reference to the visitation was intended to establish this right once and for all as unquestionable, to confirm it, to give it unimpeachable, unchallengeable authority in virtue of the ancient canons which established it.[87]

On the other hand the II Council of Chalons on the Saône (813), celebrated in the last year of the reign of Charlemagne, cautioned the bishops against the oppression of their subjects in this regard, lest they scandalize some of the brethren. It also brought to their attention that they should be satisfied with the bare costs or expenses of the visitation and that they should accept such help only in the event that they were not in a position to meet the costs themselves.[88]

85. C. 4: "... Et quando *jure canonico* episcopus circumit parochiam ad confirmandum populum, abbates et presbyteri parati sint ad suscipiendum episcopum in adjutorium necessitatis. . . ." — Hardouin, III, 1933; Hefele-Leclercq, III, 857.

86. The I German National Council (742), c. 3 — Hardouin, III, 1920; Mansi, XII, 366; Hefele-Leclercq, III, 822; the Council of Soissons (744), c. 4 — Hardouin, III, 1933; Hefele-Leclercq, III, 857.

87. Thomassin: "Il y a même sujet de croire que ces deux mots, qui sont communs et comme affectés dans ces deux canons, *jure canonico*, n'y sont employés que pour rendre ce droit de procuration incontestable par l'autorité des anciens Canons qui l'ont établi." — *Ancienne et nouvelle discipline de l'église*, part II, liv. 3, chap. 78, n. 2.

88. C. 14 — Hardouin, IV, 1034; Mansi, XIV, 96; Thomassin, *Ancienne et nouvelle discipline de l'église*, part II, liv. 3, chap. 79, n. 5.

The VI Council of Paris (829) went further in its effort to moderate the excessive demands made upon the priests and parishioners by the bishops during the visitation. It declared that the bishops were not to be a burden on the clergy and laity any longer.[89] Another council of this period, the III of Valence (855), took up the plea for moderation in the course of the diocesan visitation as expressed in the canons.[90]

A rather interesting bit of information as regards procuration is presented in certain provisional specifications in the Capitulary of Toulouse (*Capitulare Tolosanum*) which were drawn up at a meeting at Toulouse under Charles the Bald (844). They were to be effective until a general synod took up the question, since it was at the earnest importunity of the priests who claimed that the episcopal visitation was ruining their churches that the king called the meeting. Furthermore, the bishop was not as hitherto to burden any individual priest who was in charge of a church, but was to select a central place convenient for himself and for the neighboring pastors. The latter were to bring their people to this station. And each priest was to present the bishop with ten loaves of bread, half a measure of wine, a young pig worth four *denarii,* two chickens, ten eggs and a measure of oats for the horses. The resident priest was to do likewise. The bishop was not to demand anything else from him except the use of wood and implements needed to carry on the work of the ministry. The bishop also had the obligation to see that no member of his party damaged any property. The priests, moreover, incurred the expense of but one visit a year. On the other hand, if for any reason the bishops failed to make their visitation they were prohibited from demanding the aforesaid contribution or its equivalent either through themselves or any agent. Finally, if they did visit and made their stay at a house of a priest they were not to enlarge their retinue excessively or to invite the neighbours to a meal, lest they become a burden to the parish.[91]

89. Lib. 1, c. 31 — Hardouin, IV, 1317; Mansi, XIV, 559; Hefele-Leclercq, IV, 65. Cf. also Gonzalez-Tellez, *Commentaria perpetua in singulos textus quinque librorum decretalium Gregorii IX* (Venetiis, 1699), lib. III, tit. 39, cap. 6.

90. C. 17 — Hardouin, V, 94; Mansi, XV, 15; Hefele-Leclercq, IV, 208.

91. Capp. 4, 5, 6 — Hardouin, IV, 1458; Mansi, XVIII B, Baluzius II, 21, 23, 24; Hefele-Leclercq, IV, 116; Ayrinhac, *Constitution of the Church in the new code of canon law,* p. 175-176. Cf. also the II Council of Pavia (855) — c. 16, *MGH, Leges,* I, 438; Mansi, XV, 19.

CHAPTER III

FROM THE ELEVENTH CENTURY TO THE COUNCIL OF TRENT

ARTICLE 1. PURPOSE OF THE VISITATION

Toward the close of the tenth century or at the beginning of the eleventh it seems that a considerable number of bishops were rather remiss in performing their diocesan visitation. The period from the eleventh century to the Council of Trent, however, saw a revival as well as another decline of this canonical institution, just as it saw the rise and decline of Christian living and Christian thought. It was not without reason that Pope Alexander II (1061-1073) in his letter to William, King of England, paid tribute to him for his devotion to the cause of religion at a time when, as he expressed it, "mundus in maligno positus plus solito pravis incumbat studiis."[1]

Furthermore, most of the legislation of this period with respect to the episcopal visitation had to do with the abuses that occurred during the course of the visit. Universal and particular laws were enacted which dealt chiefly with procuration or the sustenance due the visitor while fulfilling his obligation.[2] Although during the eleventh, twelfth and thirteenth centuries the visitations received attention, the actual work was for the most part done by the archdeacons and not by the bishops. This is proved from the fact that at this time most of the legislation dealing in any way with visitation was addressed to archdeacons.[3]

1. Hardouin, VI, 1068.

2. This particular canonical institution failed to merit a caption in the Decretals, except incidentally by reason of the abuses that arose with regard to procuration. Cf. X, *de censibus, exactionibus et procurationibus,* III, 39; *De censibus, exactionibus et procurationibus,* III, 20 in VI°.

3. Wernz (*Ius decretalium,* II, 759, § 2) makes a statement that at the time of the Decree of Gratian (1140) and of the Authentic Compilations (the third [1210], and the fifth [1226-1227]) the obligation of visiting the diocese was *frequently* urged on the bishops. He adduces no proof in reference and an examination of the acts of the councils of that age does not bear out his contention.

Practically all the legislation, however, whether addressed to the bishops or to the archdeacons, offered some express purpose for the visitation. The constitutions of Alexander II (1067) addressed to the Church of Milan gave as one of the purposes for a semiannual visitation the investigation or inquiry into the status of Christianity, to be gauged according to the prescriptions of the canons. This, indeed, has a wide range and is inclusive of other purposes which will be treated later. The Pope included another purpose for the visitation in that church, and that was to confer the Sacrament of Confirmation.[4]

In his synodal constitutions (1268) Guido of Clermont advised his priests to have those members of their parishes prepared who were to receive Confirmation whenever and wherever he should come to dedicate a church or a cemetery or to make the visitation. This is an indication that the visitation was not considered as instituted primarily for the conferring of the Sacrament of Confirmation. The visit becomes an occasion for the administration of that Sacrament.[5]

On the other hand the Council of Würzburg (1287), due to the fact that men and women who had attained the age of sixty years were found to be unconfirmed, expressly ordered the bishops to visit their dioceses annually or at least every two years to confirm the people.[6]

Finally, when Otto, cardinal archbishop of Augsburg, announced at the Synod of Augsburg (1548) that the diocese was to be visited annually either by himself or by his suffragan, he added that the latter was also to confer the Sacrament of Confirmation.[7] Thus the visitation was again considered as an occasion for the conferring of this Sacrament.

Another purpose advanced for the visitation and stressed from time to time was preaching. The Council of Avignon (1209) advised the bishops to preach sound orthodox doctrine throughout their diocese

4. Hardouin, VI, 1084; Baronius, *Annales ecclesiastici* (36 vols., Barri Ducis, 1864-1882) vol. XVII (1067), n. 8, p. 281; in the text the purpose of confirming is mentioned first. Cf. the constitutions of Peter, archbishop of Bordeaux, c. 4 — Hardouin, VII, 553.

5. C. 5 — Hardouin, VII, 591; Mansi, XXIII, 1190.

6. C. 27 — Hardouin, VII, 1139; Hefele-Leclercq, VI, 312.

7. C. 29 — Mansi, XXXII, 1321.

more frequently and diligently, since it claimed that, had the prelates preached the evangelical discipline, heresies would not have arisen. They were allowed to have other capable men act in that capacity if that were found to be expedient.[8]

Pope Innocent III at the IV General Council of the Lateran, while treating the matter of procuration, directed those who performed the visitations to give themselves over to preaching and exhortation.[9]

Then, in his desire to eliminate the Waldensian and Albigensian heresies, he asked the bishops who, on account of the multiplicity of their duties or through sickness, were often prevented from preaching the Word of God among the people throughout the diocese, to select suitable men, capable in word and deed, who would visit the people in their stead, edifying them by word and example.[10]

The constitution "*Romana Ecclesia*" (1246) of Pope Innocent IV[11] mentions preaching (*proposito verbo Dei*) first in describing the manner in which the visitation was to be carried out. This in itself is an indication of the importance of preaching as a reason for the visitation. The Council of Albi (1254) directed the bishops while on their visitations to preach the word of God to both the clergy and the people.[12] The Provincial Council of Rouen (1445) commanded the

8. Cap. 1 — Hardouin, VI, 1986; cf. the Council of Arles (1234) for an identical law — c. 2 — Hardouin, VII, 236.

9. C. 33 — Hardouin, VII, 43; Mansi, XXII, 1019; Hefele-Leclercq, V, 1360; c. 23, X, *de censibus, exactionibus et procurationibus*, III, 39.

10. C. 10 — Hardouin, VII, 27; Mansi, XXII, 988; c. 15, X, *de officio iudicis ordinarii*, I, 31; Cf. the constitutions of Richard Poore, c. 77, which refers to archdeacons, and c. 78 — Hardouin, VII, 108, 109. The Council of Beziers (1233) directed bishops and others to appoint only such persons as archdeacons who could preach to the clergy and people. — c. 9 — Hardouin, VII, 210; cf. also the Council of London (1237), c. 22 — Hardouin, VII, 299; Mansi, XXIII, 458.

11. C. 1, *de censibus, exactionibus et procurationibus*, III, 20, in VI°.

12. Cc. 17 and 57 — Hardouin, VII, 460, 467; Mansi, XXIII, 848. At the Synod of Bayeux (1303) priests were told that they were to assemble the people to hear the sermon of the bishop, as soon as they heard that the bishop was to arrive to preach in any particular place. — c. 5 — Hardouin, VII, 1226. Cf. also the synodal statutes of Clermont (1268), c. 5 — Hardouin, VII, 591.

archdeacons to explain the word of God to the people at least in the larger parishes during the course of the visitation,[13] while the Council of Sens (1485) ordered the bishops to preach or to give salutary admonitions.[14]

The visitation was also intended as a means for the extirpation of heresy. This, in addition to preserving truth, was the direct aim of preaching sound orthodox doctrine.[15] At the time of the so-called Reformation the Council of Cologne (1549) urged upon bishops more frequent visits to banish heresies and schisms.[16]

A purpose of the visitation which will always demand attention is the correction and reformation of the clergy and laity alike.[17] The IV General Council of the Lateran (1215) charged the visitors to direct the visitations to correction and reformation in addition to preaching and exhortation.[18] The Council of Apt (1365) claimed that it was on the authority of the Fathers that bishops were obligated to visit the churches to reform evil doings and to obviate shortcomings,[19] while the Council of Sens (1485), in determining the scope of the visitation

13. C. 19 — Mansi, XXXII, 39.

14. C. 3 — Mansi, XXXII, 417; cf. also the Council of Cologne (1536), pars 14, c. 8 — Mansi, XXXII, 1291.

15. Cf. the Council of Paris (1209), c. 15 — Hardouin, VI, 2003; Mansi XXII, 823. However, church authorities also used other means to offset the evil occasioned by heretics. In each parish men were commissioned under oath to investigate and to seek out the heretics as well as their places of assembly. Their findings were to be forwarded to the bishop. These men were known as *Inquisitores.*

16. "*De quarto medio reformandi ecclesiam per visitationem,*" n. 1 — Mansi, XXXII, 1377.

17. Cf. the Council of Avignon (1209) which advised those who preached throughout the diocese to center their attention in bringing about a hatred for adultery, fornication, perjury, usury, etc. — c. 1 — Hardouin, VI, 1986.

18. C. 33 — Hardouin, VII, 43; Mansi, XXII, 1022; c. 23, X, *de censibus, exactionibus et procurationibus,* III, 39; Cf. the Council of London (1237), c. 32 — Hardouin, VII, 299; the Council of Albi (1254), c. 57 — Hardouin, VII, 467; the Council of Würzburg (1287), c. 27 — Hardouin, VII, 1139.

19. C. 9: "Cum sanctorum patrum auctoritas sit, ut dioecesanus suas visitare debet ecclesias ut male acta quaecumque reformentur et quae in eis deficiunt procurentur. . . ." — Mansi, XXVI, 449.

or the reasons for the visitation as intended by the Fathers, included the reformation of morals.[20]

Whenever required, the means used to obtain the reforms and emendations were penalties. Thus Pope Innocent IV recommended that notorious crimes which require no further examination be corrected freely by inflicting penalties on the delinquents.[21]

To effect these reforms and correct the abuses or crimes required, first of all, an inquiry into the life of the people and clergy. This, then, was an immediate object of the visitation. For example, Pope Innocent IV in his constitution "*Romana Ecclesia*" directed those upon whom the duty of visitation was incumbent to inquire into the life and deportment of the ecclesiastics stationed at churches and places dedicated to divine worship.[22]

In this regard it is to be noted that the archdeacons were under the same obligation. At the Council of Oxford (1222) the archdeacons were charged to see whether the priests knew how to pronounce the words of the Canon and of Baptism properly; and whether the lay people knew how to baptize at least in the vernacular in case of necessity.[23] Then the Council of London (1237) also directed them to find out how the nightly and daily offices were conducted.[24]

20. Art. II, c. 3 — Mansi, XXXII, 417; cf. the Council of Cologne (1536) p. 14, capp. 4, 5 — Mansi, XXXII, 1290; Hefele-Leclercq, VIII, 1246; the Council of Cologne (1549), "*De quarto medio reformandi ecclesiam*", n. 3 — Mansi, XXXII, 1377; the Provincial Council of Narbonne (1551) c. 59 — Hardouin, X, 465.

21. C. 1, *de censibus, exactionibus et procurationibus,* III, 20, in VI°.

22. C. 1, *de censibus, exactionibus et procurationibus,* III, 20, in VI° The Council of Albi (1254) included this law in its decree on the episcopal visitation, c. 57 — Hardouin, VII, 467; Mansi, XXIII, 848. Cf. also the Council of Sens (1485), art, II, cap. 3 — Mansi, XXXII, 417. The articles of inquiry adopted by the visitors made it unnecessary for the councils to make mention of the investigation, since it was taken for granted that it would be discharged, as without it there could be no true visitation. Hence the councils reminded the visitors of it whenever abuses appeared.

23. C. 23 — Wilkins, I, 589; Hardouin, VII, 121.

24. C. 20: "Et qualiter diurnis et nocturnis officiis ecclesiae serviatur. . . ." — Hardouin, VII, 298; Mansi, XXIII, 457; Wilkins, I, 654. Cf. also the Council of London (1268), c. 19, as recorded by Wilkins, II, 9; and c. 20 as listed by Hardouin, VII, 629; Mansi, XXIII, 1235.

Intimately associated with the life and ministry of a priest are the church furnishings, that is, the furniture and the equipment. Hence, the visitation was also directed to an inquiry of their existence and condition. The Council of London (1200) said that it belonged to the office of the visitor to see that each and every church had a silver chalice, a sufficient number of proper sacerdotal vestments, the necessary liturgical books and the utensils which pertain to the worship and reverence of the Sacrament.[25]

The Council of Albi (1254) expressed great concern as to the cleanliness of the priest's vestments and of the altar furnishings, especially the corporals, vases and chalices.[26] It must be remarked in this connection that the inquiry into the state of the church furnishings was the especial work of the archdeacons.[27] They were also to inquire into the financial condition of the churches.[28] Walter Kirkham, bishop of Durham, in his constitutions of the year 1255 ordered his archdeacons to find out which churches were dedicated and which were not; what endowment or dotation (*dos*) was assigned at the time of the dedication of the church ("quae dos in ecclesiae dedicatione sit assignata"); which altars were consecrated, and if they were consecrated, whether they were adorned with the cross.[29]

The III and IV General Lateran Councils both stated that the prelates while on their visitations were to seek those things *quae Jesu*

25. C. 5 — Hardouin, VII, 1959; Wilkins, I, 505, 506. This council addressed itself to both bishops and archdeacons.

26. C. 57 — Hardouin, VII, 467; Mansi, XXIII, 848.

27. Cf. the Council of Oxford (1222), c. 11 — Wilkins, I, 586; c. 10 — Hardouin, VII, 118; the Council of London (1237), c. 20 — Wilkins, I, 654; Hardouin, VII, 298; Mansi, XXIII, 451; the Council of London (1268), c. 19 — Wilkins, II, 9; c. 20 — Hardouin, VII, 629; Mansi, XXIII, 1235; the Synod of Exeter (1287), c. 40 — Wilkins, II, 150; Hardouin, VII, 1107.

28. Cf. the Council of London (1237), c. 20 — Wilkins, I, 589; Hardouin, VII, 121. Cf. also the Synod of Exeter (1287), c. 40 — Wilkins, II, 151; Hardouin, VII, 1107. The Councils of London (1237 and 1268) use the expression "*Et generaliter de temporalibus et spiritualibus inquirendo.*" — c. 20 (1237) Hardouin, VII, 298; Wilkins, I, 654; c. 19 (1268) — Wilkins, II, 9; c. 20 — Hardouin, VII, 629.

29. Wilkins, I, 705; Hardouin, VII, 489; Mansi, XXIII, 897.

Christi sunt.[30] This thought was certainly brought out in the Council of Sens (1485), in which it was specially emphasized. For the council stated that the office of visitation was wholesomely instituted by the Fathers for the glory of God, the profit and advantage of the Church in both temporal and spiritual matters, the salvation of souls,[31] the edification of the people and the reformation of their morals.[32]

Certainly all that was treated specifically with respect to the purpose of the visitation, in one way or another, falls under this generic expression of the reason for the institution of the visitation as well as for its continued existence.

Article 2. The Episcopal Visitation

Although the visitation was for the greater part performed by the archdeacon, especially during the first three centuries of this period, one does find instances in which the councils or popes imposed the visitation of the diocese upon the bishops as an obligation. However, no universal law expressly enjoined the annual visitation on the bishop.

In the constitutions of Pope Alexander II of the year 1067, which the legate of the Holy See prescribed for observance in the diocese of Milan, it was stated that the visitation was something worthy of special devotion. It charged the bishop of that diocese to visit the entire see once a year, or even twice a year if that were possible for him.[33]

The Decree of Gratian, which never obtained the force of law by official recognition, merely repeated the legislation of the Council of Tarragona (516), of the II Council of Braga (572) and of the IV Council of Toledo (633). The exception to this repetition of past

30. C. 4 — Hardouin, VI, 1675; Mansi, XXII, 219; c. 32 — Hardouin, VII, 43; Mansi, XXII, 1019.

31. Cf. the Council of London (1200), c. 5 — Wilkins, I, 506; Hardouin, VII, 1959.

32. Art. II, cap. 3: "Cum visitationis officium ad Dei honorem, et ecclesiarum in temporalibus et spiritualibus utilitatem et profectum, ad salutem animarum, ad aedificationem populi, et morum reformationem, a sanctis patribus fuerit salubriter institutum." — Mansi, XXXII, 417.

33. Hardouin, VI, 1084; Baronius, *Annales ecclesiastici*, XVII, n. 8, p. 281; Thomassin, *Ancienne et nouvelle discipline de l'église*, part II, liv. 3, chap. 80, n. 1; Wilkins, I, 326.

conciliar legislation was an excerpt from a letter of Pope Leo IV (847-855) addressed to the bishops of England, wherein he stated that the bishop was to visit his diocese whenever he deemed it necessary.[34]

Although the III and IV General Lateran Councils legislated as regards procuration, they did not by law impose any obligation on the bishop to make the visitation.[35] In the Decretals of Gregory IX (1227-1241) we have an excerpt from the letter of Pope Honorius III (1216-1227) to the bishop of Assisi, in which he enumerates among the *rights* of bishops the *annual* visitation of the diocese.[36]

The Council of London (1237) ordered the bishops to visit their dioceses at opportune times.[37] The Council of Würzburg (1287) prescribed an annual or biennial visitation.[38] In the fourteenth century (1339) Bertrand, patriarch of Aquileia, at a provincial council held in that city issued his provincial constitutions. Among other things they required the bishops to make a personal visitation, but if a just and righteous cause arose which would prevent them from making the visitation, they were to see to it that suitable men fulfilled the task. The visitation was to begin within one month's notice of the mandate or order and was to terminate six months later. If a bishop

34. C. 4, C. X, q. 1.

35. Nevertheless in the thirty-third canon of the IV General Council of the Lateran is found this expression: "visitationis officium exercentes," which refers to bishops, archdeacons and others who performed the visitation. Thus the visitation is acknowledged by the general law of the Church to be a duty attached to the episcopal office. Cf. Hardouin, VII, 43; c. 23, X, *de censibus, exactionibus et procurationibus,* III, 39. In fact the Decretals supposed that the visitation would be undertaken annually.

36. C. 16, X, *de officio iudicis ordinarii,* I, 31; cf. c. 1, *de censibus, exactionibus et procurationibus,* III, 20, in VI°. Peter, archbishop of Bordeaux, in his constitutions of the year 1263 uses the expression, "cum jura nostrae dioeceseos nos contigit visitare," c. 4—Hardouin, VII, 553. The *obligation* of the *annual* visitation was imposed by the Council of Trent.—Conc. Trident., sess. VII, *de ref.,* c. 8—Hardouin, XI, 56. Cf. also Sess. XXIV, *de ref.,* c. 3—Hardouin, XI, 155; Fagnanus, lib. III, tit. 39, cap. 21, n. 3. The Council of Apt (1365) claimed that the obligation on the part of the "dioecesani" to visit the churches was based on the *auctoritas sanctorum patrum*—c. 9—Mansi, XXVI, 449.

37. C. 22—Hardouin, VII, 299; Hefele-Leclercq, V, 1581; Mansi, XXIII, 458.

38. Cap. 27—Hardouin, VII, 1139; Hefele-Leclercq, VI, 312.

or prelate neglected to begin it within the specified time, or if upon having begun it he failed to continue, he was suspended from the execution of his pontifical office ("esse suspensos ab executione pontificalis officii") until he remedied this neglect by beginning the visitation, or continuing it, as the case might be.[39]

At the Provincial Council of Cologne (1452) it was stated that the visitations were to be made by the ordinaries as prescribed by law.[40] The Provincial Council of Sens (1485) acknowledged the obligation to be incumbent upon bishops and other prelates, while at the same time recognizing their right to commission others.[41] Another provincial council, that of Seville (1512), directed the bishops to make the visit annually, or to have it performed in their name by learned, conscientious, godfearing men.[42]

In the year 1528 the Provincial Council of Bourges demanded that visitations be made annually by the prelates themselves.[43] The Provincial Council of Sens (1528) commanded the bishop to make the visit himself or through another twice a year, or oftener if the situation demanded it.[44] The Council of Cologne (1536) ordered the bishop to make the visit through his vicar *in pontificalibus*.[45] At the Synod of Augsburg (1548) Otto, the cardinal bishop of Augsburg, announced that he would visit his diocese annually, or as often as conditions made it imperative, either personally or through his suffragan.[46]

The visitation of the diocese was classified as the fourth means for the reformation of the Church at the Council of Cologne in the year

39. C. 7 — Mansi, XXV, 1118.

40. Mansi, XXXII, 149; Hefele-Leclercq, VII, 1225.

41. Cap. 3 — Mansi, XXXII, 417.

42. Cap. 45 — Mansi, XXXII, 618.

43. C. 9: ". . . Fiant etiam visitationes a dominis prelatis singulis annis et per se, legitimo cessante impedimento, quoniam ad eos pertinet de ovibus curam solicitam agere." — Mansi, XXXII, 1143. In the *Dictionnaire des conciles*, l'Abbé Peltier refers the canon of this council to bishops: ". . . et que les évêques feront tous les ans leurs visites." — *Encyclopédie théologique*, I serie, vols. 13 and 14 — *Dictionnaire des Conciles* (Migne: Paris, 1847), I, 366.

44. Cap. 32 — Mansi, XXXII, 1197.

45. Pars 14, cap. 1 — Mansi, XXXII, 1290.

46. Cap. 29 — Mansi, XXXII, 1321.

1549. It was considered necessary for the rooting out of heresy and vices. Hence the council ordered the bishops to make their visits more often within the next three years. A notary in the person of a priest or of an unmarried cleric was to accompany the visitor.[47]

Article 3. The Archdeacon's Visitation

Since the archdeacon practically dominated the office of the visitor during the first three centuries of this period, either in the capacity of a *de jure* substitute for the bishop, as his vicar,[48] being regarded as the *oculus episcopi* as it were,[49] or in the capacity of a visitor of the diocese and especially of his own district in his own right, it is considered necessary and fitting to give a special treatment of the laws regulating his visitation. For thus, through their office of care and surveillance over the rural parishes, as well as their position with respect to the bishops, the duty naturally fell on them of making the visitation either through custom or agreement.[50]

This obligation was acknowledged by the councils, which ordered them to make their rounds. For example, the Council of Lillebonne (1080) prescribed an annual visitation throughout the archdiaconate.[51] Then the Decree of Gratian mentioned among the duties of an archdeacon the inspection of parishes at the behest of the bishop.[52]

Pope Innocent II in a letter written "Bonnensi preposito" on the 16th of December, 1139, stated that the archdeacons must (*debent*) visit the parishes and exercise diligent care of souls within their arch-

47. Nn. 1 and 2 — Mansi, XXXII, 1377. Cf. also the Provincial Council of Narbonne (1551), c. 59 — Hardouin, X, 465.

48. C. 1 and 7, X, *de officio archidiaconi,* I, 23; Hostiensis, lib. I, tit. 23, c. 1, n. 1; Panormitanus, lib. I, tit. 23, c. 1, n. 2; Fournier, *Les origines du vicaire général* (Paris, Auguste Pesard, 1922), p. 44.

49. C. 7, X, *de officio archidiaconi,* I, 23; cf. also, c. 6, D. XCIII.

50. C. 54, X, *de electione et electi potestate,* I, 54, n. 4; Hostiensis, lib. I, tit. 23, c. 1, n. 4; Panormitanus, lib. I, tit. 23, c. 6, n. 1; Fournier, *Les origines du vicaire général,* p. 47.

51. C. 6 — Hardouin, VI, 1599.

52. Cc. 1, 11, D. 25.

deaconries.[53] The III and IV General Councils of the Lateran took the archdeacon into consideration when they legislated on the subject of procuration.[54]

Pope Gregory IX incorporated into his Decretals a supposed extract from the *Liber Romani Ordinis,* which is not contained in the extant editions.[55] At the end of the citation mention is made of the archdeacon's obligation to make a visit of the entire diocese every three years if the bishop is prevented from doing so in any way.[56] The seventh chapter of title 23, *de officio archidiaconi,* includes a text taken from a letter of Pope Alexander III to the bishop of Coventry and the abbot of Chester.[57] Here the archdeacon is restricted to an annual visitation of the churches of his district unless circumstances demand otherwise. The apparent contradiction is cleared by closer scrutiny. The annual visitation is a general rule.[58] In the first instance it is a question of the entire diocese, in the second that of his archdeaconry. Hostiensis (†1271) was of the opinion that the bishop was free to send anyone in his stead. Nevertheless the archdeacon could

53. *MPL, CLXXIX,* 495; Fournier, *Les origines du vicaire général,* pp. 47, 48.

54. Cf. c. 4 of the III General Lateran Council — Hardouin, VI, 1675; Mansi, XXII, 219; c. 6, X, *de censibus, exactionibus et procurationibus,* III, 39; and c. 33 of the IV General Lateran Council — Hardouin, VII, 43; Mansi, XXII, 1019; c. 23, X, *de censibus, exactionibus et procurationibus,* III, 39; Cf. also the Council of Rouen (1189), c. 12 — Hardouin, VI, 1906; the Council of London (1200), c. 5 — Hardouin, VI, 1958; the Council of Paris (1212), cap. 15 — Hardouin, VI, 2003; Mansi, XXII, 823. Richard Poore in his constitutions (1217) for the diocese of Sarum made mention of a penalty to which an archdeacon was subject if he neglected the visitation. — C. 42 — Hardouin, VII, 102.

55. Cf. footnote n. 2, to c. 1, X, *de officio archidiaconi,* I, 23, of Richter's edition. Cf. also Fournier, *Les origines du vicaire général,* p. 44, footnote 84, where he says that the authenticity of the passage is not guaranteed, but that it is taken as an expression of a practice prevalent at a given epoch.

56. C. 1, X, *de officio archidiaconi,* I, 23.

57. C. 6, X, *de officio archidiaconi,* I, 23.

58. The authors refer to the Decree of Gratian, cc. 10, 11, C. X, q. 1, where are found the canons of the Council of Tarragona (516) and of the IV Council of Toledo (633) respectively, which, as is known, prescribed an annual visitation for the bishops.

make the visitation, if it were his custom to do so, because one visit would not impede the other.[59]

The Council of Oxford (1222) furnished the archdeacons with special points of inquiry which they were to employ while they conducted their annual visitation,[60] whereas the Council of London (1237) advised them to visit the churches faithfully and serviceably, without specifying any time period within which the visitation was to be carried out.[61] Aegidius of Bridport, bishop of Salisbury (Sarum) in his constitutions of the year 1256, accorded his archdeacon the option of visiting all the principal churches once a year,[62] while bishop Peter Quivil at the Synod of Exeter (1287) ordered an annual visitation by the archdeacons of every church of their archdeaconries.[63]

The Provincial Council of Rouen (1445) insisted on a personal visitation, although it allowed for a substitute provided the archdeacon had permission from the Apostolic See.[64] At the Provincial Council of Sens, held at Paris in the year 1528, the diocesan bishops were given permission to use archdeacons as substitutes for the visitation, which was to take place at those places wherever heresy was suspected to exist. It was to occur twice a year or oftener if conditions required it.[65]

Undoubtedly influenced by the demands for reformation at the first ten sessions of the Council of Trent, the Council of Cologne (1549) sought means to effect reforms in discipline and morals. Among the six means considered necessary for the reform of the Church, the archdeacon's visitation, together with the episcopal and archiepiscopal visitations, held the fourth place. Like the bishops, the archdeacons were asked to make frequent visitations of their archdeaconries within

59. Lib. I, tit. 23, c. 6, n. 1; c. 1, n. 1; Panormitanus, lib. I, tit. 23, c. 1, n. 2.

60. Cc. 33, 35, 36 — Hardouin, VII, 121; Hefele-Leclercq, V, 1432; c. 33 — Wilkins, I, 589.

61. C. 20 — Hardouin, VII, 298; Mansi, XXIII, 457; Wilkins, I, 654; cf. also the Council of London (1268), c. 20 — Hardouin, VII, 629; Mansi, XXIII, 1235; c. 19 — Wilkins, II, 9.

62. Hardouin, VII, 498; Wilkins, I, 715.

63. C. 40 — Hardouin, VII, 1107; Wilkins, II, 151.

64. C. 19 — Mansi, XXXII, 29. Practically all the legislation of the intervening period with reference to the archdeacon's visitation had to do with the subject of procuration.

65. C. 32 — Mansi, XXXII, 1197.

the coming three years. The council also provided for a notary to accompany the visitor.[66]

In conclusion it may be remarked that the archdeacon reached the height of his power in the thirteenth century. He exercised his office *jure ordinario.* Pope Innocent III speaks of him as a *judex ordinarius*[67] and Innocent IV in his constitution *"Romana Ecclesia"* (1246) makes reference to appeals made from his tribunal.[68] Up to the thirteenth century the archdeacon as a diocesan visitor possessed but delegated jurisdiction.[69] The fourteenth century saw the beginning of his decline in power and prestige. It became rather definite at the end of the fifteenth century. Hence from the 16th century the archdeacon of old was no longer in existence,[70] for he had become supplanted in his judicial competence by the diocesan court official and in his administrative powers by the vicar general.[71]

ARTICLE 4. OBJECTS VISITED

During this period the councils emphasized the inspection of the altar furnishings, the vestments, the liturgical books, the utensils and other necessities for the sanctuary.[72] As has been stated above, the examination and supervision of these utensils was the especial work of the archdeacon.[73]

66. *De quarto medio reformandi ecclesiam per visitationem,* nn. 1 and 2 — Mansi, XXXII, 1377. The special purpose for these frequent visits within the three year period was to eradicate heresies and schisms.

67. *Regesta,* lib. XIV, *ep.* 45 (May, 1211) — *MPL,* CCXVI, 413.

68. C. 3, *de appellationibus,* II, 15, in VI°.

69. C. 1, X *de officio archidiaconi,* I, 23.

70. Amanieu, "Archidiacre", *Dictionnaire de droit canonique* (Paris, Letouzey et Ané, 1924), I, 991.

71. The Council of Trent still accorded the archdeacon the right of visitation in those churches wherein he legitimately exercised it up to that time. Cf. sess. XXIV, *de ref.,* c. 3.

72. Cf. for example, the Council of London (1200), c. 5 — Hardouin, VI, 1959; Wilkins, I, 505.

73. C. 3, X, *de officio archidiaconi,* I, 23. Cf. the Council of Oxford (1222), c. 11 — Wilkins, I, 586; c. 10 — Hardouin, VII, 118; the Council of London (1237), c. 20 — Hardouin, VII, 298; Wilkins, I, 654; Mansi, XXIII, 457; the Council of London (1268), c. 19 — Wilkins, II, 9; c. 20 — Hardouin, VII, 629; Mansi, XXIII, 1235.

Pope Innocent IV in his constitution "*Romana Ecclesia*",[74] while treating the matter of procuration, referred to cathedral chapters and the chapters also of other churches, to the churches themselves and to other religious and pious places, to clerics and to the people as being comprised within the scope of the diocesan visitation.[75] In his constitution "*Vas electionis*" (1336), which constituted an elaborate treatment on the question of procuration, Benedict XII, besides speaking of cathedral churches, monasteries and other churches in relation to the graduated maximum payments which could be demanded, also made mention of priories, and with reference to these likewise indicated the maximum sum derivable from them in consideration of the expenses incurred through the bishop's visitation of them.[76] Cemeteries and homes were mentioned by the Council of London (1342)[77] while at the Council of Rheims (1408) reference was made to schools,[78] hospitals,[79] and religious houses.[80] The Council of Sens (1485) alluded to ecclesiastical places,[81] the Council of Seville (1512)

74. C. 1, *de censibus, exactionibus et procurationibus,* III, 20, in VI°.

75. C. 14, X, *de censibus, exactionibus et procurationibus,* III, 39. C. 17 of the same book and title declared that all exempt churches were to supply procuration to the legates of the Apostolic See unless they had a privilege to the contrary. Cf. also the Council of Aquileia (1339), c. 8 — Mansi, XXV, 1118; Hefele-Leclercq, VI, 840. The Council of Padua (1350) insisted that the bishops visit nonexempt monasteries. — c. 20 — Mansi, XXVI, 235; Hefele-Leclercq, VI, 914. For a history of the development of exemption, confer Vendeuvre, *L'exemption de visite monastique* (Dijon, 1906), pp. 19-306, and Reilly, *The visitation of religious* (The Catholic University of America, Canon Law Studies, n. 113, Washington, D. C., 1938), pp. 41-49, 50-55.

76. C. un., *de censibus, exactionibus et procurationibus,* III, 10, in Extravag. com.

77. C. 2 — Hardouin, VII, 1650.

78. *Cf. Tractatus de visitatione praelatorum et curatorum, Gersonii opera* (ed. du Pin, Antuerpiae, 1706), II, 650-651. Cf. also the Council of Cologne (1536), pars 14, cap. 2 — Mansi, XXXII, 1290.

79. Cf. also the Provincial Council of Seville (1512), cap. 45 — Mansi, XXXII, 618; and the Council of Cologne (1536), pars 14, capp. 2 and 14 — Mansi, XXXII, 1290; Reformationes cleri dioecesis Leodiensis (Liége, 1446) — Mansi, XXXII, 41.

80. Ad Remense concilium additio, *Brevis instructio* — Mansi, XXVI, 1069.

81. Art. II, cap. 3 — Mansi, XXXII, 417.

referred to hermitages,[82] and the Council of Cologne (1536) enumerated the library among the places to be visited.[83]

Article 5. Manner of Proceeding

The visitation afforded the medieval bishop an opportunity to vindicate his jurisdiction and to exercise its functions not only in the cathedral city but also throughout the entire diocese. This relation of jurisdiction with the diocesan visit is evident from the words of Pope Alexander II (1061-1073) addressed to the Church of Milan. The Pope stated that the bishop had full power throughout the diocese over all his clergy to judge and constrain them. This power extended to the laity and churches as well. And the clergy and laity in turn were to be obedient to the authority over them.[84] Thus the bishop was privileged to set up his tribunal wherever he visited within his territory.

Pope Innocent IV in his constitution "*Romana Ecclesia*" (1246) outlined how the archbishop, bishop and other visitors [*mutatis mutandis*] were to carry out their visitation and how they were to act. At the outset the bishop was to begin his visitation with the chapter of his church, followed by a visitation of all the other churches, large and small, of the episcopal city. However, not only were the clergy to receive consideration in this regard but the laity as well. To avoid inconvenience and difficulties the visitor was allowed to select a focal point in a district to which he could summon the clergy and laity from several other neighbouring parishes or churches.[85] This was proposed as a means of avoiding the neglect of any parish.[86]

82. Cap. 45 — Mansi, XXXII, 618.

83. Pars 14, cap. 2 — Mansi, XXXII, 1290.

84. Hardouin, VI, 1084; Baronius, *Annales ecclesiastici*, XVII (1067), n. 8, p. 281; Thomassin, *Ancienne et nouvelle discipline de l'église*, part II, liv. 3, chap. 80, n. 1.

85. Cf. the Capitulary of Toulouse (844), c. 4 — *MGH, Leges*, I, 379; Hardouin, IV, 1458; Mansi, XVIII B, Baluzius, II, 23; Hefele-Leclercq, IV, 116.

86. The constitution primarily considered the visitation of a province by an archbishop and thus all the stipulations or provisions laid down refer to it. Later on in the constitution it is pointed out that the same mode of action was to be adopted by all visitors, but with the understanding that the necessary changes and adaptations be made.

After the bishop had visited his own city, he was then to visit the monasteries, churches, and other religious and pious places throughout the entire diocese. The constitution cautioned the bishop that he was to go about the entire diocese before returning to any particular church or part of the diocese, unless conditions at a particular place or district demanded the immediate attention of the bishop. On his arrival at a church or place the visitor was to begin with a sermon. Then he was to make an inquiry into the life and deportment of the ecclesiastics stationed at the church or oratory as well as into all other things which pertained to an ecclesiastic's office. Furthermore, in his endeavour to bring about the correction and reformation of the ministers he was not to force them to take an oath or to demand that they do so, but was to give salutary advice,[87] its nature to be determined according as his prudence would dictate to him. If any persons were laboring under infamy, then as he thought it expedient he was to see to it that a solemn inquiry would be made with reference to the reason and basis for such infamy. Moreover, with regard to notorious crimes which required no examination or investigation he was to proceed freely in correcting them and in inflicting due and proper penalties.[88] Pope Honorius III (1216-1227) explicitly directed the visitors to act in a paternal and conciliatory manner in making the corrections which proved necessary. Furthermore, the admonitions and corrections were to be made in secret.[89] Thus the insistence was on the paternal manner of action in the investigation and correction of abuses.

In the seventh canon of the IV General Lateran Council (1215) Pope Innocent III, while ordaining that prelates make a prudent and earnest

87. Cf. also the Council of Albi (1254), c. 57 — Hardouin, VII, 467; Mansi, XXIII, 848.

88. C. 1, *de censibus, exactionibus et procurationibus,* III, 20, in VI°. For the mode of action with respect to the procuration confer the article dealing with it, *infra,* pp. 48-57.

89. "... Ut iuxta illius supremi post Christum pastoris edictum pastor forma factus gregis ex animo dignoscitur, non dominandi libidine sed amore recte regendi debet illum salubriter visitare, sic excessus delinquentium quantum potest corripiens ne revelet, sic increpans ne confundat, quia, quum iuxta sapientis edictum secreto sit arguendus amicus, amicitiae legem violare videtur si e contra palam arguat exprobrando." — c. 17, X, *de officio iudicis ordinarii,* I, 31.

effort to correct the excesses and reform the morals of their subjects, especially the clergy, decreed that no custom or appeal was to thwart their efforts, unless the visitors exceeded the bounds or limits of authoritative intervention that the particular case demanded. However, the prelates were not to make the occasion of such a correction a source of personal profit or gain, or the cause of a just complaint on the part of the party concerned.[90]

The Parochial Synod

Usually the visitation began in the morning with the singing of a High Mass. Next in order was the inspection of places and things. Following this came the personal investigation or the synod properly so called. It was the principal part of the visitation. It was carried out in the manner outlined by Regino of Prüm.[91] This form of procedure was in use till the sixteenth century,[92] when it began to die out. Nevertheless in Germany the practice did not cease completely till the nineteenth century.[93]

In England, especially during the thirteenth century, there appeared a number of "Visitation Articles" which bishops and archdeacons used in their visits.[94] In their answers to the questions proposed to them at the parish synod the *testes synodales,* as is attested by documents

90. C. 13, X, *de officio iudicis ordinarii,* I, 31. The council did not forbid the bishop to impose fines or monetary penalties, but it did disallow the appropriation of the same to their own personal uses in opposition to the ancient practice which allotted these fines to pious causes or the relief of the poor. Cf. Panormitanus, lib. I, tit. 31, c. 13, n. 1; Schroeder, *Disciplinary decrees of the general councils,* p. 248.

91. Cf. above p. 22. Cf. also "Une visite synodale dans l'ancien archidiaconé de Carden au moyen age", an article by Victor Carrière in *Revue des questions historiques* (*RQH*) XCII (1912), 120. This informative article (pp. 117-141) is a detailed descriptive account of an archdeacon's visitation made in the year 1475 in the diocese of Treves. Information as to the visitatorial practice obtained from visits in 1512 and 1516 is also interspersed throughout the article.

92. Auerbach, *De visitationum ecclesiasticarum progressu, a primis temporibus usque ad concilium Tridentinum* (Francofurti ad Moenum, 1862), p. 25.

93. Carrière, "Une visite synodale au moyen age", *RQH,* XCII (1912), 120.

94. Cf. Wilkins, I, 627, and Cutts, *Parish Priests and their People in the Middle Ages in England,* pp. 280-281.

contained in episcopal registers, revealed not only the impressions and knowledge they had concerning the clergy, but also their own acquaintance in general with the happenings of ecclesiastical matters. As the testimony which was furnished at Bishop Stapledon's visitations of the year 1310 in the diocese of Exeter shows, these witnesses were not reluctant in pointing out the failings or virtues of the clergy. For example,[95] "*Branscombe.* — Thomas, the Vicar, conducts himself well in all things and preaches willingly (*libenter*) and diligently does all things which belong to the office of a priest. . . . . *Culmstock.* — William, the Vicar, is a man of good life and honest conversation . . . and well instructs his parishioners. In the visitation of the sick and baptizing the children, and in all things which belong to his office, they know nothing to be found fault with in him, with the exception that he makes too little pause between the matins and mass on festival days. *Coylton.* — Sir Robert, the Vicar, is a good man (*probus homo*), and preaches to them so far as he knows (*quatenus novit*) but not *sufficienter* as it seems to them. They say also that his predecessors were accustomed to call the friars to instruct them about their souls' salvation, but he does not receive them nor give them entertainment (*viatica*); whereof they pray that he be admonished. . . . At a later visitation in 1330, the synodsmen of Coylton complain that their vicar had been struck with leprosy, but continued to come to communion with the parishioners at the risk of contaminating the whole flock, which was a scandal. . . . They complain that the vicar chooses his own clerk at his own pleasure and will not '*manucipere pro eodem*'. They say that the clerks of the church used by custom to ring the curfew at the elevation of the *Corpus Domini. Colebrook.* — Hugh de Coppelestone and other trustworthy men of the parish, lawfully requisitioned and examined, say that Sir William, the Vicar, preaches after his own fashion (*suo modo*); also he expounds to them the Gospels on the Lord's Days so far as he knows (*quatenus novit*); but concerning the Articles of Faith, the Commandments of the Decalogue, and the mortal sins, he does not teach them much. And he does not say his matins with note on the more solemn days and only celebrates on

95. Quoting from Cutts, *Parish priests and their people in the Middle Ages in England*, p. 285.

the weekdays every other day. He is defamed of incontinency with Lucia de la Stubbes, a married woman (*conjugata*). . . ."[96]

Testimonies such as these furnish proof of the zealous participation of the laity in work which is designated for the advancement of religion and of the parish itself. Given the opportunity to act, the laity will inevitably respond to the call. It is to be admitted with Gasquet "that one of the great differences between ecclesiastical life in the Middle Ages and modern times lies in the fact that then people had no chance 'of going to sleep'."[97] For an institution such as the bishop's visitation of a parish inspired the people to a lively interest in the liturgy and in spiritual things.

Finally, it is to be observed with Claude Jenkins[98] that "few departments of episcopal activity illustrate more vividly the difference between medieval and modern conditions than that of visitation. If the medieval bishop or archbishop said a great deal less and did a great deal more than his later successors, as is undoubtedly the case, that is not a ground in itself for disparaging comparisons. For them a visitation was not only an obligation of pastoral care: it was vindication of jurisdiction and a very definite exercise of its functions."

Ceremonial Specifications

Although the Pontificals of that time and age contained the order of ceremonies for the visitation of parishes, there are but a few ceremonial references in the acts of the synods and councils. For example, at the Synod of Bayeux (1300) the priests were instructed to meet the bishop together with the people with a cross at their head,[99] while the Council of Ravenna (1314) legislated that whenever the bishop made a visitation of his diocese the bells were to be rung as a reminder to the people to come and receive his blessing.[100] Then the Council of

96. Cutts, *Parish priests and their people in the Middle Ages in England*, pp. 285-288.

97. *Parish life in medieval England* (New York, Cincinnati, Chicago: 1906), p. 220.

98. In an essay entitled "The medieval bishops" in the work, *Episcopacy ancient and modern* (Macmillan, London: 1930), pp. 79-80.

99. C. 5 — Hardouin, VII, 1226.

100. C. 6 — Hefele-Leclercq, VI, 734; Hardouin, VII, 1384.

Sens (1485) declared that, after the bishop had been garbed in the proper ecclesiastical dress and the candles had been lighted, the Blessed Sacrament was to be visited.[101] The Council of Seville (1512) made the visit to the Blessed Sacrament on the part of the visitor an essential requisite or the *conditio sine qua non,* for if he failed to comply with this stipulation the church was not considered visited and the rector (*praefectus*) or person in charge of the church was not obligated to offer anything in procuration. In other words, the visit was null and void of juridical effect without this ceremony. If the rector perchance had paid the procuration, his act could not be officially recognized, nor could it be honored as an act which fulfilled the law's requirement concerning the payment of the procuration.[102]

Article 6. Procuration

It seems that no council of any note[103] enacted any law on procuration during the early part of this period. The first general law appeared in the year 1179. Then for the first time the Church intervened to correct an abuse that had arisen with the canonical institution of the visitation. The fourth canon of the III General Lateran Council was a stinging indictment of the extravagance of some of the prelates in its lament over the events that occurred. The seriousness of the situation can be gauged from the acknowledgment made in the canon itself. For after citing the example of the Apostle St. Paul, who in no way burdened those to whom he preached, this canon stated that such excessive demands were made at times that the church ornaments had to be offered for sale to cover the cost of the procuration. This was due to the sumptuous banquets which were exacted for the large retinue that accompanied the prelates as well as to the lavish

101. Art. II, cap. 3: "... Sacramenta, praesertim eucharistiam, cum habitu ecclesiastico honesto, accensis luminaribus, devote visitent...." — Mansi, XXXII, 417.

102. Cap. 45 — Mansi, XXXII, 619.

103. An exception is the Council of Lillebonne (1080) which allowed the archdeacon to accept food for a period of five days if that were expedient, at each of the three places or stations designated by the bishop, from the priests who came to the appointed place during a period of three days. C. 6 — Hardouin, VI, 1599; Hefele-Leclercq, V, 279.

equipage, caparison and display which attended their escort. Wherefore it was ordained that archbishops visiting their dioceses were to employ in their entourage not more than forty or fifty horses according to the different conditions of the provinces and the resources of the churches; cardinals, not more than twenty-five; bishops not more than twenty or thirty; archdeacons, five or seven; and deacons delegated by the bishops were to be content with two.[104] Furthermore, the prelates were forbidden to take hunting dogs or birds along with them.[105] Finally, the council points out that the above-mentioned provisions were to obtain only in places where the revenues and the resources of the church were more abundant. Therefore, in poorer places the prelates were not to come with an augmented train even though they were allowed to do so by the terms of this law, for the rule was to be observed that by the coming of many the few were not to be burdened.[106]

The Provincial Council of Rouen (1189) in addressing itself to the archdeacons commanded them to refrain from accepting the procuration from any cleric lacking a suitable income. If the archdeacon could not make his stay at a particular parish because of existing conditions, he was to receive but three solidi in compensation. However, on the other hand, if other circumstances demanded his stay at a poor cleric's home, the four or five neighbouring clerics enjoying a benefice were to shoulder the burden.[107]

If the visitor's retinue exceeded the number determined by the III General Lateran Council, then, so Pope Clement III (1187-1191) declared, the places visited were liberated from paying the procuration which was in excess of what could be rightfully demanded. Moreover,

104. Many of the ensuing particular councils emphasized this point in bringing the general law to the attention of the prelates.

105. The Councils of London (1321 and 1342) both make mention of prelates going hunting instead of fulfilling their obligations when going around their districts. — cc. 2, 7 — Hardouin, VII, 1458; and VII, 1650.

106. C. 4 — Hardouin, VII, 1675; Mansi, XXII, 219; Hefele-Leclercq, V, 1091. This continued to be the chief law on the matter of procuration. Later general laws were in the main but modifications of this one. Cf. c. 6, X, *de censibus, exactionibus et procurationibus*, III, 39.

107. C. 12 — Hardouin, VI, 1906; Hefele-Leclercq, V, 1159.

if the visitor passed sentence against his subjects (for example, an excommunication) because of their failure to comply with his request, it was of no effect.[108]

The Council of London (1200) claimed that if the visitor did not exercise his duty in the proper manner he was forbidden to ask for the procuration or its equivalent.[109] The Council of Paris (1212) took up the matter of visitation as affecting the archdeacons. If they failed to visit personally or if they did not fulfill their obligation at a particular church[110] they were not to demand the procuration or its equivalent. If anyone had acted against this prescription and, after having been warned, failed to amend, the aforesaid procuration was to be forfeited by him. Then if he still persisted in his evil way, he was to be excommunicated.[111]

At the IV General Lateran Council (1215) procuration was acknowledged as something due the bishops and others who performed the visitation.[112] At this council the conditions posited by the Capitulary of Toulouse (844) and reaffirmed by the Council of Paris (1212) received official approbation and obtained the force of universal law. According to the thirty-third canon of the council the prelates were to be entitled to a moderate procuration, but only when they made the visit personally and abided by the provisions of the III General Lateran

108. C. 7, X, *de excessibus praelatorum et subditorum,* V, 31.

109. C. 5: "... Sane ad praecidendum tam avaritiae quam negligentiae vitium, auctoritate Toletani Concilii subnixi, praecipimus, ut visitator ab ecclesia, in qua visitationis officium debito modo non exercet, procurationem aut procurationis redemptionem exigere non praesumat". The reference to the Council of Toledo could not be traced. Which of the Councils of Toledo is referred to cannot be determined, for none of the canons of the Toledo Councils treated the subject in this manner unless the reference is merely to the fact that the VII Council of Toledo (646) legislated against the avarice manifested by some of the visitors. Cf. *supra,* p. 25. Cf. also c. 6 of the Provincial Council of Tours (also called Angers, 1448) for similar legislation — Mansi, XXXII, 82.

110. Cf. also the Council of Saumur (1253), c. 9 — Hardouin, VII, 442; Hefele-Leclercq, VI, 75.

111. C. 15 — Hardouin, VII, 2003; Mansi, XXII, 823; Hefele-Leclercq, V, 1310.

112. Subsequent councils added the same expression: "procurationes quae visitationis ratione debentur episcopis", or its equivalent.

Council (1179) with regard to the limited numbers allowed for their entourage. If anyone infringed upon this law, he was bound to make restitution.[113]

The Council of Oxford (1222) forbade the archdeacons to invite strangers to the procurations provided for them although it allowed the rectors of churches to do so out of respect for the dignitaries.[114] The Council of Chateau-Gonthier (1231) anticipated the legislation of Pope Innocent IV (1243-1254), for it prohibited prelates from taking the procuration in the form of money, that is, from accepting money in lieu of the provisions, stating that this practice was contrary to the *statuta* of the General Council.[115] The Council of London (1237), over which Otto, the legate of the Apostolic See, presided, warned the visitors against collusion and particularly the practice of accepting bribes

113. C. 33 — Hardouin, VII, 43; Hefele-Leclercq, V, 1360; c. 23, X, *de censibus, exactionibus et procurationibus,* III, 39. The Councils of London (1237 and 1268) and the councils of a later date emphasize the matter of restitution; c. 20 (1237) — Wilkins, I, 654; Hardouin, VII, 298; Mansi, XXIII, 457; c. 19 (1268) — Wilkins, II, 9; given as c. 20 — Hardouin, VII, 629; XXIII, 1235.

114. C. 22 — Wilkins, I, 588; c. 21 — Hardouin VII, 119; Hefele-Leclercq, V, 1432. Cf. also the Council of London (1237), c. 20 — Hardouin, VII, 298; the Synod of Worcester (1240), c. 25 — Hardouin, VII, 339; the Council of London (1268), c. 20 — Hardouin, VII, 629. The diocesan Synod of Exeter (1287) suspended clerics who forced themselves on a procuration and ordered a temperate rebuke to be given to lay persons who violated the law in this regard with the admonition that they refrain from doing so in the future — c. 40 — Hardouin, VII, 1107; the Council of Marsiac (1326) forbade the archdeacon to invite anyone to partake of the procuration if by so doing the procuration were to exceed the amount set for it in its monetary value of thirty solidi in Tours currency — c. 38 — Hardouin, VII, 1525.

115. C. 13 — Hardouin, VII, 193; Hefele-Leclercq, V, 1531. Cf. also the diocesan Synod of Worcester (1240), c. 25 — Hardouin, VII, 339. Obviously the reference is to the III (1179) or IV General Lateran Council (1215), but no explicit terms outlawing money were used either in the thirty-third canon of the latter or in the fourth canon of the former of these two councils. Nevertheless, the fourth canon does speak of the sumptuous meals which were not to be exacted. Thus the interpretation of this canon by the Council held at Chateau-Gonthier was that the procuration was to be provided only in kind and not in its monetary value.

from interested parties in an effort to escape detection, correction and punishment in the course of the visitation.[116]

In 1246 another general law appeared on procuration in the constitution "*Romana Ecclesia*" of Pope Innocent IV.[117] It decreed that procurations were to be received according to what was determined in the canons. However, neither the visiting prelate nor any attendant was to accept any money, notwithstanding any contrary custom, or any other claim based on the plea of some service or presented under any other guise or pretext. They were to receive the procuration in kind.[118] Furthermore, neither the prelate nor any attendant was to presume to accept any gift,[119] whatever it might be or in whatever manner it was offered. The recipient who made himself guilty by accepting such a gift incurred a curse (*maledictio divina*) from which he was not freed until he gave back twice as much as he received or demanded.[120]

The Council of Albi in 1254 emphasized the fact that the churches themselves had to be visited,[121] either by the bishop or by one who was prudent and honest. Moreover, since the visitor was not to delay without a reasonable cause, it restricted the stay at a church to one day.[122] In the province of Tours, France, the amount of food to be served received special consideration, for at the Provincial Council of Nantes (1264) it was decided that the prelates were to receive but two courses of food. Whatever surplus was prepared without the per-

116. C. 20 — Hardouin, VII, 298; Hefele-Leclercq, V, 1581; for a similar law cf. the Council of Apt (1365), c. 9 — Mansi, XXVI, 449; Hefele-Leclercq, VI, 956; and the Council of London (1268), c. 20 — Hardouin, VII, 629; Hefele-Leclercq, VI, 144.

117. C. 1, *de censibus, exactionibus et procurationibus,* III, 20, in VI°.

118. Cf. the Council of Saumur (1253), c. 9 — Hardouin, VII, 443; and the Council of Albi (1254), c. 57 — Hardouin, VII, 467.

119. Cf. Council of Albi (1254), c. 57 — Hardouin, VII, 467.

120. C. 24 — Hardouin, VII, 716; Mansi, XXIV, 97; Hefele-Leclercq, VI, 202. "The threatened penalty," as Schroeder remarks, "meant no more than that the prohibition bound *sub peccato mortali,* and was not likely, therefore, to put an end to the abuse." — Schroeder, *Disciplinary decrees of the general councils,* p. 354.

121. Cf. also the Council of London (1268), c. 19 — Hardouin, VII, 628; Hefele-Leclercq, VI, 144.

122. C. 60 — Hardouin, VII, 467.

mission of the prelates was to be given to the poor.[123] The Council of London (1268), over which cardinal Ottoboni, the legate of the Apostolic See, presided, stated that bishops and other inferior prelates should not burden their subjects with expenses exceeding in quantity and number such as were determined in the constitution of Pope Innocent IV.[124]

At the II General Council of Lyons (1274), the fourteenth general council, it was expressly acknowledged in the twenty-fourth chapter ("*Exigit*") that the law of Innocent IV ("*Romana Ecclesia*") was not being obeyed. To enforce it, Pope Gregory X (1271-1276) introduced a sanction. Thus the law of this council was a mere confirmation of the constitution of Innocent IV, to which Pope Gregory added penalties. Hence, the law ordained that anyone who demanded money, or even accepted it from one who willingly offered it, or presumed to violate the constitution itself by receiving gifts[125] either in accepting the procuration in consumable goods without fulfilling the visitation or in availing himself of anything else on the occasion of the visitation, would be bound within a space of one month to make restitution in double the amount to the church from which he obtained the money or the gift. Then in stating the sanction Pope Gregory X made a distinction by reason of the rank of the visitor. Patriarchs, archbishops and bishops would incur the interdict *ab ingressu ecclesiae,* if they did not comply with the conditions stated above with respect to the amount and the time within which the restitution was to be made, while inferior

123. C. 5 — Hardouin, VII, 557; Hefele-Leclercq, VI, 118.

124. C. 19: "... Episcopi vero et alii inferiores praelati cum visitant, in superflua comitia, seu evectionum numero, vel alias in expensis, gravare subditos non praesumant, ultra quantitatem et numerum determinatum in constitutione felicis recordationis Innocentii Papae IV. . . ." — Hardouin, VII, 628; Hefele-Leclercq, VI, 144. As has been seen, the constitution "*Romana Ecclesia*" of Pope Innocent IV made no mention of any *definite* amount with regard to procurations (". . . . sed in victualibus expensas tantum recipiat moderatas. . . ." — c. 1, *de censibus, exactionibus, et procurationibus,* III, 20 in VI°), unless perhaps a special constitution was addressed to the English Church on this point.

125. Cf. the Council of Nogaro (1303), c. 11, by the terms of which any attendant who accepted a gift was excommunicated *ipso facto,* as long as he did not make restitution in double the amount. — Mansi, XXV, 1114. Cf. also the Council of Marsiac (1326), c. 38 — Hardouin, VII, 1525.

prelates or the clergy of lower rank were suspended from their office and benefice.[126]

The Council of Langeais (1278) in the province of Tours, France, made an exception to the universal law. It approved the acceptance of money from places where it had been a custom or practice of long standing and wherever through force of circumstances the place visited was not in a position to give the visiting prelate the procuration in consumable goods. However, one was bound to visit the places before he could accept the procuration in its monetary value.[127]

In 1298 Pope Boniface VIII effected a change in the existing law. He was impelled to do so because his experience had taught him how inconvenient it was for the visitor and visited alike to comply with the actual law. Therefore he allowed patriarchs, archbishops, bishops and others who were bound in the line of their official duty to perform the visitations to accept money in lieu of the procuration from the rectors or persons in charge of the churches and places visited, if

126. C. 2, *de censibus, exactionibus et procurationibus,* III, 20, in VI°; c. 24 — Hardouin, VII, 716; Mansi, XXIV, 97; Hefele-Leclercq, VI, 202. As to the meaning of the clause in the text *"visitationis officio non impenso"*, Schroeder quotes Duranti, fol. 83, who says: "Respicit praecedentia ac sequentia, punitur ergo hic, qui procurationes recipit in pecunia vel etiam aliis a locis non visitatis et haec fuit mens papae, prout saepe ab ipso audivi, licet littera ista confuse loquatur." — *Disciplinary decrees of the general councils,* p. 354, n. 65. Schroeder also writes in the following manner concerning the clause, *"ingressum sibi ecclesiae sentiant interdictum"*; "that is, they are forbidden to enter a church, to celebrate the divine offices therein, or even to assist passively at the service. This penalty does not come under the head of suspension, unless for the sake of giving it a name, we understand it in a very broad sense. It is rather a form of punishment that is distinct from and independent of every other form. Suspension can be imposed on clerics only, whereas the *interdictum ab ingressu ecclesiae* can be imposed also on laymen (c. 15, C. XXXII, q. 2). Moreover, suspension deprives a cleric either totally or partially of the exercise of the power of orders, office, or benefice, but it does not deprive him of those rights that he has in common with the laity; it does not exclude him from the reception of the sacraments, from the passive participation of divine services, etc., whereas the *interdictum ab ingressu ecclesiae* deprives him of both. Sometimes the prohibition is called *suspensio* (c. ult. VI°, *De off. ordinarii,* I, 16), but that does not mean that they are alike in penal content." Kober, *Die suspension,* pp. 237 ff. — Schroeder, *op. cit.,* p. 353, footnote 60.

127. C. 1 — Hardouin, VII, 759; Hefele-Leclercq, VI, 240.

these were willing to make money payments. Nevertheless, this obtained only on the day they made the visit personally, and on that day they were allowed but one procuration, despite the fact that they visited several places or even though the places visited were economically able to supply an entire procuration or its monetary equivalent.[128] The Council of London (1321), legislating against archdeacons, superiors and other ordinaries who, while they were supposed to be making their canonical visit, instead devoted themselves to hunting or other pastimes, claimed that no one of the above-mentioned was to presume to accept any procuration unless he personally scrutinized and inspected all that was subject to an inquiry.[129] The Council of Marsiac (1326) legislated against the anticipated procuration obtained in view of a future visitation. The penalty of suspension was placed on those who did not comply with this regulation.[130]

Acting on the advice of his fellow-bishops, Pope Benedict XII (1334-1342), in his effort to forestall future abuses, issued his constitution "*Vas electionis*" in 1336.[131] This was an itemized account according to which the payment of the procuration was to be gauged throughout the Catholic world. He divided the then known Christian world into four parts or regions. For each of these regions the Pope made out a list of fixed taxes, beyond which no one could make any rightful claim, graded according to the ranks of the visiting prelates and the classes of churches, monasteries and other moral persons to be visited. Thus, elaborate definite scales or standards were furnished to point out the limits within which alone all lawful demands for the procuration, whether it was paid in consumable goods or in money, could be made. If, because of an apostolic privilege,

128. C. 3, *de censibus, exactionibus et procurationibus*, III, 20, in VI°. Cf. the Provincial Council of Seville (also known as the Spanish Council, 1512), cap. 45 — Mansi, XXXII, 618.

129. C. 2 — Hardouin, VII, 1458; cf. also the Council of Marsiac (1326), c. 38 — Hardouin, VII, 1525, and the Council of London (1342), c. 7 — Hardouin, VII, 1649.

130. C. 38 — Hardouin, VII, 1525.

131. C. un., *de censibus, exactionibus et procurationibus*, III, 10, in Extravag. com. Pirhing claims this constitution was never put into general practice and as a result fell into desuetude (lib. III, tit. 39, n. 69).

prelates used substitutes to make the visitations, the corresponding procurations were considerably lowered. Moreover, if in view of a prevalent custom to the contrary or as a result of existing pacts the standards in certain localities were lower than those determined by this constitution, the prelates and places concerned were to abide by the custom and pacts. However, no pretext of custom or of any other sort justified a higher sum. Furthermore, in addition to the renewal of the penalties of the II General Council of Lyons (1274) for the acceptance of gifts and the exaction of excessive procurations, the constitution imposed penalties on the members of the retinue who were guilty of such practices. A cleric was to be suspended from his office and benefice, whereas a lay person was to be under interdict *ab ingressu ecclesiae* and at the same time barred from the reception of the Eucharist.[132]

In 1365 the bishops of three provinces in the south of France met in council at Apt near Avignon. The council placed the procuration for metropolitans and suffragans alike at four florins, which the places visited would either pay or supply in kind.[133] The council also prohibited the bishop or his vicar from entering into any kind of pact with a person in charge of a church or benefice whereby the places to be visited would be exempt from a visitation in consideration of the annual or biennial procuration. Those in possession of such an unlawfully paid procuration at the time the law was passed were bound to restitution within a month's time after the promulgation of this law. Thus the law was retroactive. If they failed to make restitution they were to be compelled to pay double the amount.[134]

The Provincial Council of Seville (also known as the Spanish Council, 1512) decreed that neither the visitor nor his notary were to be entertained (*hospitentur*) at the homes of the rectors (*praefecti*) or administrators of the churches, under penalty of the loss of a

132. Cf. also the Council of Sens (1485), art. II, cap. III — Mansi, XXXII, 418.

133. C. 10 — Mansi, XXVI, 449; Hefele-Leclercq, VI, 956. It was but a tentative arrangement, an experiment, for the law was to last but four years.

134. C. 9 — Mansi, *loc. cit.;* Hefele-Leclercq, *loc. cit.* Cf. the Council of London (1237), c. 20 — Hardouin, VII, 298; Hefele-Leclercq, V, 1581; and the Council of London (1268), cap. 20 — Hardouin, VII, 629; Hefele-Leclercq, VI, 144.

thousand *morapetini*,[135] to be sustained by him who received them into his house. The visitor and the notary on the other hand were to be deprived of their emoluments and in addition were to be fined to the amount of two thousand *morapetini*. Moreover, if the church was to be considered as visited, it was necessary for the visitor to enter the church and pay a visit to the Blessed Sacrament; otherwise the church was officially adjudged as not visited and the rector of the church was not to make any payment to the visitor. If he did, it was regarded as not paid.[136]

135. One of which was worth five or six solidi.
136. Cap. 45 — Mansi, XXXII, 619.

CHAPTER IV

FROM THE COUNCIL OF TRENT TO THE CODE OF CANON LAW

Article 1. Purpose of the Visitation

In setting forth the general law for the visitation the Council of Trent also included its aim. It stated that the principal object of the visitation was to secure sound and orthodox doctrine by the eradication of heresies, to maintain good morals, and to correct by admonition and exhortation such as were evil, to animate the people to religion, peace and innocence, and to initiate whatever else might be prompted by the prudence of the visitor for the benefit of the faithful according as time, place, and opportunity would allow.[1]

In the seventh session the council declared that ordinaries in their annual visitation of the churches were to make sure by suitable legal remedies that whatever needed repairs was to be repaired and that wherever the churches were deficient in their pastoral service the proper care of souls was to be effected.[2] In the twenty-first session it prefaced the treatment of the visitation of commendatory monasteries and benefices with the statement that in the diocese the ordinary was to take care of whatsoever pertained to the worship of God, and wherever there was any other spiritual need, he was to provide for the same.[3] The twenty-second session directed the bishops to take cognizance of and to see to the performance of all things instituted for the worship of God, for the salvation of souls, and for the support of the poor.[4]

The particular councils either repeated the very words of the Council of Trent, or stated the same in substance. At the IV Provincial Council of Milan (1576), St. Charles Borromeo (1538-1584) stated as one of the purposes of the visitation the restoration of primitive Christian

1. Conc. Trident., sess. XXIV, *de ref.*, c. 3.
2. Conc. Trident., sess. VII, *de ref.*, c. 8.
3. Conc. Trident., sess. XXI, *de ref.*, c. 8.
4. Conc. Trident., sess. XXII, *de ref.*, c. 8.

discipline among the clergy and the laity.[5] Some of the particular councils specified the conferring of the Sacrament of Confirmation.[6] Hence the administration of the Sacrament of Confirmation held an important place in the purpose of the visitation. Evidence is had to this effect in the text of the laws of the particular councils. For example, the Council of Quebec (1863) used the expression "besides the administration of the Sacrament of Confirmation" in conjunction with the expression of the purpose as stated by the Council of Trent.[7]

On the other hand, the II Plenary Council of Baltimore (1866) reminded the bishops that they were to visit their dioceses not merely to administer the Sacrament of Confirmation, but that they might know their flock, and might better provide for their spiritual welfare.[8] At the III Plenary Council of Baltimore (1884) the emphasis was shifted. The council declared that the bishop was to visit his diocese not only that he might know his flock, but also that through the administration of the Sacrament of Confirmation he might strengthen the faithful who were exposed to so many dangers of losing their faith. It also stressed the need of making an inquiry into the temporal administration of the churches.[9]

With a wealth of experience behind him, Pope Benedict XIV well expressed the scope of the visitation in the words: "There are many things concerning which the bishop will be ignorant, many things will escape his attention, and again many things will come to his knowledge too late for any effective action, unless he betake himself to all parts

5. Pars III, cap. III, *de visitatione* — Hardouin, X, 901.

6. I Provincial Council of Milan (1565), pars III, cap. XXX — Hardouin, X, 673; V Provincial Council of Milan (1579), cap. VIII — Hardouin, X, 977; the Provincial Council of Bordeaux (1583), tit. XXXII — Hardouin, X, 1375; the Provincial Council of Aix (1585), tit. *de visit.* — Hardouin, X, 1550; the Provincial Council of Aquileia (1596), rubrica XIII — Hardouin, X, 1910.

7. Decr. VI, par. 2 — *Coll. Lac.*, III, 674; cf. also the Council of Rheims (1849), tit. XIII, cap. II — *Coll.* Lac., IV, 132; the Council of Toledo (1850), tit. I, cap. II, decr. X — *Coll. Lac.*, IV, 1036.

8. N. 86 — *Concilii plenarii Baltimorensis II, acta et decreta* (Baltimorae, 1868) — *Coll. Lac.*, III, 427.

9. N. 14 — *Acta et decreta concilii plenarii Baltimorensis III* (Baltimorae, 1886).

of his diocese, and unless he *personally* view every place and hear all things, and ascertain which evils are to be cured, what have been their causes, and in what manner their reappearance can be providently averted."[10]

Article 2. The Obligation of the Bishop

The Council of Trent considered the episcopal visitation as a means of reforming the Church and of eradicating heresies. The twenty-fourth session set forth the general law on the subject. At this session the council declared that patriarchs, primates, metropolitans, and bishops were not to fail to visit their respective dioceses personally or, if they were lawfully hindered, through their vicar general or visitor. Furthermore, they were to make the visit annually unless the extent of the diocese forbade this, whereupon they or their visitors were to visit the greater part of the diocese within one year so that the whole would be completed within two years.[11]

The Provincial Council of Toledo (1565) obliged the bishops who could not visit their entire dioceses in person to devote at least three continuous or uninterrupted months a year to a visitation of a part of the diocese outside the cathedral city. It claimed that the bishop was not to be excused by any impediment. Then it gave an interpretation of the clause "if lawfully hindered". Only an urgent necessity involving either the public or his own private welfare, spiritual or corporal, was to prevent him from making the visitation personally.[12]

The Council of Bordeaux (1624) ordered the bishops to make a visit of their dioceses at least once every three years.[13] Fagnanus testifies that the Sacred Congregation of the Council ordered the word

10. Ep. Encycl. "*Ubi Primum*", 3 dec. 1740, n. 5 — *Fontes*, n. 304; Lucidi, *De visitatione sacrorum liminum* (3. ed., Romae, 1883), I, 151.

11. Conc. Trident., sess. XXIV, *de ref.*, c. 3. The provincial and national councils of this period made efforts to enforce this law. Some of the councils merely repeated certain parts of the law of the Council of Trent, either verbatim or in substance, while others modified or enlarged on its terms. Reference will be made to one or the other of the particular councils whenever a particular point will warrant it.

12. Act. II, 2 — Hardouin, X, 1148.

13. C. 8 — Hardouin, XI, 108.

biennio to be inserted instead of *triennio* in conformity with the Tridentine law.[14]

In a constitution Pope Clement XII (1730-1740) reminded the cardinal bishops of the six suburbicarian sees that they had the obligation of making the visitation of their dioceses in conformity with the sacred canons and the decrees of the Council of Trent. This law bound them even if they assisted the Pope in the Roman Curia.[15] Pope Benedict XIV (1740-1758) in an encyclical letter commanded the bishops to visit their dioceses personally, unless a grave and legitimate cause prevented them from doing so, but failed to specify any time within which the visitation was to be fulfilled.[16] The bishops of Ireland were advised to visit their dioceses frequently,[17] while the bishop of Peking was charged personally to perform this duty outside the city limits as well as within the episcopal city.[18] Pope Pius IX (1846-1878) told the bishops of the Austrian Empire that they were to consider nothing more important committed to their care than the visitation of their dioceses.[19] Then he warned the bishops of Portugal not to dispense with the diligent visitation of their diocese.[20]

The Council of Aquitaine (1851) declared that a notable part of the diocese should be visited every year so that the visitation be completed within a few years (*paucis annis*).[21] The II Plenary Council of Baltimore (1866) brought the attention of the bishops to the fact that they had a strict obligation to visit their dioceses frequently and regularly. If they could not visit all their churches annually, either because of their number or because of great distances between them, they were to visit the larger parishes, and those nearer the episcopal city. However, they were to arrange their visits so that they would complete the visitation of the entire diocese within two years in conformity with the law of the Council of Trent, or, if that were not possible, at least within

14. Lib. II, tit. 24, cap. 4, n. 78.

15. "*Pastorale officium*", 10 ian. 1731 — *Fontes*, n. 295.

16. "*Ubi primum*", 3 dec. 1740, n. 5 — *Fontes*, n. 304.

17. S. C. de Prop. Fide, instr. (ad Archiep. Hiberniae), 25 iun. 1791 — *Fontes*, n. 4631.

18. S. C. de Prop. Fide (C. P.), 14 ian. 1798 — *Fontes*, n. 4659.

19. Ep. Encycl. "*Singulari quidem*", 17 mart. 1856 — *Fontes*, n. 521.

20. Ep. "*Quo graviori*", 8 iul. 1862 — *Fontes*, n. 535.

21. Tit. II, cap. II, decr. 34 — *Coll. Lac.*, IV, 1176.

every three years.[22] The III Plenary Council of Baltimore (1884) renewed the prescription in requiring the bishops to visit the entire diocese at least every three years.[23]

According to the First Schema of the Vatican Council (1870) the bishop was to complete his pastoral visitation within three years. But if the extent of the diocese made this impossible, he was to visit the greater part of it within this period so that he would complete the entire visitation of the diocese within five years.[24] The Ruthenian Provincial Council held at Lwow (1891) allowed the bishops a period of five years within which they were to make a visitation of their entire dioceses. It made this concession primarily because of the vastness of the dioceses. Another reason advanced was that the rural deans, acting as vicars of the bishops, made an annual visitation of the parishes within their territory.[25]

The Plenary Council of Latin America held at Rome (1899) directed the bishops to visit their entire dioceses. However, no time was specified. Allowing for the extent of the dioceses, and nevertheless realizing the utility of the personal visit on the part of the bishop, the Council decided that the bishop to the best of his ability was to see to it that at an opportune time he was to make a visitation of the places visited by his delegate. To accomplish this the more easily, the diocese was to be divided into regions and each one was to be successively visited by the bishop, so that within a certain number of years the whole diocese would be visited.[26] A similar arrangement was decreed

22. N. 86 — *Concilii plenarii Baltimorensis II, acta et decreta;* cf. also the Council of Westminster (1852), decr. 29 — *Coll. Lac.*, III, 791.

23. N. 14 — *Acta et decreta concilii plenarii Baltimorensis III.* The Plenary Council of Australia held at Sydney (1885) adopted the three-year period. — *Acta et decreta concilii plenarii Australasiae* (Sydney, 1887), n. 22.

24. Sec. I, cap. III — Martin, *Omnium concilii vaticani documentorum collectio* (2. ed., Paderbornae, 1873), p. 130. In the *postulata* of the bishops of Germany, there was a plea that, wherever possible, the dioceses should be circumscribed, since because of the vastness of many dioceses the bishops were unable to fulfill even the most important tasks of their office. Sec. II, n. 2. — *op. cit.*, p. 175.

25. Tit. VII, cap. 3, n. 2 — *Acta et decreta synodi provincialis Ruthenorum Galiciae* (Romae, 1896).

26. N. 200 — *Acta et decreta concilii plenarii Americae Latinae* (Typis Vaticanis: Romae, 1902), p. 99.

by the First Plenary Council of Quebec (1909). However, this council definitely stated that the whole diocese was to be visited within a four year period.[27]

In a pastoral letter of the year 1905 the bishop of Harrisburg informed his priests that a visitation of the diocese was in order. For he stated that the cardinal prefect of the Propaganda, in a letter dated May 22, 1905, had called his attention to the fact that the canonical visitation of the diocese had never been made. Hence, in compliance with this notice, he instructed his clerics to make preparations for the visitation.[28]

Whereas Pope Clement XII recalled to the minds of the bishops of the six suburbicarian sees that they had the obligation of visiting their churches, Pope Pius X (1903-1914) declared that the cardinal bishops had the right of visitation which was to be exercised at their own discretion.[29]

In a decree of the Sacred Consistorial Congregation, which was obligatory upon all bishops not subject to the Congregation of the Propagation of the Faith, it was pointed out that the *Ad Limina* Visit and Report to the Holy See were not to be confused with the law on the diocesan visitation. The law for the latter as prescribed by the Council of Trent in the twenty-fourth session continued to be in force.[30]

Co-Visitors

The sixth session of the Council of Trent, while treating of the visitation of the chapters of cathedrals and other larger churches, granted the bishop the privilege of visiting them alone or in the company of those whom he thought fit to accompany him.[31]

27. *Acta et decreta concilii plenarii Quebecensis I* (Quebec, 1912), n. 101.

28. *American ecclesiastical review,* XXXIII (1905), 184. The diocese of Harrisburg was established in 1866. Cf. Guilday, *The history of the councils of Baltimore* (The Macmillan Company, New York, 1932), p. 22.

29. Const. "*Apostolica*", 15 apr. 1910, n. XVI — *Fontes,* n. 686.

30. *A remotissima,* 31 dec. 1909, c. VII — *Fontes,* n. 2064.

31. Conc. Trident., sess. VI, *de ref.,* c. 4. Pope Honorius III (1216-1227) required the bishop to have two or three canons as companions in the visitation of monasteries; c. 17, X, *de officio iudicis ordinarii,* I, 31. For a discussion of this point, cf. Fagnanus, lib. I, tit. 31, c. 17, n. 37 sq.

At the IV Provincial Council of Milan (1576) it was decided that the bishop could on his visitation avail himself of one or two canons or other ecclesiastics as aides in carrying out his work.[32] In a reply of the Sacred Congregation of the Council, of the 27th of May, 1713, it was stated that the bishop could select one or two canons of the cathedral church for the duration of the visitation of the cathedral city and diocese.[33] Another reply directly affecting the vicar capitular advised that the latter was to be guided by the deceased bishop's mode of action. Therefore, if the bishop had used co-visitors, he was to do likewise; if not, he was also to refrain from doing so.[34] The Council of Avignon (1725) charged the bishops to select clerics as their companions for the visitation.[35] The III Plenary Council of Baltimore (1884) directed the bishop to have one or two co-visitors to be chosen from among the priests excelling in knowledge and experience as administrators.[36] By the decree of the Sacred Consistorial Congregation of the year 1909, one of the co-visitors was required to sign the quinquennial report.[37] This legislation was in effect even at the promulgation of the Code, which permits co-visitors, but does not require them.[38] The legislation of the Code is in harmony with the new formula for making the report, wherein no mention is made of the signature of any co-visitor. Although this new formula was issued on November 4, 1918, it did not go into effect until the year 1921.[39]

ARTICLE 3. OBJECTS VISITED

The sixth session of the Council of Trent declared that the chapters of the cathedrals and other larger churches were subject to the visitation of the bishop notwithstanding exemptions, contrary customs,

32. Pars III, cap. 3 — Hardouin, X, 900; cf. also the Council of Aix (1585), tit. *de visit.* — Hardouin, X, 1553; the Council of Toledo (1590), pars IV, cap. 8 — Hardouin, X, 1826.

33. Pallottini, IX, p. 327. .

34. S. C. C. 13 sept. 1721 — *Fontes*, n. 3232.

35. Tit. XI, cap. 4 — *Coll. Lac.*, I, 493.

36. N. 14 — *Acta et decreta concilii plenarii Baltimorensis III.*

37. "*A remotissima*", 31 dec. 1909, capp. 3 and 4 — *Fontes*, n. 2064.

38. C. 343, § 2.

39. S. C. Consist., 4 nov. 1918 — *AAS*, X (1918), 487.

judgments, oaths or agreements.[40] The next session declared that ecclesiastical benefices with the care of souls which had been always united and annexed to cathedrals, collegiate or other churches, to monasteries, colleges or other pious places, were to be visited annually by their ordinaries.[41] The Council likewise stated that, empowered with apostolic authority, local ordinaries were to visit all churches, no matter in what manner they were exempt.[42]

It was also determined that no cleric under any pretext whatsoever was exempt from the correction, punishment and visitation of the bishop.[43] Furthermore, it was pointed out that honorary titles and particular privileges would not derogate in any way from the right of bishops over the persons bearing them.[44] The twenty-first session enjoined the bishops as delegates of the Holy See to visit annually commendatory monasteries, as also abbeys, priories and provostries wherein a regular observance was not in effect, as well as all regular or secular benefices even though they were exempt and without the care of souls.[45] In the decree concerning the things to be observed and avoided in the celebration of Mass the ordinaries were reminded that they were to visit all oratories which were dedicated solely to divine worship.[46]

After referring to the legislation mentioned above concerning the visitation of benefices, the council at the twenty-fourth session commanded the bishop of the nearest cathedral to visit those secular churches which were said to be in no one's diocese (*nullius dioecesis*). If the bishop concerned could not do so, then the bishop whom the prelate of such a territory selected at the provincial council was obligated to make the visitation.[47] In monasteries or houses of men or women charged with the care of souls of persons other than those of the household, the individuals, whether regulars or seculars, who exercised that care were immediately subject to the jurisdiction, visita-

40. Conc. Trident., sess. VI, *de ref.*, c. 4.
41. Sess. VII, *de ref.*, c. 7.
42. Sess. VII, *de ref.*, c. 8.
43. Sess. XIV, *de ref.*, c. 4; sess. VI, *de ref.*, c. 3.
44. Sess. XXIV, *de ref.*, c. 11.
45. Sess. XXI, *de ref.*, c. 8.
46. Sess. XXII, *in decret. de observ. et evit. in celebrat. missae.*
47. Sess. XXIV, *de ref.*, c. 9.

tion and correction of the bishop in those things that pertained to that care and to the administration of the sacraments.[48] The observance of this prescription was demanded by Pope Gregory XV (1621-1623) in his constitution "*Inscrutabile*",[49] while Pope Benedict XIV made an effort to put an end to all doubts in this matter.[50]

The twenty-second session of the Council of Trent decreed that the bishops, as delegates of the Apostolic See, had the right to visit all hospitals, colleges, schools and confraternities of laymen, with the exception of those under the immediate protection of the kings. These, however, could be visited with their permission. Moreover, this right extended to charitable institutions and all other pious places no matter how designated, even though they were in the care of laymen or enjoyed a privilege of exemption. In the visitation they were to take cognizance of every phase of the work connected with the worship of God, the salvation of souls and the support of the poor, regardless of contrary custom, privilege or statute.[51]

The decree on the establishment of seminaries instructed bishops to visit their seminaries often, particularly for the purpose of ascertaining the observance of the internal rule.[52]

The provincial councils of this period renewed the prescriptions of the Council of Trent while the Roman Congregations settled controversies with regard to rights and exemptions.

Article 4. Manner of Proceeding

The thirteenth session of the Council of Trent stated that in causes relative to visitation and correction there could be no appeal from any interlocutory sentence or other grievance prior to the definitive sentence, unless such grievance could not be righted by the definitive

48. Sess. XXV, c. 11; cf. sess. VII, *de ref.*, c. 7.

49. 5 febr. 1622, ad 2, 4 — *Fontes*, n. 199.

50. Const. "*Firmandis*", 6 nov. 1744 — *Fontes*, n. 349. For a fuller treatment of the visitation of religious cf. Reilly, *The visitation of religious*, pp. 58-70.

51. Sess. XXII, *de ref.*, c. 8.

52. Sess. XXIII, *de ref.*, c. 18.

sentence or unless an appeal from the definitive sentence itself could not be interposed.[53] Then, with respect to the visitation of benefices and commendatory monasteries, the council in the twenty-first session decreed that regardless of any appeals whatsoever, or of privileges, or of contrary customs, even of such as were immemorial in their existence, or also of the injunctions of judges, the bishop had the right to provide suitable measures to assure that the required renovations and repairs be made, and that the care of souls as well as all other duties be diligently fulfilled.[54]

In the twenty-fourth session, after the council declared the principal object of the visitation, it admonished those who had the right of visitation to treat all with a fatherly love and Christian zeal in order that the end intended could be more easily realized.[55]

Nevertheless, that they might the more effectively keep the people dutiful and obedient, bishops were in all matters concerning visitation and the correction of morals accorded the right and power, even as delegates of the Apostolic See, to ordain, regulate, correct and execute, in accordance with the enactments of the canons, whatever in their prudence seemed necessary for the betterment of their subjects and for the good of their dioceses. Moreover, no exemption, injunction, appeal or complaint, even though addressed to the Holy See, would in any way bar or suspend the execution of those things which the bishops commanded, decreed or adjudged in connection with the visitation and the correction of morals.[56] Pope Benedict XIV reaffirmed the legislation of the Council of Trent and at the same time clarified it in many respects.[57]

Fagnanus testifies that on the first of February, 1607, the Congregation of the Council advised the bishop of Tournai to make no special judicial inquiry, to start no judicial process and to pass no judicial sentence in the course of the visitation, but to settle matters relating

53. Sess. XIII, *de ref.*, c. 1.

54. Sess. XXI, *de ref.*, c. 8.

55. Sess. XXIV, *de ref.*, c. 3.

56. Sess. XXIV, *de ref.*, c. 10. Cf. also Gregory XV, const. "*Inscrutabili*", 5 feb. 1622 — *Fontes*, n. 199.

57. Const. "*Ad militantes*", 30 mart. 1742, nn. 6, 10, 19, 21 — *Fontes*, n. 326.

to correction and the amendment of morals without any vestige of a judicial process.[58]

In regard to the manner of carrying out the visitation or the investigation proper the particular councils gave specific directions in this matter. The Councils of Milan[59] under the presidency of St. Charles Borromeo were especially significant in this respect. His influence can be seen in the acts of the particular councils from his time on.

On the seventh of March, 1904, the Sacred Congregation of the Council published rules for the apostolic visitation throughout Italy.[60] The next day the Sacred Congregation of the Apostolic Visitation issued norms which were to be used in the apostolic visitation of the city of Rome.[61]

Article 5. Procuration

With the view that the visitation produce salutary effects and yield invaluable results, the Council of Trent advised the bishops to be content with a modest train of horses and servants, and to try to complete the visitation as speedily as possible. During the visitation they were to be careful not to be troublesome or burdensome to anyone by useless expenses. Furthermore, neither the bishop nor any member of the entourage was to receive anything under the guise of procuration, be it money or a gift of any kind, notwithstanding contrary customs, even though these were immemorial. However, frugal and moderate *victualia* were to be furnished to the entire company, but only during the time necessary for the visitation and no longer. Those who were visited nevertheless had the option of either supplying the *victualia* or of paying the procuration in money according to the fixed assessment which they had been wont to give.

This law on procuration did not affect the pacts entered into with monasteries or other pious places or nonparochial churches, whose

58. Lib. I, tit. 3, cap. 26, n. 46; cf. also Van Espen, *Ius ecclesiasticum universum*, pars I, tit. XVII, cap. IV, n. 6. Fagnanus also goes into a lengthy discussion to prove that ordinary causes were not to be heard during the visitation; lib. I, tit. 3, cap. 26, nn. 26-46.

59. I Provincial Council of Milan (1565), pars II, cap. 30; IV Provincial Council (1576), pars III, cap. 3; V Provincial Council, pars III, cap. 10 — *Acta ecclesiae Mediolanesis*, I, 81, 431, 687.

60. *ASS*, XXXVI (1904), 563-565, 607-609.

61. *ASS*, XXXVII (1904), 202-221, 275-289, 403-410.

rights remained inviolate. Then, too, the custom according to which no procuration under any form was received by the visitor who performed his work gratis was to continue in force in those places where it obtained.

Anyone who presumed to receive anything more than what was allowed in the above cases was bound to restore within a month's time double the amount received, otherwise he became liable to the penalties of the constitution *"Exigit"* of the Second General Council of Lyons (1274),[62] and also to the other penalties which provincial councils had decreed to inflict.[63]

At the I Provincial Council of Milan (1565) it was decreed that only two courses of food were to be served.[64] The Council of Aix (1585) went further in its determination of the food to be served. It stated that only one of the foods was to be served with gravy, and allowed but two kinds of fruits.[65] The Council of Bourges (1584) allowed censures to be inflicted as a means of compelling the payment of the procuration.[66]

At the I Provincial Council of Milan (1565) it was decided that the entourage of the bishop was to consist at the most of eight men and six horses,[67] while the IV Provincial Council of Milan (1576) allowed seven horses and ten men, counting the person sent before the bishop to announce his coming and to make preparations for the visit.[68] In this connection the Sacred Congregation of the Council would not commit itself. In its replies it merely repeated the words of

62. C. 24 — Harduin, VII, 716; Mansi, XXIV, 97; Hefele-Leclercq, VI, 202; c. 2, *de censibus, exactionibus et procurationibus,* III, 20 in VI°. Cf. Schroeder, *Disciplinary decrees of the general councils,* p. 353, for an English translation of this canon.

63. Conc. Trident., sess. XXIV, *de ref.,* c. 3.

64. Hardouin, X, 675; cf. also the Council of Toledo (1590), cap. VIII, n. 5 — Hardouin, X, 1826.

65. Tit. *de visit.* — Hardouin, X, 1553.

66. Tit. XXXIII, can. 6 — Hardouin, X, 1492.

67. Cap. XXX — Hardouin, X, 675.

68. Pars III, cap. III — Hardouin, X, 900; cf. also the Council of Aix (1585), which allowed from eight to ten horses and twelve to fourteen men, tit. *de visitatione* — Hardouin, X, 1550; and the Council of Avignon (1594), which permitted seven or eight men, tit. II — Hardouin, X, 1837.

the Council of Trent, and added that the more specific determination was left to the discretion and moderation of the bishop.[69]

The III Plenary Council of Baltimore (1884) declared that diocesan synods were to decide concerning the defrayal of expenses for the bishops and their co-visitors.[70] This position was also adopted by the Plenary Council of Australia (1885).[71]

However those who were visited were not obliged to supply for the expenses of the journey from one place to another.[72] And whoever demanded this inordinate emolument incurred the penalties prescribed by the Council of Trent.[73]

The penalties determined in the constitution "*Exigit*"[74] against those who presumed to demand more than a moderate procuration were omitted by the constitution "*Apostolicae Sedis*".[75] Only the prescription of the Council of Trent,[76] which left it to the discretion of the provincial council to impose a penalty on the offenders without any hope of obtaining leave or permission to the contrary continued in force until the promulgation of the Code of Canon Law.[77]

69. Pallottini, IX, p. 523, n. 217. Most of the particular councils also contented themselves with using the terminology of the Council of Trent.

70. N. 14 — *Acta et decreta concilii plenarii Baltimorensis III.*

71. *Acta et decreta concilii plenarii Australasiae*, n. 22.

72. *In Tarentina Procurationis,* 18 febr. 1826, ad IV — Pallottini, IX, 521-522, nn. 205-215; *Thesaurus Resolutionum Sacrae Congregationis Concilii* (Romae, 1718-1908), LXXXVI (1826), 74 (hereafter this collection will be cited as *Thesaurus*).

73. Pallottini, IX, p. 522, n. 214.

74. C. 2, *de censibus, exactionibus et procurationibus*, III, 20 in VI°; II Council of Lyons (1274), c. 24 — Hardouin, VII, 716; Mansi, XXIV, 97; Hefele-Leclercq, VI, 202.

75. Pius IX, const. "*Apostolicae Sedis*", 12 oct. 1869 — *Fontes*, n. 552.

76. Sess. XXIV, *de ref.*, c. 3.

77. Sebastianelli, *Praelectiones iuris canonici* (*De personis*), (2 ed., Romae, 1905), p. 224, n. 215.

HISTORICAL CONCLUSION

This historical study gives confirmation to the view that the first explicit legislation on the canonical visitation was not passed until the sixth century, when it was acknowledged as a custom of long standing. From that time on the particular councils renewed the obligation with an expression of the purpose of the visitation. The general aim of the visitation remained practically constant during the different periods. Nevertheless at various intervals the emphasis shifted to different items. Although no general law ever included the administration of the Sacrament of Confirmation, particular councils from the eighth century onward considered it as one of the main reasons for the visitation.

The obligation to make the visitation was always considered to be primarily incumbent on the bishop. However, it was not required that it be always personally fulfilled by the bishop. If he was impeded he was to delegate a person to perform the visitation. Although the episcopal visitation was regularly considered as an annual obligation, no universal law expressly declared it as such until the Tridentine legislation made its appearance. The latter, however, was of a conditional character. For if the extent of the diocese made it impossible to perform the visitation of the whole annually then the time allotted was a period of two years.

The material object of the visitation always included persons, places and things, though the early councils did not particularize in this respect.

With the appearance of the parochial synod during the Carolingian period the personal visitation took on an aspect of a judicial procedure. For the visitor functioned as a judge while the synodal witnesses acted as accusers. Nevertheless, the stress of the universal law throughout was on the fatherly or paternal method of proceeding in the course of the investigation. Hence the judicial method was exceptional.

From the earliest times some form of procuration was allowed the visitor. Divers amounts were permitted for the visitors and the entourage. Limits were determined for the latter. The procuration as a rule was made in consumable goods until the time of Pope Boniface VIII (1298). From that time on the places visited had the option of offering hospitality or giving the equivalent in money. The penalties against exorbitant demands inflicted by Pope Innocent IV

(1246), and by the Council of Lyons (1274), and confirmed by the Council of Trent, were revoked by the constitution "*Apostolicae Sedis*" (1869).

PART II

CANONICAL COMMENTARY

CHAPTER V

THE PURPOSE OF THE VISITATION

Canon 343, § 1: Ad sanam et orthodoxam doctrinam conservandam, bonos mores tuendos, pravos corrigendos, pacem, innocentiam, pietatem et disciplinam in populo et clero promovendam ceteraque pro ratione adiunctorum ad bonum religionis constituenda, . . ."

The visitation of the diocese like every canonical institution has its definite purpose. Thus the Code declares that the bishops have the obligation of making the diocesan visitation to preserve sound and orthodox doctrine, to maintain good morals, to correct such as are evil, to promote peace, innocence, piety and discipline among the people as well as among the clergy, and to establish other means for the good of religion as the nature of the circumstances demands.[1] This statement of the purpose is almost a literal reproduction of the words of the Tridentine Council which expresses it in this manner: "The principal object of all these visitations shall be to lead [men] to sound and orthodox doctrine by banishing heresies, to maintain good morals, and to correct such as are evil; to animate the people by exhortations and admonitions to religion, peace and innocence, and to establish such other things as to the prudence of the visitor shall seem for the profit of the faithful, according as time, place and opportunity shall allow."[2]

As is evident, the Council of Trent explicitly states this to be the main purpose of the visitation, whereas the Code refrains from making note of this point. The main purpose, then, is to maintain order with respect to the internal condition or status of the Church. One of the means at the bishop's disposal for the preservation of truth, the maintenance of good morals and the promotion of genuine Christian living

1. C. 343.

2. Sess. XXIV, *de ref.*, c. 3 — Hardouin, X, 155; Mansi, XXX, 111, 158; Hefele-Leclercq, X, 155; Waterworth, *Canons and decrees of the Council of Trent* (London, 1848), p. 209.

is preaching the word of God. This was urged upon the bishops throughout the history of this institution. The IV General Council of the Lateran, for example, charged the bishops to seek the things of Jesus Christ (*quae Jesu Christi sunt*) by preaching and exhortation.[3] Authors who refer to this matter claim that the bishop is bound to preach unless he be legitimately excused.[4] Furthermore, the bishop cannot realize the purpose of the visitation to any extent if he fails to inquire into the existence of possible heresies, or of superstitious, irreligious and unbecoming practices or devotions. Likewise, to give admonitions and make corrections he must investigate the life and conduct of the clergy and the laity, for otherwise peace, discipline, innocence and piety cannot flourish. Hence the bishop has three principal duties during the visitation, to preach, perform an investigation and correct the erring.

Throughout the historical treatment of the visitation the administration of the Sacrament of Confirmation has been adduced as a purpose for the visitation, but no universal law has expressly declared it so. Today, while treating of the Sacrament of Confirmation, the Code singles out the time of the diocesan visitation as an instance when the request for its administration can especially be considered reasonable.[5]

The investigation into the material condition of the church, its appointments and the financial status of the parish necessarily comes under the words *"ceteraque pro ratione adiunctorum ad bonum religionis instituenda"*. For, with the latitude offered by these words, the Code takes cognizance of the fact that a variety of immediate reasons may arise why a bishop will make the visitation. The Roman Pontifical states concretely that the reasons for the bishop's arrival are a) to give the absolution of the dead; b) to know and see how the church is governed spiritually and temporally and if it be necessary to make corrections; c) to punish excesses and delicts; d) to absolve penitents

3. C. 33 — Hardouin, VII, 43; c. 23, X, *de censibus, exactionibus et procurationibus*, III, 39.

4. Monacellus, *Formularium legale practicum fori ecclesiastici* (4 vols., Venetius, 1706-1715), tom. I, form. 2, tit. 5, n. 51; Panormitanus, lib. I, tit. 31, c. 15, n. 1; Piasecius, *Praxis episcopalis*, pars 2, c. 3, a. 1, n. 3.

5. "Episcopus obligatione tenetur sacramentum hoc subditis rite et rationabiliter petentibus conferendi, praesertim tempore visitationis dioecesis." — C. 785, § 1.

from reserved sins; e) to administer the Sacrament of Confirmation; f) to lead the people to penance and to instruct them in the faith and in the avoidance of evil.[6]

As indicated above, the II Plenary Council of Baltimore (1866) reminds the bishop to visit his diocese not only to administer the Sacrament of Confirmation but also that he may acquire a knowledge of his people so as to make better provisions for their spiritual good.[7] But the III Plenary Council of Baltimore (1884) stresses the administration of the Sacrament of Confirmation as an aid against the dangers to which the Catholics of this country are exposed. It also indicates that an accurate inquiry be made into the temporal administration of the churches.[8]

In closing it is rather fitting at this juncture to quote the words of Pope Pius IX (1846-1878), addressed to the bishops in Portugal:

> Cum autem ad spirituale Dioecesium bonum procurandum, earumque mala avertenda Pastorum oculi magnam vim habere soleant, idcirco, dilecte Fili noster ac Venerabiles Fratres, ne omittatis vestras Dioeceses accurate invisere et Cleri populique mores sedulo agnoscere, atque omni diligentia et studio quae corrigenda sunt emendare et convellere, et flagitia, si quae sint, eliminare pravasque amputare consuetudines, peccandique occasiones tollere, et ubique locorum christianam institutionem, et sacramentorum usum, quo nihil christiano populo est salubrius, promovere, et dierum festorum cultum, ac templorum reverentiam inculcare, et

6. "[Episcopus] versus ad populum sedens, proponit populo causas adventus sui quia sacri canones et ecclesiasticus ordo hoc fieri praecipiunt propter multa. Primo ad absolvendas animas defunctorum. Secundo, ut sciat et videat qualiter ecclesia ipsa spiritualiter et temporaliter gubernetur;...ut ex officio inquisitionis suae per eum, si qua in premissis corrigenda fuerint, corrigantur et emendentur. Tertio ad adulteria, fornicationes, sacrilegia, divinationes et similia publica in populo punienda....Quarto propter casus qui de iure vel consuetudine ad Episcopum dumtaxat pertinere noscuntur, qui in Constitutionibus synodalibus continentur in quibus nullus alius se intromittere potest;... Quinto ad exhibendum sacramentum Confirmationis,...Deinde inducit diligenter populum ad poenitentiam, et instruit in Ecclesiasticis Sacramentis, et in articulis Fidei, et qualiter debent declinare a malo et facere bonum; fugere vitia, et sectari virtutes; alteri non facere quod sibi fieri nolunt." — § § 3, 4, 5, 6, 7, 8, tit. *Ordo ad visitandas parochias*.

7. Acta et decreta, n. 86.

8. Acta et decreta, n. 14.

> Clerum ad propria officia sedulo obeunda excitare, et populum ad omnes Christianas exercendas virtutes inflammare. Atque episcopali, uti par est, fortitudine, iis omnibus resistite quae contra Ecclesiam, eiusque veneranda iura et leges istic impune patrantur.[9]

9. Ep. *Qui graviora,* 8 iul. 1862 — *Fontes,* n. 535.

CHAPTER VI

THE OBLIGATION TO PERFORM THE VISITATION

Canon 343, § 1: . . . tenentur Episcopi obligatione visitandae quotannis dioecesis vel ex toto vel ex parte, ita ut saltem singulis quinquenniis universam vel ipsi per se vel, si fuerint legitime impediti, per Vicarium Generalem aliumve lustrent.

§ 2: Fas est Episcopo clericos duos etiam e Capitulo sive cathedrali sive collegiali sibi adsciscere visitationis comites atque adiutores; eosque, quos maluerit, eligere, reprobato quocumque contrario privilegio vel consuetudine.

§ 3: Si obligationi de qua in § 1, Episcopus graviter defuerit, servetur praescriptum can. 274, nn. 4, 5.

After determining the purpose of the visitation canon 343 makes reference to the obligation of the bishop to perform the visitation. First it states the nature of this duty as to the time when and within which it is to be fulfilled. Then it places the condition under which a delegate may be substituted. In the second paragraph it considers the use of co-visitors. And in the third paragraph provision is made for the case wherein the bishop is guilty of serious neglect in the fulfillment of the law.

Article 1. Nature of the Obligation

The obligation to perform the visitation is binding on the residential bishop by reason of his office, for he has ordinary jurisdiction over the subjects in the territory allotted to him. When a bishop, endowed with the power of orders and the power of jurisdiction, takes possession of the diocese assigned to him, he is bound to watch over his subjects, to guard, guide, and direct them to their final end. For this is the purpose of the episcopal office and dignity. However, he cannot fulfill this task unless he come in contact with his people, know their troubles and failings, discover and realize their dangers and perils from the enemies of the faith.[1] Furthermore, as the leader and shepherd of his flock he must devise ways and means of helping his

1. *"Qui tenetur ad finem, tenetur ad media finis."*

people, of advising and correcting them, as well as of checking any form of waywardness. But the best means of accomplishing all this is to make a visitation, a personal tour of the territory entrusted to his care. Without it he cannot have firsthand information of conditions in his diocese.

Besides, the common good of the Church requires that the bishop make a visitation of the diocese from time to time, for without it discipline, faith, and morals would be weakened. Hence it is that the basis for the law on visitation is both the nature of the office of the bishop, and the common good of the Church.

Some authors claim that the obligation is based on the divine law.[2] They adduce the text from the book of Proverbs: "Be diligent to know the countenance of thy cattle and consider thy own flock".[3] But here Solomon is addressing himself to the *paterfamilias,* as Cornelius à Lapide puts it,[4] and symbolically or metaphorically the text can refer to any one who has a charge, who has to exercise a care over subjects. Thus it would include the heads of the state as well as prelates.[5]

Patriarchs, primates, and metropolitans have a similar duty in their respective dioceses.[6] By the same token prelates and abbots of independent jurisdictions are responsible in this regard.[7] Vicars and prefects apostolic are likewise obligated within their own territories.[8] A permanently instituted apostolic administrator, inasmuch as he possesses the same rights and obligations as a residential bishop, is also bound by this duty.[9] The same is true of a coadjutor assigned to a bishop who is entirely incapacitated.[10] Major religious superiors are required to act in a similar rôle with respect to their religious houses, provided the constitutions designate them as visitors.[11] It is to be noted

2. Fagnanus, lib. III, tit. 4, cap. 8, nn. 38, 39; Monacellus, *Formularium,* tom. I, form. 2, tit. 5, n. 1.

3. Proverbs, XXVII, 23.

4. *Commentaria in scripturam sacram* (Parisiis, 1850), tom. VI, pp. 355, 357.

5. *Loc. cit.*

6. C. 273.

7. C. 323, § 1; 215, § 2.

8. C. 301, § 2.

9. C. 315, § 1.

10. C. 351, § 2.

11. C. 511.

that the term "major superiors"[12] embraces major superioresses, among whom are included the ruling abbesses.[13]

The vicar general does not enjoy the right of visitation in his own right but must be delegated by the bishop.[14] This is evident from the law itself which mentions the vicar general as a suitable substitute for the bishop.[15]

The Council of Trent acknowledged the right of the cathedral chapter to make the visitation, a right which may have arisen out of prescription, or because of a privilege. Hence, according to canon 4, if a cathedral chapter enjoyed the privilege before the Code, such a privilege is still in effect. But the council stipulated that those who were selected (*visitatores*) to make the visitation had to be approved by the bishop.[16] The visitors, however, had to be approved only when the right of visitation was confined exclusively to the cathedral chapter.[17]

A temporary apostolic administrator can make the visitation even though the see be occupied.[18] Upon the death of the bishop, or when the see becomes vacant for any other reason acknowledged by law,[19] the government of the diocese redounds to the cathedral chapter,[20]

12. C. 490.

13. Larraona, "Commentarium codicis" — *CpR,* VIII (1927), 356, note 462; Reilly, *The visitation of religious,* pp. 76, 77.

14. Azorius, *Institutiones morales* (Brescia, 1617), pars II, lib. III, cap. 45, q. 4; Barbosa, *De officio et potestate episcopi,* alleg. 73, n. 28; *idem., Ius eccl. univ.,* lib. I, cap. 14, n. 7. Campagna, *Il vicario generale del vescovo* (Catholic University of America, Canon Law Studies, n. 66, Washington, D. C., 1931), p. 130.

15. C. 343, § 1.

16. Sess. XXIV, *de ref.,* c. 3; Azorius, pars II, lib. III, cap. 40, q. 8; Barbosa, *De officio et potestate episcopi,* alleg. 73, n. 26; *idem., Ius eccl. univ.,* lib. I, cap. 14, n. 14.

17. "...quod quidem locum habere ubi, soli Capitulo absque Episcopo competit jus visitandi refert decisum Armend. in addit. ad Recopil. legum Navar. lib. I, tit. 18, 1. 7 de Episc. num. 110." — Barbosa, *Ius eccl. univ.,* lib. I, cap. 14, n. 15.

18. C. 315, § 2, 1°.

19. C. 430, § 1.

20. C. 432.

or to the diocesan consultors.[21] With the election of the vicar capitular[22] or the diocesan administrator,[23] the ordinary jurisdiction of the bishop in spiritual as well as temporal matters is transferred to the vicar capitular or the diocesan administrator,[24] except in those instances in which the law expressly states otherwise. On that account the vicar capitular or diocesan administrator has the right and obligation to perform the visitation. But he may not act in the capacity of a visitor until a year has passed from the day of the last visitation made by the since deceased bishop, although it must be admitted that today in the Code there is no restriction in this regard; just as there is no express mention that the vicar capitular has the right of visitation.[25] Ordinarily, owing to the modern policy of filling vacant sees as soon as possible, this duty will not be incumbent on the vicar capitular or diocesan administrator.

Blat[26] and Toso[27] are of the opinion that the vicar capitular does not have the right of visitation. They base their argument on canon 315, § 2, 1°, which states that the temporary apostolic administrator has the same rights and duties as the vicar capitular, but that even though the see be occupied he can make a visitation of the diocese according to the prescriptions of law. Obviously they work on the assumption that a complete parity exists between the apostolic administrator and vicar capitular except as regards the provision mentioned

21. C. 427.

22. C. 432.

23. Cc. 427, 432.

24. C. 435.

25. S. C. C., 13 sept. 1721—*Thesaurus,* II, 77-79, cf. *Fontes,* n. 3232; Azorius (*Institutiones Morales*) pars II, lib. III, cap. 38, q. 14; Barbosa, *De officio et potestate episcopi,* alleg. 73, n. 24; *idem., Ius eccl. univ.,* lib. I, cap. 14, n. 8; Monacellus, *Formularium,* pars III, tit. I, form. 4, n. 2; Ferraris, *Prompta bibliotheca,* v. "Visitatio", n. 9; v. "Vicarius Capitularius", art. 2, n. 11; Benedict XIV, *De synodo dioecesana,* lib. II, c. 9, n. 6; lib. X, c. 10, n. 6; Bouix, *Tractatus de capitulis* (Parisiis, 1882), pp. 73-78; Castillo, *La potestad del cabildo en sede vacante o impedida del vicario capitular* (Catholic University of America, Canon Law Studies, n. 4, Washington, D. C., 1919), p. 84.

26. *Commentarium textus codicis iuris canonici,* II, *De personis* (2. ed., Romae, 1921), n. 333.

27. *Ad codicem iuris canonici commentaria minora,* II, *De personis* (Romae, 1923), p. 137.

above, when, as a matter of fact, the canon seems to point out a distinction between them. For the administrator is given the right to make the visitation even though the episcopal see be occupied, which presupposes, not that the vicar capitular lacks the right of visitation, but that *a fortiori* the apostolic administrator[28] enjoys it when the see is vacant. Moreover, as stated above, nowhere does the Code debar the vicar capitular from making the visitation.

When provicars or proprefects assume office in vicariates and prefectures apostolic, they each have full authority in the government of their own districts.[29] Therefore, the right of making the visitation comes within the scope of their power.

Under the old law every prelate who enjoyed jurisdiction and administrative power had the right and faculty to make the visitation.[30] Hence the legate *a latere* had the right and obligation by reason of the commission entrusted to him by the Holy See.[31] Today the legate has only delegated jurisdiction.[32] Then the *legati nati,* who enjoyed the apostolic *commission* by reason of the dignity in which they were constituted, also had this right and obligation.[33] Now the *legati nati* are residential bishops who in virtue of the see they occupy retain but an honorary title.[34] The *legati missi* or nuncios needed a special delegation unless an urgent necessity arose.[35] The present law neither

28. "Cui licet quod est plus, licet utique quod est minus" — Reg. 53, R. J., in VI°.

29. C. 309, § 2.

30. "... Hanc autem visitandi formam ab universis, etiam episcopis aliisque praelatis, ordinario jure suos subjectos visitantibus plene observari praecepimus." — C. 1, X, *de censibus, exactionibus et procurationibus,* III, 20, in VI°; Azorius, *Institutiones morales,* pars II, lib. III, cap. 40, q. 6; Barbosa, *De officio et potestate episcopi,* alleg. 73, n. 20.

31. "... quare visitare possunt ac debent jure ordinario ... legati a latere ex officio legationis sibi a Sede Apostolica demandatae." Azorius, *loc. cit.*

32. C. 266.

33. "... item legati pontificii qui non sunt a latere sed dicuntur nati quibus legatio apostolica competit ratione dignitatis in qua sunt constituti." Azorius, *loc. cit.;* Barbosa, *loc. cit.*

34. "Legati nati qui sunt episcopi residentiales qui ratione sedis episcopalis quam occupant, quoque saeculis transactis ius legationis exercuit in determinatis ecclesiis, nunc titulum sine re retinent." — Coronata, *Institutiones iuris canonici,* I, 410.

35. Azorius, *loc. cit.;* Barbosa, *loc. cit.*

acknowledges a right, nor expresses an obligation in the case of nuncios, internuncios and apostolic delegates to perform the visitation. Thus, although these offices include the duty of vigilance in the territory assigned, they do not embrace the right of visitation.[36]

The bishop is obliged to visit the diocese, or at least a part of it, annually, so that the entire diocese is visited within a five year period. Hence a bishop may visit his entire diocese every year if he so wishes, and if it can be done properly. In fact, the writer ventures to state that in small dioceses which could be visited entirely within a year's time the bishop would be obliged to do so. This seems to be borne out by the words of the canon "*tenentur* Episcopi *obligatione* visitandae *quotannis* dioecesis *vel ex toto* vel ex parte." Otherwise, the legislator would have limited the obligation to a partial visitation. Hence, for larger dioceses the limit within which the visitation must be completed is set at five years. However, instances will arise which may warrant more than one investigation a year. Therefore, it will rest with the bishop to decide whether it is necessary or whether it would be useful to make another visitation.[37] But he may not within the same year revisit any particular object unless some contingency arise.[38]

36. Cc. 267, § 1, 2°; 267, § 2. The right of vigilance and visitation, as the terms are used in the Code, are, while not the same, very similar and the precise distinction between them is difficult to define. Both rights imply a certain amount of jurisdiction.... Visitation, however, is the broader term and the right of visiting signifies that one may go to a place (or person) and subject the place (or person) to an investigation. The right of vigilance does not extend so far. When the Code wishes to include visitation under vigilance the former is expressly mentioned (e. g., c. 1515, § 2). However, when one has the right of visiting a place in reference to a certain matter, it is certainly legitimate for him while there to exercise a right of vigilance in regard to other points. In such cases it is at times all but impossible to show wherein visitation and vigilance differ.—Reilly, *The visitation of religious,* pp. 124, 125. "*Visitatio* est forma solemnis ac plena jurisdictionis. Non est confundenda cum *vigilantia,* nec cum *jure exigendi rationem* de aliqua re, nec cum *simplici dependentia* seu *subiectione* quoad aliqua."—Larraona, "Commentarium codicis," *CpR,* XIII (1932) 31, note 549.

37. Fagnanus, lib. I, tit. 31, cap. 16, n. 34; lib. III, tit. 39, cap. 21, n. 3.

38. S. C. C., *Segobricen.*, 24 aug. 1605 ad 8—*Fontes,* n. 2358; Pallottini, IX, 564.

Coronata[39] is of the opinion that the text of canon 343, § 1, does not require a visitation of a part of the diocese every year, but only a visitation of the entire diocese every five years. He fails to produce any arguments, and he admits the opposite opinion is more common.

Here in our own country the stipulation of the III Plenary Council of Baltimore (1884)[40] is still in effect.[41] Therefore the visitation of the entire diocese is to be completed within an interval of three years. But in accord with the text of the Code a part of every year is to be devoted to this particular duty of the bishop. However, if he has a very large diocese and circumstances require a thorough investigation, it would be unreasonable under the circumstances to hold the bishop to a triennial visitation.

Since the law cautions the bishop to act diligently and to avoid useless delays in the performance of the visitation,[42] he is not to divert his attention in the course of the visitation to matters that are extraneous or irrelevant to it.[43] It is to be observed that the administration of the Sacrament of Confirmation is not an act outside the sphere or domain of the visitation.[44] Furthermore, a bishop is by no means bound to conclude the visitation within a set period of time. The matter rests with his discretion and honest judgment.[45] Wherefore no set number of days or any specific period of time is to be defined for the bishop.[46] Hence, the bishop is also to determine the length of time he is to spend at any particular church. Nevertheless

39. I, 465, nota 6.

40. *Acta et decreta,* n. 14.

41. Barrett, *A comparative study of the Councils of Baltimore and the Code of Canon Law* (Catholic University of America, Canon Law Studies, n. 83, Washington, D. C., 1932), p. 65; Ayrinhac, *Constitution of the Church in the new code of canon law* (Benziger, New York, 1925), p. 179.

42. C. 346.

43. Cf. S. C. C., *Segobricen.,* 24 aug. 1605; *Boianen.,* 14 nov. 1654 — Pallottini, IX, 568; Fagnanus, lib. I, tit. 31, cap. 16, n. 36.

44. Cf. S. C. C., *Amalphitana,* 18 iulii, 1699 — Pallottini, IX, p. 568, n. 48.

45. Cf. S. C. C., *Segobricen.,* 24 aug. 1605; *Asturicen seu Dubrium,* 1620 — Pallottini, IX, 568, n. 49; *S. Marci plurium,* 19 dec. 1722, 16 jan. 1723 ad 6 — *Thesaurus,* II, 262.

46. Cf. S. C. C., *S. Marci,* anno 1609; *Boianen.,* 14 nov. 1654—Pallottini, IX, 568, n. 50; *S. Marci plurium,* 19 dec. 1722, 16 jan. 1723 ad 6 — *Thesaurus,* II, 257, 262.

the Sacred Congregation of the Council claimed that the visitation should be carried out continuously and not intermittently unless some just cause exist to the contrary.[47] In this connection it may be recalled that the Provincial Council of Toledo (1565) decided that the bishops who could not visit their entire dioceses annually were to expend three continuous or uninterrupted months of a year for the visitation of a part of a diocese outside the cathedral city.[48]

According to canon 338, § 3, the bishop is not to be absent from the cathedral church during Advent, Lent, Christmas, Easter, Pentecost or Corpus Christi, except for a grave and urgent reason. Therefore, may a bishop visit his diocese, say for instance, during Advent or Lent? The answer seems to be in the affirmative. Today with the modern means of transportation he can easily go back and forth. Furthermore, the visitation itself is certainly a solid and urgent reason. In confirmation of this view is a reply of the Sacred Congregation of the Council wherein it is stated that a bishop complies with the Tridentine law on residence at the cathedral even though his episcopal duties call him elsewhere.[49]

Despite the law on the visitation obliging the bishops to this duty, there is no penalty attached for the failure to comply in any way with the present legislation. However, its importance and gravity are indicated by the obligation placed on the bishop to provide for a substitute whenever he cannot comply with the law personally.

With respect to the vicar and prefect apostolic the Code states that the visitation is to be made by them whenever they deem it necessary,[50] whereas the temporary apostolic administrator must comply with the prescriptions of the law in every respect.[51]

47. "Unde Sacra Congregatio declarat continuate et non interpollate fieri debere visitationem ab Episcopo, ut quamprimum, justo impedimento cessante, perficiatur." S. C. C., *In Dubium* ad cap. 3, sess, 24, Posit. 77 — Pallottini, IX, 567.

48. Art. II, 2 — Hardouin, X, 1148.

49. Verum haudquaquam satisfacit suae obligationi residendo in dioecesi et non in cathedrali temporibus in cap. 1, sess. 23, *de ref.*, praescriptis vers. "Eosdem interim admonet", *nisi tunc temporis episcopalia munia eum alio vocent.* — S. C. C., *In Dubium,* 24 sept. 1622, Pallottini, IX, 539, n. 25.

50. C. 301, § 2.

51. C. 315, § 2, 1°.

The Use of a Substitute

The present law, as contained in the Council of Trent, uses the clause "*si fuerint legitime impediti*" to indicate when the bishop is excused from making a personal visitation. But, when is a bishop legitimately impeded and who is the judge in the matter? A bishop cannot *tuta conscientia* satisfy the obligation through a delegate unless he himself is legitimately impeded.[52]

The IV National Council of Toledo (633)[53] mentioned sickness and the preoccupation with other duties or engagements as valid excuses for employing a substitute.[54] But the nature of the work or of the other duties must be urgent,[55] or their importance must at least be proportionate to this charge.[56] The Provincial Council of Toledo (1565) also interpreted the clause "if they be lawfully impeded" by stating that only an urgent necessity with resultant harm, whether spiritual or corporal, to the public or the private welfare of the bishop, excused a bishop from the personal visitation.[57] Hence if the bishop experiences difficulties in traveling, the use of a substitute would be warranted.[58] The plea of old age would also lawfully excuse a bishop from performing the entire visitation. However, if he were to perform his other duties regularly, there is no reason why he should desist entirely. In a very large diocese it is reasonable to suppose that a bishop and one of his delegates may visit different parts of the diocese at different intervals according as their respective duties make no demands on their time.

52. Bargilliat, *Praelectiones juris canonici* (37. ed., 2 vols., Parisiis apud Baston, Berche et Pagis, 1923), I, p. 502, n. 727; Cocchi, *Commentarium in codicem iuris canonici*, III (4. ed., Taurinorum Augustae: Marietti, 1931), 215.

53. C. 36. Bruns, I, 233; Hardouin, III, 587; Mansi, X, 629; Hefele-Leclercq, III, 272.

54. "Quod si ipse aut languore detentus aut aliis occupationibus implicatus et explere nequerit, presbyteros probabiles aut diacones mittat."

55. Augustine, *A commentary on the new code of canon law*, II (5. ed., Herder, St. Louis, Mo., 1928), 369.

56. Toso, *Commentaria minora*, II, 173.

57. ". . . ut nisi maximo cum detrimento vel publicae vel propriae salutis spiritualis vel corporalis, per seipsos eam visitationem exsequi non valeant." — art. II, n. 2 — Hardouin, X, 1148. Cf. *supra*, p. 60.

58. Ferreres, *Institutiones canonicae* (2. ed., 2 vols., Barcinone, 1920), I, 248.

As to the lawfully impeding cause the bishop is not obliged in any way to reveal its character. In fact, his assertion to that effect suffices. Furthermore, the impediment need not be continuous for the entire period stipulated for the visitation. The conscience of the bishop is to be his guide.[59]

On the other hand, the bishop certainly cannot use a substitute all the time. For it is hard to see how he would be prevented from making a visitation of at least a part of the diocese throughout the three or five year period. He certainly will not gain an intimate knowledge of the people, which is intended by the legislator and which the very nature of his office demands. Then, too, he will be acting counter to the very spirit of the law. Furthermore, the obligation is primarily a personal one, for the care of the diocese is entrusted to the bishop.[60] Hence it is only when the bishop is not in a position to comply with the obligation in person that he is privileged to use the services of some other person. And it is only then that the rules of law concerning the possibility of a supplied agency[61] are applicable in this matter. Moreover, it must be observed that this delegation is not simply optional with the bishop. It is of obligation whenever he cannot perform the visitation in person. This is evident from the clear statement of the law, which demands that the visitation be carried out by the bishop either in person or through a substitute.

59. S. C. C., *Portugallien.*, 15 et 29 ian. 1701—*Fontes*, n. 2982; Pallottini, IX, 563.

60. "Numquam enim [episcopi] Tridentini decreto satisfacient, nisi personaliter ad oves accedere curent, et ad instar boni Pastoris bonas foveant, errantes vero quaerant, et ad Ovile, qua fortiter, qua suaviter clamando et agendo, tandem aliquando perducant.... *Ipsismet* enim, non Ministris, Gregum suorum cura concredita est: *Ipsis* peculiaris Spiritus Sancti gratia: *Ipsis* et Charismatum dona fuere promissa. Ex quo fit, ut oves proprii Pastoris multo libentius, quam Vicarii vocem audiant, et a proprii Pastoris quam a Vicarii manu salubria alimenta fiducialius petant ac laetiori animo suscipiant, tanquam a manu Domini, cuius in Episcopis suis venerantur personam; quae omnia, praeter hactenus dicta, ipsa enim rerum magistra experientia satis superque confirmat." —Leonis Papae XII *Epistola Encyclica ad omnes Patriarchas, Primates, Archiepiscopos et Episcopos*, 3 maii 1824 (Romae, Ex Typographia Rev. Camerae Apostolicae, 1824), p. 5. Cf. also the words of Pope Benedict XIV quoted on pp. 59, 60.

61. "Potest quis per alium quod potest facere per seipsum." "Qui facit per alium est perinde ac si faciat per se ipsum." —Regg. 68, 72, R. J., in VI°.

At this point it is opportune to recall that the first written law to acquaint us with the use of substitutes for the visitation considered priests and deacons of an upright character as suitable choices for this undertaking.[62] The present law advises the use of the vicar general or some other qualified person, unquestionably an ecclesiastic, in view of the legislation with respect to jurisdictional power.[63]

Although the Code mentions the vicar general expressly, the bishop is under no obligation in virtue of any positive law to show priority to his vicar general. If a bishop has a coadjutor or an auxiliary he may employ him also in the capacity of a visitor.[64] The fact that the legislator mentions only the vicar general is a manifest indication that in ordinary circumstances he considers him the proper and logical choice. It is very fitting that the vicar general be the visitatorial substitute of the bishop owing to his ordinary jurisdiction in the entire diocese,[65] and because of his competence as deduced from the requisites of a candidate for his office.[66] By using the expression *aliumve* the Code does not limit the selection to the vicar general.[67] However, it is reasonable to suppose that by making mention of the vicar general the Code thus indirectly indicates some of the qualifications that the delegate should possess. Still, according to the strict letter of the law one cannot agree with Blat[68] that the visitor must be a priest because of the use of the word *vicarium*.

The use of this word proves nothing in itself. For, although the vicar general must be a priest,[69] the expression *aliumve* does not necessarily refer to a priest but to any ecclesiastic. As stated above, the reference to the vicar general perhaps intimates the required nature of the competency for this task. But it would rather refer to capacity than to status. And since the law allows any cleric the exercise of

62. The IV National Council of Toledo (633), c. 36—Hardouin, III, 587; Mansi, X, 629.

63. C. 118.

64. Toso, *Commentaria minora,* II, 173.

65. C. 366, § 1.

66. C. 367; Toso, *Commentaria minora,* II, 173.

67. The Council of Trent used the phrase "aut Visitatorem".

68. "... per vicarium generalem aliumve sibi benevisum *sed sacerdotem* ob expressum 'Vicarium' ..." *Commentarium,* II, n. 368.

69. C. 367, § 1.

jurisdiction,[70] it would not be outside the realm of possibility for a bishop to use a deacon, for example, as his substitute.

If for any purpose the Holy Father were to appoint a special visitor in a diocese or province, the respective bishops or bishop would not thereby be deprived of the exercise of their right during that interval. For one visitation would not impede another. And a general delegation of this kind is not derogatory to the ordinary jurisdiction enjoyed by the bishop, unless the Holy Pontiff expressly forbids the visitation on the part of the bishop.[71]

Finally, the bishop's right of visitation is not subject to prescription,[72] for it is a *ius publicum.* If persons, places and things were no longer subject to the visitation, the Christian commonweal would suffer, since the visitation is intended for the salvation of souls, the correction of the morals of the people and the reformation of discipline in the churches.[73] This, however, has reference to the so-called *extinctiva praescriptio,* whereby the subjects would not come under the jurisdiction of any prelate with respect to the visitation and obedience. Hence the way remains open for the *praescriptio translativa,* by the force of which one prelate can acquire the right of visitation by prescription against another prelate.[74]

Article 2. Use of Co-Visitors

The Code extends to the bishop the right to select two clerics as co-visitors, that is, as companions and aides in determining the condition of the parishes, churches and institutions. The old law permitted but never required this practice.[75] Obviously this does not signify that the

70. C. 118.

71. Fagnanus, lib. I, tit. 30, cap. 2, n. 8.

72. C. 1509, n. 7.

73. Pirhing, lib. II, tit. 26, n. 23. By the same token a bishop cannot expressly or by a pact forego this right of visitation.

74. Vermeersch-Creusen, *Epitome juris canonici,* II (5 ed., Mechlinae-Romae, H. Dessain, 1934), 580; cf. also cc. 12, 16, X, *de praescriptionibus,* II, 26.

75. C. 1, *de officio iudicis ordinarii,* I, 7, Extravag. com.; Piasecius, *Praxis episcopalis,* pars II, cap. 2, art. II, n. 2; Barbosa, *Ius eccl. univ.,* lib. I, cap. 14, n. 38.

law allows the bishop to have two clerics as simultaneous visitors with himself in different parts of the diocese.[76]

It would seem that the co-visitors or aides are limited to two in number, but it certainly does not mean that the bishop may not enlarge his entourage if he deems it feasible. What is evidently meant is that no more than two persons may take an active part with the bishop in the investigation proper. Furthermore, these co-visitors may even be chosen from a cathedral or collegiate chapter, irrespective of any privilege or custom to the contrary.[77]

Likewise, if a bishop decides to have two members of a collegiate or cathedral chapter as his co-visitors, no contrary custom or privilege restricting his right of choice is recognized in law. He alone has the right to select his companions. On the other hand the bishop is not required to choose his co-visitors from the members of the cathedral chapter, or of some collegiate chapter in the diocese. Furthermore, a custom in contravention of the disposition of the law may not arise in the future.[78] Then, too, although the bishop may employ the services of exempt religious he cannot force them to accompany him in this undertaking.[79]

Suffice it to say that these men should be blameless in character, versed in a knowledge of ecclesiastical affairs and excelling in experience as administrators.[80] The legislation of the III Plenary Council of Baltimore (1884) with respect to co-visitors is no longer of obligation, as it contravenes the ruling of the Code which makes the use of these co-visitors optional.[81]

76. Blat, *Commentarium*, II, n. 368.

77. Cf. also S. C. C., *Anagnina*, 27 maii, 1713 — *Fontess*, n. 3120. The canons who accompany the bishop in the visitation of the diocese are excused from choir duty but have the right to get both the income of the prebend and the daily distributions. — C. 420, § 1, n. 12.

78. Cc. 5, 27.

79. Cf. c. 615; Beste, *Introductio in codicem* (Collegeville, Minn., St. John's Abbey Press, 1938), p. 270; Vermeersch-Creusen, *Epitome iuris canonici*, I (6. ed., Mechlinae-Romae, H. Dessain, 1937), 346.

80. Lucidi, De visitatione sacrorum liminum, I, 156; *Acta et decreta concilii plenarii Baltimorensis III*, n. 14.

81. *Acta et decreta*, n. 14. However, the use of these co-visitors was conditional as the council used the clause, "*si fieri potest.*"

Article 3. Provision in Case of Neglect

In case a bishop is gravely negligent in fulfilling his obligation, i. e., if he fails to make a visitation within the specified period of time prevailing in the respective territory, the metropolitan is to notify the Roman Pontiff of this neglect.[82] If the Holy See gives its approval, he may then proceed to make a visitation of the diocese in question.[83] The metropolitan can fulfill this duty not only with regard to his suffragans, but also with respect to a bishop immediately subject to the Holy See, to an archbishop without a suffragan and an abbot or prelate of an independent territory provided they have selected him as their metropolitan in accord with canon 285. This view (relative to the last three mentioned), as is evident, is based on an analogy of law.[84]

No explicit provision is made in the law concerning the neglect of the metropolitan in his own diocese. To draw a parallel from the law on residence,[85] it would seem that the senior suffragan[86] should notify the Holy See of the matter and perhaps action would be taken to have him make the visitation.

Herein it may be stated that as early as the year 397 archbishops were advised to visit the churches of their province.[87] Up until the time of the Council of Trent the metropolitans had the right to visit the dioceses of their suffragans without approval, regardless of whether negligence existed or not.[88] The Council of Trent declared that a metropolitan could not perform the visitation in the diocese of his suffragan before he made a visitation of his own diocese. Moreover, the metropolitan required the approval of a provincial council before he could proceed in the visitation.[89] Today the metropolitan need not visit his own diocese previous to visiting his suffragan's.

82. C. 274, n. 4.
83. C. 274, n. 5.
84. C. 20; Blat, *Commentarium,* II, n. 368.
85. C. 338, § 4.
86. That is, he who was first promoted to a suffragan diocese of the province. —c. 284.
87. The Council of Turin (397), c. 2—Bruns, II, 114; cf. also *Canones Ecclesiae Africanae,* c. 52—Bruns, I, 167.
88. Cc. I, 5, *de censibus, exactionibus et procurationibus,* III, 20, in VI°.
89. Sess. XXIV, *de ref.,* c. 3.

CHAPTER VII

THE MATERIAL OBJECT OF THE VISITATION

Canon 344, § 1: Ordinariae episcopali visitationi obnoxiae sunt personae, res ac loca pia, quamvis exempta, quae intra dioecesis ambitum continentur, nisi probari possit specialem a visitatione exemptionem fuisse ipsis ab Apostolica Sede concessam.

§ 2: Religiosos autem exemptos Episcopus visitare potest in casibus tantum in iure expressis.

Canon 344 states the material object of the visitation. In the first paragraph, after giving the general rule concerning the right and obligation of the bishop to make a visitation of his entire diocese, it also adduces the norm for proving the exception to the rule. In the second paragraph it further qualifies the general statement by alluding to the extent of the subjection of exempt religious to the jurisdiction of the bishop in this matter.

As is evident, the present law on the material object of the episcopal visitation is rather brief. But it is pointed and clear even in its generality. Accordingly, the bishop as the governing head of the diocese enjoys a presumption of law with respect to the right of visiting all persons, places and things within the confines of the diocese. Thus, as a general rule, subject to the contrary proof of a special exemption, any person, place or thing, even though exempt, but under ecclesiastical authority, is amenable to this particular manifestation of the exercise of the episcopal office.[1]

Hence, the bishop's visitatorial jurisdiction extends over all, irrespective of any general exemption, for the latter is not sufficient in itself in the eyes of the law to include the privilege of immunity from the periodic or ordinary episcopal visitation. A special exemption from the visitation itself granted by the Holy See is the only effective means

1. Blat, *Commentarium,* I, n. 369; Sipos, *Enchiridion juris canonici* (3. ed., Pecs [Hungary] ex Typographia Haladas R. T., 1936), p. 263.

of establishing an exception to the general law enjoyed by any particular person, place or thing. This was also the teaching of the authors and of the Roman Rota.[2]

In regard to exempt religious, however, the canon declares that the bishop can visit them only in the cases expressly indicated by the law.[3] Thus the ambit of the bishop's visitation is not all-extensive.

The visitation according as its object is a person, a thing, or a place, can be classified as personal, real or local. The latter will be considered first.

ARTICLE 1. LOCAL VISITATION

Churches

Logically, the local visitation embraces in the first place the examination and inspection of churches,[4] namely, the cathedral, and the parochial and nonparochial churches which are not exempt. Secular churches, even though they be in the hands of religious or joined to a religious house, are nevertheless subject to the visitation of the bishop.[5] Likewise religious churches of exempt and nonexempt pon-

2. Barbosa, *De officio et potestate episcopi,* pars III, alleg. 74, n. 6.

3. C. 344, § 2. The visitation of religious will not receive separate treatment. It will be indicated in the general discussion of the three forms of the object of the visitation. For an *ex professo* treatment on matters religious the reader may consult Reilly, *The visitation of religious,* pp. 84 ff.

4. "Secundo ut sciat et videat qualiter Ecclesia ipsa . . . gubernetur" — Pontificale Romanum, *Ordo ad visitandas parochias,* § IV.

5. A parish may be either religious, or secular, although it be under the care of religious or incorporated with a religious house. A religious parish is one united *pleno iure* with a religious house (cc. 1425, § 2, 452, 471, § 1), while a secular parish is one united with a religious house with regard to the temporalities alone (*quoad temporalia tantum,* c. 1425, § 1) or which is in the care of clerical religious in spiritual matters. It is to be noted that the Code does not identify a religious parish with a religious church. The church may be secular even though the parish is religious. For a further treatment of these points, cf. Maroto, *CpR,* VII (1926), 438; Vermeersch-Creusen, *Epitome,* II, nn. 476, 869; Nebreda, "Studia Canonica" — *CpR,* VII (1926), 116, 263, 330; Reilly, *The visitation of religious,* pp. 130-133.

tifical congregations as well as those of diocesan congregations are completely within the ambit of the ordinary's visitatorial rights.[6] This is also true of the churches or chapels of nuns subject to the local ordinary or immediately subject to the Holy See.[7]

The churches of regulars, however, are not under the jurisdiction of the local ordinary except in the cases expressed in law.[8] The Council of Trent obligated the local ordinaries to visit all ecclesiastical benefices charged with the care of souls, regardless of whether these benefices were exempt or attached to monasteries.[9] Although the present law fails to mention expressly the subjection of these churches to the local ordinary's visitation, still it does not deny him the right of visiting them. Furthermore, the bishop or local ordinary is the pastor of the entire diocese and thus is charged with the care of all the souls of the faithful. Hence he also has jurisdiction over things that pertain thereto. Moreover, the legislator subjects the religious pastor or vicar to the visitation, correction, and entire jurisdiction of the local ordinary in the same manner as secular pastors, even though the ordinary residence of the major religious superiors be in the house or place where he exercises his ministry.[10] (Before the Code, however, the parochial churches where the major superiors of regulars resided were exempt from the visitation of the ordinary.)[11] Therefore, the exemption of regulars spoken of in canon 615, when it is considered with reference to parochial or quasi-parochial churches, must be interpreted in the light of the old law.[12] In this manner whatever is intimately bound up with the parochial office (i. e., the care of souls) will necessarily fall under the ordinary's visitatorial powers. Consequently herein apply the points determined by Benedict XIV in his

6. C. 512, § 1, n. 2, § 2, n. 2.
7. C. 512, § 1, n. 1.
8. C. 615.
9. Sess. XXV, *de regularibus,* c. 11; sess. VII, *de ref.,* c. 7.
10. C. 631, § 1.
11. Conc. Trid., sess. XXV, *de regularibus,* c. 11; const. "*Firmandis,*" 6 nov. 1744, §§ 13-16 — *Fontes,* n. 349.
12. C. 6, nn. 2, 3, 4. Vromant, *Ius missionariorum, De personis* (2. ed., Louvain: Museum Lessianum, 1935), n. 85.

constitution "*Firmandis*"[13] for the visitation of the parochial churches of regulars.[14]

During the visitation of the church the bishop is to see to it that decorations, ornaments and repairs which are out of harmony with Catholic tradition and Catholic art be rectified.[15] He may inquire about the consecration or blessing of the church,[16] the annual observance of its titular feast,[17] its violation or desecration,[18] the conducting of serv-

13. 6 nov. 1744, § 7. This constitution states that the bishop may visit that altar and tabernacle where the Blessed Sacrament is reserved, the baptismal font, the confessional of the pastor, the pulpit, the sacristy with respect to the place where the *sacra suppelex* (sacred vestments, sacred vessels) used in the administration of the sacraments is kept, the sepulchres and the cemetery for the faithful departed, the campanile if the bells belong to the parish, and finally, all the sacred vessels in which the consecrated particles, the holy oils, the baptismal water or the holy water for the parishioners is kept.—*Fontes*, n. 349.

14. C. 6, n. 6. There is but one instance when the law empowers the local ordinary to visit the nonparochial churches of regulars. According to canon 1261 he is to exercise vigilance concerning the faithful observance of the general precepts on divine worship, and he is to eliminate all abuses connected with their violation. Moreover, if he passes particular laws on matters relative to divine worship, all religious, even though they be exempt, are obliged to observe them, and the ordinary has the right to visit their churches and public oratories for this purpose. As President of the Pontifical Commission for the Interpretation of the Code, Cardinal Gasparri gave an interpretation of this right of the bishop in the form of a private reply. It stated in effect that the local ordinary is accorded the right of visitation in view of his laws which constitute more than a mere affirmation of the general law; and that *this visitation* performed by him in view of the particular laws he has enacted *is not* of the same nature as his quinquennial visitation in his diocese. Finally, as a reason which alone will justify the making of a visitation there must be present a positive knowledge on the part of the bishop that his laws are not being observed in the churches of these exempt regulars.—Rome, 8 apr., 1924. The text may be found in Wernz-Vidal, *Ius canonicum ad codicis normam exactum*, tomus III, *De religiosis* (Apud Aedes Universitatis Gregorianae, Romae, 1933), p. 429, nota 32; cf. also Coronata, *Institutiones iuris canonici*, II, p. 154, nota 4; Marcellus, "De exemptione ecclesiarum regularium a canonica episcopi visitatione"—*CpR*, IX (1928), 243, 244; Reilly, *The visitation of religious*, p. 126.

15. C. 1164.

16. C. 1165. A record of this function must be kept in the parochial archives. (C. 1158.)

17. C. 1168, § 2.

18. C. 1172.

ices before its reconciliation,[19] the use of the basement of the church for profane or secular purposes,[20] the length of time the church is kept open during the day for the people to frequent it[21] and the subjection of the church itself to anything incongruous with the nature of the place, for example, to meetings and social gatherings.[22] He should also insist that cleanliness pervade the entire structure as is befitting to the house of God,[23] that proper care and custody be given it against possible profanation, thefts and damage,[24] and that no admission fee be charged for entrance.[25]

Oratories

Next in importance on the roster of the local visitation are the oratories. The bishop may visit all three classes of oratories, that is, public, semipublic and private oratories.[26] Like churches they are dedicated to divine worship.[27] Hence it behooves the bishop to see that all liturgical requirements are fully complied with, and that no abuses are present. Public oratories are governed by the same laws as churches.[28] The ordinary may not grant permission for the canonical erection of semipublic or private oratories before he or some other delegated ecclesiastic has visited the structure and found it properly equipped.[29]

19. C. 1173.
20. S. R. C. *Taurinen.*, 4 maii 1882 — *Decr. Auth.* n. 3546; *Fontes*, n. 6135.
21. C. 1266; S. R. C. *Compostellana*, 15 nov. 1890, ad 1 — *Decr. Auth.* n. 3739; *Fontes*, n. 6205.
22. C. 1178.
23. C. 1178.
24. S. C. Consist. *De relationibus dioecesanis, Formula*, 4 nov. 1918, n. 21; S. C. Sacr. Instructio, 26 maii 1938, § 5 — *AAS*, X (1918), 491; XXX (1938), 202, 203.
25. C. 1181; *Acta et decreta*, n. 288.
26. Claeys Bouuaert-Simenon, *Manuale iuris canonici*, I (4. ed., Gandae et Leodii: 1934), 486.
27. Cc. 1188, § 1; 1191, § 2; 1196, § 2.
28. C. 1191, § 1.
29. Cc. 1192, §§ 1, 2; 1195. The word "ordinary" in canon 1192, § 1, includes the major superiors of clerical exempt institutes (c. 198, § 1). There are three kinds of private oratories: a) domestic oratories erected for the convenience of private persons (cc. 1188, 1195); b) private oratories of cardinals and bishops (c. 1189); and c) private oratories erected in cemeteries. (c. 1190).

With respect to religious, the bishop has a right to visit the public and semipublic oratories of nuns immediately subject to the local ordinary or to the Holy See.[30] He may likewise visit the oratories of men and women religious of diocesan approval,[31] but, although he may visit the public oratories of clerical exempt and nonexempt religious of pontifical approval, he may not visit their semipublic oratories.[32] There is no difficulty concerning the semipublic oratories of clerical exempt religious as canon 344, §2, distinctly states that the bishop may visit exempt religious only in the cases expressly stated by the law. But the semipublic oratories of nonexempt clerical religious do not enjoy this exemption. Then, too, canon 344, § 1, which deals with the general visitation of the diocese declares that all pious places even though exempt are subject to the bishop's visitation unless they enjoy a *special* exemption from the Holy See. However, in canon 512 which treats of a particular phase of the general diocesan visitation — the local ordinary's visitation of religious — the legislator while giving a taxative enumeration of the places subject to the visitation of the bishop fails to allude to semipublic oratories. Hence if the lawgiver wished to include the semipublic oratories he certainly would have made mention of them especially since he expressly refers to public oratories. Therefore the silence of the Code is to be construed as an indication that the legislator wishes to exclude semipublic oratories from the visitatorial jurisdiction of the bishop. What has just been said applies equally as well to semipublic oratories of lay congregations of pontifical approval for the provisions for the local visitation in these congregations as contained in canon 512, § 2, 3°, are identical with those for the visitation of clerical exempt and nonexempt religious. The fact

30. C. 512, § 1, n. 1.

31. C. 512, § 1, n. 2.

32. C. 512, § 2, n. 2. Goyeneche, "Consultationes" — *CpR,* III (1922), 335, 336; Vromant, *De personis,* n. 88; Schaefer, *De religiosis* (3. ed., S. A. L. E. R., Romae, 1940), p. 311; Blat, *Commentarium textus codicis iuris canonici, Ius de religiosis et laicis iuxta codicis ordinem* (3. ed., Romae, 1938), n. 157. Coronata on the other hand favors the subjection of semipublic oratories of nonexempt clerical religious since they would not come under the jurisdiction of any visitor: *Institutiones iuris canonici,* I, p. 648, note 2. As a rule the chapels of religious institutes are semipublic oratories — Creusen, *Religious men and women in the code* (3 ed., Milwaukee: Bruce, 1940), p. 102.

that these semipublic oratories are not subject to the visitation of an ecclesiastical superior is of no consequence. The legislator was certainly aware of this fact when he framed the legislation. Neither does the inquiry into the internal discipline of lay congregations of pontifical approval necessitate the visitation of their semipublic oratories. For this inquiry into the internal discipline on matters connected with their semipublic oratories can be effected without visiting the latter. The public and semipublic oratories of nuns subject to regulars only may not be visited unless the regular superior has failed to make the required visitation.[33]

Before the Code most of the authors were of the opinion that, once the preliminary visitation prior to the approval which was required for its canonical erection had been carried out, the bishop could no longer visit the private oratory. It was claimed that such a place could not be brought under the category of a sacred, or of a religious, or of a pious place. Furthermore, only that which was public, and not private or domestic, could be visited.[34] And the only causes calling for a revisit were an accusation of carelessness in its upkeep (*indecenter teneatur*) or the failure to comply with the provisions of the indult of the Holy See.

On the other hand, Gattico aptly pointed out that no law or precept of the Apostolic See forbade the ordinary to revisit the private oratories. Hence he conceded a visitation at some time during the general visitation of the diocese. He also correctly stated that the text cited by the dissenting authors[35] did not prohibit the ordinary from making a visitation. Nevertheless he admitted that in the practice of his time it was indeed a rare event for an ordinary to visit an oratory once its canonical erection had received his approval, unless he prudently suspected that the provisions of the indult were being exceeded or that abuses

33. C. 512, § 2, n. 1.

34. Hostiensis, lib. III, tit. 39, cap. 27, n. 1; Panormitanus, lib. III, tit. 39, cap. 27, n. 1; Fagnanus, lib. III, tit. 39, c. 27, nn. 2, 7, 8, 9, 29; Ferraris, *Bibliotheca*, ad v. "Oratorium," n. 25; Pignatelli, *Consultationes canonicae* (Coloniae Allobrogum: 1700), tom. I, consult. 93, n. 24; Melchers, *De canonica visitatione* (Coloniae ad Rhenum, 1893), p. 15.

35. C. 27, X, *de censibus, exactionibus et procurationibus*, III, 39.

existed.[36] Today, however, there seems to be no difficulty. Although the nature of a private oratory does not fit the definition of a *locus sacer*,[37] nevertheless its inclusion in the section of the Code which treats of sacred places reveals the regard of the legislator for it. And the latitude offered by the term *loca pia*,[38] as well as the failure of the Code itself to make an exemption in its favor, presents sufficient proof that a private oratory is also subject to the visitation of the bishop. This manner of reasoning receives confirmation through an inference made from the fact that a cardinal's private chapel or oratory (*sacellum*) is exempt from the visitation of the ordinary.[39] Moreover, the recent instruction of the Sacred Congregation of the Sacraments on the custody of the Blessed Sacrament charges the bishops to make a diligent inquiry in the course of their diocesan visitation even in private oratories concerning the care manifested in the custody of the Blessed Sacrament.[40] As a concluding remark let it be said that in the visitation of the oratories the bishop should see to it that the liturgical laws relative to their equipment are minutely observed and that cleanliness is maintained.

Cemeteries

Cemeteries for the faithful as *loca sacra*[41] are likewise subject to the episcopal visitation.[42] Cemeteries common to the faithful and exempt religious come under the jurisdiction of the local ordinary,[43] whereas

36. *De oratoriis domesticis et de usu altaris portatilis* (Romae, 1746), cap. XXIV, n. XI.

37. C. 1154.

38. C. 344.

39. C. 239, § 1, 18°.

40. "Praesertim dum sacras peragunt dioecesium visitationes, sed etiam extra easdem, quoties casus ferat, per se aut per idoneos ac prudentes ecclesiasticas personas diligenter inquirant animadvertantque de visu quomodo in singulis nedum paroeciis sed et ecclesiis, oratoriis, *etiam privatis*, hoc iure fruentibus provisum sit securitate custodiae Ssmae Eucharistiae." — S. C. Sacr., Instructio, 26 maii 1938, § 9 — *AAS*, XXX (1938), 205.

41. Cc. 1205, 1154.

42. Cf. Pontificale Romanum, *Ordo ad visitandos parochias*, § XI.

43. Leo XIII, const. "*Romanos Pontifices*," 8 maii 1881, n. 17 — *Fontes*, 582; Benedictus XIV, const. "*Firmandis*," 8 nov. 1744, n. 7 — *Fontes*, n. 349.

cemeteries dedicated to the interment of exempt religious alone do not.[44] Although the Code[45] claims that only exempt religious can have their own cemetery as distinct from the common cemetery, nevertheless if any nonexempt religious of pontifical approval have their own cemetery by special indult it also is exempt from the jurisdiction of the ordinary.[46]

In the visitation of the cemetery the ordinary will be concerned about its violation or desecration;[47] its enclosure and custody.[48] Then he will see that it has a special plot for clergy and clerics;[49] a separate section for infants;[50] unconsecrated ground for those to whom ecclesiastical burial is not granted,[51] such as unbaptized infants, apostates, condemned excommunicates, suicides, duellists unto death, persons who directed that their bodies be cremated, public and manifest sinners.[52] He is likewise to see to the exclusion of epitaphs, panegyric inscriptions, decorations and ornaments which are out of harmony with the Catholic religion.[53] While visiting the cemetery the bishop is also to inspect the chapels or private oratories erected in it.[54]

Schools

Canon 1382 declares that the local ordinary may visit, either personally or through a delegate, schools of every kind (*quaslibet*) and examine them on the things which bear on moral and religious instruction. Thus the ordinary need not be legitimately impeded in order to use a substitute. No mention is made of the frequency of the

44. Leo XIII, const. "*Romanos Pontifices,*" 8 maii 1881, n. 17 — *Fontes,* n. 582; cf. cc. 512, § 2, n. 2; 1209, § 1; 1228, § 2.
45. C. 1208, § 2.
46. Cf. c. 512, § 2, n. 2, which does not mention the cemetery as one of the objects to be visited. Cf. Vromant, *De personis,* n. 85, p. 97, note 2.
47. C. 1207.
48. C. 1210.
49. C. 1209, § 2.
50. C. 1209, § 3.
51. C. 1212.
52. Cc. 1239, 1240.
53. C. 1211.
54. C. 1194.

visitation. The presumption is that it is to be performed during the general visitation of the diocese.[55]

Moreover, in addition to its mention of schools, the text of the canon includes mention of centers where mental diversion and spiritual guidance are offered the young (*oratoria*), recreation or convalescence centers (*recreatoria*), and orphanages or institutes for unbefriended youths (*patronatus*).[56] Since the legislator included these institutions with the schools it is an indication that he proposed to extend the right to all such institutions where the young and the old are accepted, and where they obtain some moral or religious training in addition to the material benefits which answer their temporal needs.[57] On the other hand, the bishop may not visit universities which are under the immediate protection or supervision of the Holy See. Only the Pope, or his lawful representative, has this right.[58]

55. The catechetical decree of the Sacred Congregation of the Council, issued January 12, 1935, charges the pastor to see to it that when the pastoral visitation takes place the children be prepared to pass an examination in catechism in the presence of the bishop. The latter is then to make the required corrections with respect to parish catechetical instructions. On the other hand, the ordinaries have the obligation to appoint suitable priest visitors annually whose duty is to inspect all the classes of religion in the diocese, and to make a complete report on the findings, the progress, or the defects of the religious instruction given.—S. C. C., decr. 12 ian. 1935, II d, III, 2—*AAS*, XXVII (1935), 150, 151; cf. also Benedict XIV, ep. encycl. "*Etsi minime,*" 7 febr. 1742, n. 16—*Fontes*, n. 324.

56. Cf. Augustine, *A commentary on the new code of canon law*, VI, 426, note 31: *oratoria* and *recreatoria* are almost identical in nature. They denote asylums for the poor or aged, and conservatories for boys and girls. In the *oratoria*, besides the time which is given to recreation and relaxation, some time is devoted to intellectual pursuits and the practice of piety. Cf. Coronata, *Institutiones iuris canonici*, II, 312.

57. Cf. Vermeersch-Creusen, *Epitome*, II, n. 718; De Meester, *Juris canonici et juris canonico-civilis compendium*, III (Nova editio, Brugis, Desclée de Brouwer et S[i]: 1926), n. 1331; Boffa, *Canonical provisions for Catholic schools* (Catholic University of America, Canon Law Studies, n. 117, Washington, D. C., 1939), p. 178; Cocchi, *Commentarium in codicem iuris canonici*, VI (3. ed., Taurinorum Augustae: Marietti, 1933), n. 56, p. 133.

58. S. C. C. *Conimbricen.*, 18 aug., 1 sept. 1888—*ASS*, XI, 674 ff.; *Fontes*, n. 4274; *Thesaurus*, CXLVII, 601-618, 637.

In the legislation of the Council of Trent[59] the acknowledgment was made of the bishop's right to visit hospitals, colleges, and schools of every kind, regardless of whether they were exempt, or whether they were in the care of laymen. Immemorial customs, privileges, or statutory enactments to the contrary were of no consequence. The only exceptions to the law were institutions under royal protection, but even these could be visited provided the ruler's permission had been obtained. Pope Benedict XIV confirmed this law and declared that the legislation tolerated no appeal.[60]

At present the scope of the right of visitation with respect to all schools is not so broad as that of the former law, for the right of visitation is limited to matters involving religious and moral training. Because of the nature of the Church's right in regard to the education of youth, the stipulation that schools and similar institutions be erected or approved by ecclesiastical authority is not made a necessary prerequisite for the exercise of the bishop's right. All that is required is that they be erected for Christians — for the mental, religious and moral education of the faithful.[61] In reality, because of state or federal control of education in many countries, the bishops can exercise their right only over schools which are directly under the control of ecclesiastical authority.[62]

The III Plenary Council of Baltimore enjoined bishops to set up a School Commission or Board as required by the diversity of locality and language. These Boards were to consist of one or more priests. Their purpose was to examine the state of affairs in urban and rural schools. To effect this they were to make an annual or semiannual visitation of every school in their district. Thereupon they were to hand in an accurate report to the chairman of the Diocesan Board, who in turn was to forward it to the bishop. The bishop could then take action according to the disclosures of the survey.[63] This law does

59. Sess. XXII, *de ref.*, c. 8.

60. Const. "*Ad militantis,*" 30 mart., 1742, § 5, 31 — *Fontes*, n. 326.

61. Coronata, *Institutiones iuris canonici,* II, 312; Najera, *Derecho docente de la iglesia, la familia y el estado* (Linares: Impr. "El Noticiero," 1934), p. 440.

62. Coronata, *loc. cit.*

63. *Acta et decreta,* n. 204.

not contravene any law of the Code and therefore must be regarded as *praeter codicem.*[64]

The purpose of this law is realized under the existing diocesan school system with its diocesan school board. The superintendent of schools, acting in the name of the ordinary, makes a visitation of the schools of the diocese. This is also in conformity with the present legislation, which affords the bishop the choice of making the visitation in person or through others.

The existence of schools other than those belonging to the diocesan school system calls for an explanation as to the extent of the right of the bishop. The canon states that the bishop's right is limited to matters concerning religious and moral education. Obviously, however, the bishop has complete authority over the diocesan schools since he is their superior. His position is similar in regard to schools of diocesan religious.[65] Hence, the choice of teachers, the curricula, the disciplinary and pedagogical methods, in short, the entire scholastic administration and pedagogical system come under his jurisdiction.[66]

Furthermore, all Catholic elementary schools — known in England as schools of the poor — are of their very nature religious schools.[67] On that account they come under the surveillance and vigilance of the bishop even though they be in the hands of regulars.[68] Consequently

64. Pope Leo XIII in a letter to the Hungarian bishops exhorted them to institute school inspectors for each diocese and deanery. In a joint annual meeting the bishops and inspectors were to consider the state and condition of the schools, as well as matters bearing on morals and the care of souls. Ep. encycl. "*Constanti Hungarorum,*" 2 sept. 1893, n. 6 — *Fontes*, n. 620.

65. C. 492, § 2.

66. Creusen, "L'école catholique" — *NRT*, LIII (1926), 192.

67. Pius IX, ep. "*Quam non sine,*" 14 iul. 1864, n. 4 — "In hisce potissimum scholis omnes cuiusque e populo classis pueri vel a teneris annis sanctissimae nostrae religionis mysteriis ac praeceptionibus sedulo sunt erudiendi et ad pietatem morumque honestatem et ad religionem civilemque vivendi rationem accurate formandi, *atque in iisdem scholis religiosa praesertim doctrina ita primarium in institutione et educatione locum habere ac dominari debet,* ut aliorum cognitiones, quibus iuventus ibi imbuitur, adventitiae appareant." — *Fontes*, n. 539.

68. Leo XIII, const. "*Romanos Pontifices,*" 8 maii 1881, nn. 18, 19 — *Fontes*, n. 582.

the bishop has a right to visit such schools under the care of regulars with regard to all matters of school supervision.[69]

The situation is different concerning their intermediate schools and colleges, for their acquired rights or privileges remain inviolate.[70] The implication of paragraph 20 of the constitution *"Romanos Pontifices"*, if considered with reference to the last sentence, seems to be that these schools of regulars are not subject to the visitation in all things (*quoad omnia*) as are the elementary schools. This interpretation harmonizes with the text of the Code. However, if by the *privilegia* a complete exemption from the visitation of the bishop, even in what pertains to faith and morals, is meant, then naturally they are not subject to the visitation.[71] This is equally true of other religious, provided they can prove that their exemption was granted them directly.[72] Therefore, if regulars or other religious have no acquired rights or privileges exempting their intermediate and higher schools from the episcopal visitation, then these same schools are subject to the visitation of the bishop in matters concerning religious and moral training.

The canon adduces but one exception to the law. It cites the *scholae internae* of exempt religious. By this term are understood

69. "... Nos probantes declaramus: Episcopos ius habere quoad omnia visitandi huiusmodi scholas pauperum in missionibus et paroeciis regularibus aeque ac in saecularibus." Leo XIII, *ibidem*, n. 19.

70. "Alia profecto causa est ceterarum scholarum et collegiorum, in quibus religiosi viri secundum ordinis sui praescripta iuventuti catholicae instituendae operam dare solent; in hisce enim et ratio postulat, et nos volumus *firma atque integra privilegia manere* quae illis ab Apostolica Sede collata sunt. ..." — Leo XIII, *ibidem*, n. 20.

71. C. 4.

72. C. 613, § 1. Fanfani, *De iure religiosorum* (Edito altera, Taurini-Romae: Marietti, 1925), p. 450, n. 444; Coronata, *Institutiones iuris canonici*, II, 312; Blat, *Commentarium textus codicis iuris canonici*, III, *De rebus* (Editio secunda, Romae: Institutum Pontificium Internationale Angelicum, 1934), n. 275 (p. 371). Vermeersch *endeavors* to prove in virtue of the constitution *"Romanos Pontifices"* of Pope Leo XIII, the reply of the Sacred Congregation for the Propagation of the Faith (S. C. de Prop. Fide, 18 ian. 1886 (C. G.), ad 4 — *Collect. S. C. de P. F.*, n. 1651) and canon 63 that exempt clerical religious enjoy an immemorial privilege of exemption from the visitation of the ordinary even regarding matters referring to moral and religious training. Cf. "De Permanente vi C. Romanos Pontifices, 8 maii 1881, post c. 1382" — *Periodica*, XV (1926-1927), 57-61.

schools for the professed members of an exempt religious institute.[73] The exempt religious, therefore, are clerical exempt religious in virtue of canons 512, § 2, n. 3, and 618, § 2, n. 2.[74] But schools for postulants, apostolic schools or scholasticates do not come under this exemption.

Canon 1381, § 3, states the right of the bishop to approve books of religion. Moreover, according to canon 1336 the local ordinary has the right to regulate everything that pertains to the teaching of Christian doctrine to the people in his diocese. Even exempt religious are bound to obey his orders when there is question of teaching nonexempt persons. Hence the choice of textbooks of Christian doctrine rests with the bishop.[75] However, in schools which are not under his immediate authority he cannot impose a particular textbook in lieu of another which is unobjectionable as to its dogmatic content.[76] It seems that in such a case there is no basic reason for making the change. The sole reason would consist in the prelate's own preference and perhaps in his desire for uniformity. Besides, the effecting of a change would be inequitable and would place an unnecessary burden on those concerned.[77] The ordinary may also determine the time and the method of the instruction.[78] Nevertheless, with respect to the latter one can distinguish the essential from the nonessential or strictly psychological

73. The so-called schools for novices are not included. In fact, the law cautions against a situation where the novices are required to devote their time to study. C. 565; S. C. de Religiosis, *Instr.*, 3 nov. 1921—*AAS*, XIII (1921), 539.

74. Vromant, *Ius missionariorum*, II, *De personis*, (Louvain: Edition Du Museum Lessianum, 1929), p. 153, n. 179; cf. also the second edition (1935) of this work, p. 115, n. 100.

75. Wernz, *Ius decretalium*, III, 76; Creusen, "L'école catholique"—*NRT*, LIII (1926), 189; Jansen, *Canonical provisions for catechetical instruction* (Catholic University of America, Canon Law Studies, n. 107, Washington, D. C., 1937), p. 60.

76. Cruesen, *loc. cit.* Boffa (*Canonical provisions for catholic schools*, p. 163) is of the opposite opinion. Cf. also Jansen, *loc. cit.*

77. Since the Baltimore Catechism did not receive official approval as stipulated by the decree of the III Plenary Council (n. 219) and since contrary custom through the use of other texts has rendered the decree null, it cannot be considered the official text of this country. *HPR*, XXXIII (1933), 1198-99; Jansen, *op. cit.*, p. 48.

78. Wernz, *Ius decretalium*, III, 76; Jansen, *op. cit.*, p. 60.

elements. Hence the bishop can prescribe the quantity and the order of the matter to be taught, but should let the detailed pedagogical approach be determined by the experienced teachers in charge.[79] What is more, the ordinary has not only the right and duty to approve books of religion, but he also has the right to forbid books on secular topics which are at variance with Christian truths and morals (c. 1381, § 3). Such books are texts on philosophy, literature, history, biology, physics and the other sciences, which may be said to have a bearing on revealed truths and the rules of morality.

The Code also states that the bishop has the right to approve the teachers of religion.[80] Therefore the bishop has the right to test the aptitude of a candidate by an examination.[81]

The III Plenary Council of Baltimore commanded the bishops to establish a Board of Examiners, composed of one or more priests experienced in educational matters. It was the duty of this Board to examine prospective secular teachers or members of diocesan religious organizations. If the candidates passed the examinations successfully, they were to receive a diploma or certificate attesting to their fitness for a period of five years. Then at the expiration of the five year period they were to undergo another examination. This was final, provided the teachers did not fail.[82] The general aim of this law is realized under the present diocesan school system. For the superintendent of schools, acting in the name of the bishop, gives his approval to the competence of the parochial school teachers.

In the higher schools conducted by religious the bishop cannot claim the right of naming or choosing the teachers,[83] but only of giving them his approbation.[84] He may demand the removal of a teacher of

79. Creusen, *loc. cit.* — It is to be noted that the bishop's right extends to other than elementary schools. (C. 1381, § 3; Wernz, *Ius decretalium*, III, 81; Jansen, *loc. cit.*)

80. C. 1381, § 3.

81. Wernz, *Ius decretalium*, III, 77, 81.

82. *Acta et decreta*, n. 203. This law is *praeter codicem* and therefore is still binding.

83. Cf. c. 1381, § 3; Vromant, *De personis*, n. 98; Creusen, *Religious men and women in the code*, p. 70.

84. Wernz, *op. cit.*, p. 81.

religion or of secular subjects whose presence is detrimental to the interests of religion and morality among the students.[85] Moreover, he may insist on the expulsion of students if the moral education of the rest of the student body or particular local conditions require this.[86] Hence, while making the visitation the bishop will attend to the matters bearing on the religious and moral education of youth. Moreover, with respect to religious of congregations which are pontifically approved he may inquire about funds given in consideration of a certain school within the diocese.[87] As regards institutes of diocesan approval, the ordinary enjoys this right of inquiry whether the intention of the benefactor is directed to a particular school, to the institute's schools in general, or to the institute itself.[88]

Seminaries

Relative to the visitation of schools it is opportune to make mention of seminaries. The diocesan seminary naturally comes under the direct supervision of the ordinary.[89] He therefore has the obligation to visit it. The seminary, or house of studies of exempt religious institutes, on the other hand, is not subject to the bishop's visitation, for it is naturally destined for the sole use of the professed members.[90] The bishop, nevertheless, can visit their minor seminaries in whatever concerns religious and moral instruction.[91] He also has the right to visit the seminary of diocesan religious or that of nonexempt religious of pontifical approval. In the latter, however, the visitation is restricted to the religious and moral training of the students.[92]

A diocesan seminary entrusted by the ordinary to regulars enjoying an exemption from the visitation of the bishop is not thereby released

85. C. 1381, § 3.
86. Vromant, *loc. cit.*
87. Cc. 535, § 3, n. 2; 533, § 1, n. 4. Vromant, *loc. cit.*, cf. also c. 630, § 4.
88. C. 535, § 3, n. 1. Vromant, *loc. cit.*
89. C. 1357.
90. C. 1382.
91. Pejska, *Ius canonicum religiosorum*, p. 164.
92. C. 1382.

from the jurisdiction or visitation of the ordinary.[93] Pope Benedict XV (1914-1922) favored the Sulpicians with the privilege of accepting from the bishops the care and administration of diocesan seminaries. However, the superior and the members of the seminary depend on the ordinary of the diocese, and must render an account annually of the revenues of the foregoing year to the ordinary in the presence of two canons of the cathedral church of the diocese.[94]

The Code charges the bishop to make frequently a personal visitation of the diocesan seminary.[95] Evidently this obligation is distinct from that included in the general visitation of the diocese.[96] Nothing however will forbid the bishop to make the visitation of the seminary in the course of the general diocesan visitation serve to help fulfill the law with regard to this particular obligation. The insistence on frequency is practically identical with the law of the Council of Trent, for the latter used the word *saepius*,[97] while the Code uses *frequenter*. St. Charles Borromeo at the II Provincial Council of Milan (1569) commanded the bishops to visit the seminary at least every three months unless a just cause prevented them,[98] whereas Prospero Lambertini (Benedict XIV, 1740-1758), as archbishop of Bologna, was of the opinion that the bishop should make the visitation every month.[99] The Sacred Congregation of the Council stated that a bishop could visit the diocesan seminary as often as he pleased. The same holds true for

93. Vromant, *Jus missionariorum*, II, *De personis* (1929), p. 154; Coronata, *Institutiones iuris canonici*, II, 290. The bishop of Concepción, Chile, South America, wished to entrust his seminary to the Jesuits, and asked the Sacred Congregation of the Council for permission. To the doubt: "An et quomodo petitis sit annuendum?" the Congregation answered in the following manner, "Pro facultate; ita tamen ut alumni nominentur ab Episcopo, et seminarium sit sub patrocinio, protectione et subiectione episcopi." *Thesaurus*, II (1721-23), 189 et sq. Cf. also Benedict XIV, *De synodo dioecesana*, lib. v, cap. 11, n. 9.

94. Ep., 23 dec. 1921 — *AAS*, XIV (1922), 37.

95. C. 1357, § 2.

96. Cc. 343, § 1; 344.

97. "Quae omnia atque alia . . . opportuna et necessaria episcopi singuli . . . constituent, eaque ut semper observentur saepius visitando operam dabunt." — Sess. XXIII, *de ref.*, c. 18.

98. Tit. II, decr. 25 — Hardouin, XI, 746.

99. *Institutiones ecclesiasticae*, II, 233, cons. LIX, n. 16.

a vicar capitular or for the administrator of a vacant see.[100] If a bishop visits the seminary three or four times a year he certainly fulfills the prescription of the law. This visitation spoken of in canon 1357 is more of a private character and informal, while the visitation made on the occasion of the general visitation of the diocese usually takes on a more solemn note.[101]

The visitation of the seminary affords the bishop an opportunity of exercising vigilance over the material direction and supervision of the seminary, its financial management, and the mental and moral training of the students. In this visitation he can likewise satisfy himself as to the observance of seminary discipline, attendance at religious exercises and the compliance with its statutory regulations. It may also serve him in acquiring a more intimate knowledge of the students.[102] Cox[103] doubts the practicality of interviewing individual students on the occasion of the visitation, and would rather have the bishop rely on the rector or spiritual director for his knowledge. Nevertheless, in the New Formula for the Quinquennial Report in chapter six the question is asked: "An servatae sint regulae can. 1357 circa visitationem alumnorum et regulas internas?"[104]

Moreover, besides examining the students the bishop should question the rector and his immediate assistants as well as the deans or nonstudent prefects on the performance of their duties in the enforcement of discipline. It would also serve a useful purpose for the bishop to call a meeting of the board of discipline with the professors, the rector and his immediate assistants in attendance. Here ways and means could be devised for the improvement of discipline and study among the students. Then, too, the bishop may take occasion to interview the spiritual director on the conscientious fulfillment of his office and on matters pertaining to the official duties and the piety of the students.

100. S. C. C., *Viglevanen.*, 13 et 27 ian. 1714, ad 6, 7 — *Fontes,* 3130.

101. Lucidi, *De visitatione sacrorum liminum,* II, 411, 412.

102. C. 1357.

103. *The administration of seminaries* (Catholic University of America, Canon Law Studies, n. 67, Washington, D. C., 1931), p. 66.

104. S. C. Consist., *De relationibus dioecesanis, Formula,* 4 nov. 1918, n. 43 — *AAS,* X (1918), 494.

Likewise, the bishop may question the teachers and professors as to their spiritual life and clerical deportment, the fulfillment of their obligations, the method of their instruction and their orthodoxy in faith and morals. Indeed, he may take the opportunity of attending some of the classes to gain some firsthand information, though a thorough, true, and fair evaluation can scarcely be acquired in this manner alone.

Finally the bishop should make an inspection of the material condition of the seminary, giving due consideration to cleanliness, order, necessary repairs and improvements. Besides, the temporal administration of the seminary and its financial status should be discussed at a meeting attended by the procurator and the board for the temporal administration of the seminary.

The Sacred Congregation of Studies issued a decree on February 2, 1924, which obliges the ordinaries to make a report every three years on the condition of the seminary in accordance with a formula appended to the decree. The three year periods are determined from January 1, 1924. In that same year the report was to be made by the ordinaries of Italy, France, Spain, and the adjacent islands; in 1925 by the ordinaries of the other countries of Europe, and in 1926 by the ordinaries of America. This year, 1941, therefore, the report must again be made by the American bishops. It must be made in Latin; must bear the exact date of its writing and the signature of the ordinary himself. All the questions in the formula must be answered exactly and completely. Then, if any of the texts used in the courses in Philosophy, Theology, Sacred Scripture, and Canon Law are withdrawn during the period following the report, such facts are to be reported to the Sacred Congregation immediately. The fulfillment of this obligation of making a triennial report on the condition of the seminary does not thereby relieve the ordinary of the obligation of filing a report on the seminary as demanded by the decree on the Quinquennial Report. The formula consists of forty-one questions classified under seven headings.[105]

On April 24, 1931, Pope Pius XI issued a *Motu Proprio* on the canonical visitation of seminaries in Italy. By it he established an office incumbent on an ecclesiastic to be known as the Ordinary Visitor.

105. S. C. Stud., 2 feb. 1924 — *AAS,* XVII (1925), 547-551.

Once a year he is to make an inspection of all regional, interdiocesan, and diocesan seminaries.[106] Vermeersch thinks that the words of the pontiff indicate an intention of establishing a similar office for seminaries elsewhere.[107]

Pious Ecclesiastical and Lay Institutions

In Canon 1491 the Code explicitly acknowledges the bishop's right and at the same time imposes the obligation on him to visit institutions such as hospitals, orphanages, and the like. Before any further comments are made, a few explanatory remarks are necessary.

An institution is classified as a pious or secular (*profanum*) institution according to the nature of its *raison d'être.* If the latter consists in religion or charity as based on the love of God it is a pious institution, but, if the reason for its existence consists in the natural love of humanity or in mere philanthropy it is a secular institution.

Moreover, a pious institution may be ecclesiastical or lay: it is ecclesiastical if it is erected or approved by ecclesiastical authority; it is lay if it is founded by private persons without ecclesiastical approval or authority. Consequently in the latter instance its temporal goods cannot be considered as ecclesiastical goods,[108] and the laws on the temporal goods of the Church do not affect it.[109] The pious place which is under ecclesiastical control is known as an *institutum ecclesiasticum,* an ecclesiastical institution or house,[110] whereas the canonical nomenclature for an institution free from ecclesiastical control is *domus pia* (pious place or house).

The canon in question refers to pious ecclesiastical institutions. It obliges the local ordinary to visit all institutions of this kind, i. e.,

106. *AAS,* XXIII (1931), 151.

107. *Periodica,* XXI (1932), 13.

108. C. 1497.

109. Cf. S. C. C., *Corrienten. iurisdictionis,* 13 nov. 1920, which treats of the extent of the ordinary's jurisdiction with respect to the Society of St. Vincent de Paul and the nature of its pious works. — *AAS,* XIII (1921), 135-144.

110. Cf. Coronata, *Institutiones iuris canonici,* II, 428, note 1. Augustine (*A commentary on the new code of canon law,* VI, 546) retains the nomenclature of the decretals (X, *De religiosis domibus, ut episcopo sint subiectae,* III, 36). However, in canon 488, § 5, the Code has canonized the generic term *domus religiosa* to mean the residence of a religious organization.

those which are canonically erected regardless of the manner of their exemption.[111] Noncorporate institutions entrusted to a religious institute of diocesan approval are entirely subject to the jurisdiction of the bishop.[112] Therefore, the bishop has full visitational rights over them. But if a noncorporate institution is in the hands of religious of pontifical approval, the local ordinary lacks the right of visitation. The institution is then subject only to the ordinary's supervision or vigilance in all that concerns the teaching of religion, moral conduct, pious exercises, and the administration of the sacraments.[113] *A fortiori* a similar situation exists with respect to noncorporate institutions of regulars.[114] The provisions of the canon are very logical and in harmony with canon 512. For when an institution is devoid of juridic personality but is joined to an ecclesiastical moral person the nature of its subjection or exemption as regards the visitation will correspond to the status enjoyed by the moral person to which it is attached.

The Code fails to take into consideration pious lay institutions. However, as the bishop is the custodian of the faith and morals in his diocese,[115] and since pious places without exception are subject to his periodical visitation, unless they have a special privilege to the contrary,[116] he has the right to visit also pious lay institutions to

111. The visitation under consideration is the real juridical or canonical visitation, which includes the right of inspection, interrogation, correction and the right of inflicting penalties. Coronata, *Institutiones iuris canonici,* II, 433.

112. C. 1491, § 2. Although the Code speaks only of institutions in charge of a religious institute, they may also be entrusted to a chapter, parish, or a diocese. Coronata, *Institutiones iuris canonici,* II, p. 433, n. 3; Claeys-Bouuaert-Simenon, *Manuale iuris canonici,* III, p. 177, n. 245.

113. C. 1491, § 2. The distinction between the right of visitation and of vigilance is again emphasized. Coronata thinks a visitation would be warranted if anything reprehensible on the points mentioned should come to the knowledge of the ordinary. (II, *op. cit.,* p. 433, note 5.) But, it may be asked, on what grounds? Certainly the very purpose of the distinction in the law seems to be to deprive the ordinary of the right of visitation. Then, too, the insistence that the visitation is a species of vigilance is of no value as the Code expressly indicates whenever the bishop's vigilance is to bear the aspect of a visitation.

114. Coronata, *op. cit.,* II, 433. As is evident the determinant factor is the status of an institution. If it is a juridical entity enjoying juridical personality the bishop has the right of visitation whether or not the institution is controlled by exempt or nonexempt religious of pontifical approval.

115. C. 336.

116. C. 344, § 1.

preclude the occurrence of anything against faith and morals. If any abuses do occur he should correct them.[117] Under the old law it was understood that the bishop had the right to visit such places.[118] But if a hospital was under royal protection, the bishop required the king's permission to visit it.[119] While visiting pious lay institutions the local ordinary has the right to exercise vigilance over pious bequests,[120] because he is the executor of all donations and bequests (*piarum voluntatum*) made in favor of religion or charity.[121]

ARTICLE 2. THE VISITATION OF THINGS

Holy Eucharist

When the church or oratory is inspected, naturally its contents or furnishings receive particular consideration.[122] The Roman Pontifical directs the bishop to begin the visitation with the Holy Eucharist.[123] Hence he will investigate whether the Blessed Sacrament is properly and habitually reserved at but one altar which by its ornamentation is easily distinguishable from the others;[124] whether a sufficient number of consecrated particles is on hand;[125] whether fresh hosts are consecrated and renewed frequently;[126] and whether mass is celebrated at

117. Vermeersch-Creusen, *Epitome,* II, 815; Coronata, *op. cit.,* II, 434. Cf. S. C. C., *Corrieten. iurisdictionis* — *AAS,* XIII (1921), 144.

118. Barbosa, *De officio et potestate episcopi,* pars III, alleg. 75, nn. 6, 7, 11, 14.

119. Conc. Trid., sess. XXII, *de ref.,* c. 8; Barbosa, *ibid.,* n. 16.

120. C. 1515, § 2.

121. C. 1515, § 1.

122. "Secundo ut sciat et videat qualiter Ecclesia ipsa spiritualiter et temporaliter gubernetur; quomodo se habeat in ornamentis . . ." — Pontificale romanum, tit. *Ordo ad visitandas parochias,* § IV.

123. ". . . incipit visitationem a sanctissima eucharistia; ad baptisterium, inde ad sancta olea, ad sacras reliquias, tum ad altaria et capellas, et sacras imagines; item ad sacristiam se confert." — *Ibid.,* § XIII.

124. C. 1268, § 1, § 4.

125. C. 1270.

126. C. 1272; S. C. Sacr., *SS. Eucharistiae,* 7 dec. 1918 — *AAS,* XI (1919), 8; Rituale Romanum, tit. 4, cap. 1, n. 7; c. 815.

least weekly.[127] Then he will see that the tabernacle is immovable and secure,[128] and that it is adorned interiorly and exteriorly in conformity with liturgical prescriptions.[129] A further matter requiring his observation is that the tabernacle be not converted into a storehouse for such things as purified pyxes, ciboria or chalices, holy oil stocks, relics of the True Cross or of the saints, keys or other extraneous articles. He is likewise to inquire whether sufficient care is expended in forestalling any sacrilegious profanation or thievery, especially during the night,[130] and whether the key of the tabernacle is diligently guarded by the rector of the church.[131]

The bishop also examines the ciborium, lunette and pyx as to their material and condition. Moreover, he is not to tolerate relics, statues, flowers, candles, crucifix or any design whatsoever before the door of the tabernacle,[132] electric lights at the place of exposition,[133] or statues,

127. C. 1265, § 1.

128. C. 1269, § 1, § 2; S. C. Sacr., Instructio, 26 maii 1938, § 4 — *AAS,* XXX (1938), 199.

129. C. 1269, § 2; S. R. C., *Romana,* 20 iun. 1899, ad IV — *Decr. Auth.,* n. 4035; *Fontes,* n. 6298; Rituale Romanum, tit. IV, c. 1, n. 6.

130. C. 1269, § 2; S. C. Sacr., Instructio, § 5 — *AAS,* XXX (1938), 200-203.

131. C. 1269, § 4. The rector of the church should either keep the key of the tabernacle in the parish house, carry it on his person, or keep it locked in a safe and secret place in the sacristy provided he takes proper care of the second key — S. C. Sacr., Instructio, § 6 — *AAS,* XXX (1938, 203-204. In churches or oratories of nuns and sisters the key must be deposited in a safe, strong, and secret receptacle with a double lock; one of the keys is to be kept by the superioress, the other by some other nun or sister, ordinarily the sacristan. In oratories of seminaries, ecclesiastical colleges and institutes, as well as in hospitals, the key should be kept by the rector or moderator, if he be a priest, otherwise by the spiritual director usually assigned to perform sacred functions. In private oratories that enjoy the apostolic indult of reserving the Blessed Sacrament the family will ordinarily have charge of the key which is to be kept in the sacristy. Instructio, § 7, 8, 9.

132. S. R. C., *Congregationis Montis Coronae,* 22 ian. 1701, ad 10 — *Decr. Auth.,* n. 2067; *Decretum Generale,* 3 apr. 1821, ad 6 — *Decr. Auth.,* n. 2613; *Fontes,* n. 5841; *Sancti Angeli in Vado,* 6 sept. 1845 — *Decr. Auth.,* n. 2906; *Mexicana,* 10 sept. 1898, ad 1 — *Decr. Auth.,* n. 4000; *Fontes,* n. 6286; *Ordinis FF. Minorum Provinciae Portugalliae,* 11 iun. 1904, ad 2 — *Decr. Auth.,* n. 4136. *Fontes,* n. 6331.

133. S. R. C., *Dubium,* 28 iul. 1911 — *Decr. Auth.,* n. 4275.

flowers, relics on top of the tabernacle.[134] Finally, he should satisfy himself that the Sanctuary Lamp is kept burning uninterruptedly and that olive oil, beeswax or some vegetable oil, is used for this purpose;[135] that the law concerning the frequency of public exposition is observed,[136] and that devotion to and frequent visits to the Blessed Sacrament are urged upon the faithful.[137]

Baptistry

According to the Code every parochial church is to have a baptismal font.[138] In the examination of the baptistry, therefore, the bishop should focus his attention on the material and the condition of the baptismal font, especially with respect to hygiene,[139] the presence of a sacrarium, the holy oils and the ambry for the holy oils, and the other liturgical requisites for the administration of the Sacrament of Baptism.[140]

134. S. R. C., *Adnotationes super decreto generali,* 3 apr. 1821, ad dub. VI — *Decr. Auth.,* n. 2613; *Fontes,* n. 5841; *Tridentina,* 12 mart. 1836, ad 1 — *Decr. Auth.* n., 2740; *Fontes,* n. 5880; *Cadurcen.,* 31 mart. 1887, ad 2 — *Decr. Auth.,* n. 3673. According to a decree of the Sacred Congregation of Rites the top of the tabernacle is not to be used as a support for a permanent canopy of the Exposition of the Blessed Sacrament — *Westmonasterien.,* 27 maii 1911, ad 4 — *Decr. Auth.,* n. 4269; *Fontes,* n. 6386.

135. C. 1271.

136. C. 1274.

137. C. 1273.

138. C. 774.

139. The font is to be under lock and key — Rituale Romanum, tit. II, cap. 1, n. 46.

140. Rituale Romanum, tit. II, cap. I. It should be noted that the *Benedictio Fontis Baptismalis* must take place twice a year, and that only on the Saturdays before Easter and Pentecost, contrary customs notwithstanding. — S. R. C., *Lucana,* 12 apr. 1735, ad 1 — *Decr. Auth.,* n. 2436; *Fontes,* n. 5798; *Urbevetana,* 7 dec. 1844 — *Decr. Auth.,* n. 2878; *Fontes,* n. 5927; *Sancti Hippolyti,* 13 apr. 1874 — *Decr. Auth.,* n. 3331; *Fontes,* n. 6064; S. C. C., resol., 10 iun. 1922 — *AAS,* XV (1923), 225. (Cf. Bouscaren, *Canon law digest,* I, 252-253.) A church which prior to the Code had the exclusive right to a font over other parish churches now retains but a cumulative right with these churches which by virtue of canon 774, § 1, acquire the right to a font. — *AAS,* XIV (1922), 662; cf. Bouscaren, *ibid.,* p. 345.

Holy Oils

In the visitation the ordinary will observe whether the holy oils are kept under lock and key in a safe and becoming place in the church,[141] preferably in an ambry or press on the wall of the sanctuary, on either side of the main altar,[142] though they may be placed behind the altar or even in the sacristy.[143] The holy oils may not be kept in the parish house unless necessity or a reasonable cause makes it imperative, and the permission of the ordinary has been obtained.[144] Mere convenience is not a sufficient reason, whereas a great distance from the church would make such a practice justifiable.[145]

Confessionals

In connection with the visitation of confessionals the bishop is to see that they are in a conspicuous place[146] and that all are equipped with grilles.[147] Moreover, he is also to inspect them with regard to

141. C. 735; S. R. C., *Gandaven.*, 16 dec. 1826, Suffragia et adnotationes super decreto, ad dubium quaestionis tertiae. — *Decr. Auth.*, n. 2650; *Fontes*, n. 5850.

142. S. R. C., *Ariminen.*, 16 iun. 1663 — *Decr. Auth.*, n. 1260; *Fontes*, n. 5539.

143. S. R. C., *Gandaven.*, 16 dec. 1826, Suffragia et adnotationes super decreto ad dubium quaestionis tertiae. — *Decr. Auth.*, n. 2650. These *adnotationes* also state that the holy oils are not to be kept in the tabernacle, nor in the baptismal font, nor in the reliquary, and that when they are kept in the ambry the latter should bear an inscription.

144. C. 735; S. R. C., *Toletana*, 31 aug. 1872, ad 5 — *Decr. Auth.*, n. 3276; *Fontes*, n. 6047; *Compostellana*, 15 nov. 1890, ad 2 — *Decr. Auth.*, n. 3739; *Fontes*, n. 6205; *Lauden.*, 23 iun. 1892, ad 7 — *Decr. Auth.*, n. 3779; *Fontes*, n. 6216.

145. S. R. C., *Gandaven.*, 16 dec. 1826, ad tertiam facti speciem, ad 1 — *Decr. Auth.*, n. 2650; *Fontes*, n. 5850.

146. C. 909, § 1.

147. C. 909, § 2; Pont. Comm. Intr., 24 nov. 1920 — *AAS*, XXII, (1930), 576. This reply points to the need of a fixed screen with small perforations between the penitent and the confessor not only in reference to the hearing of women's confessions, but also for the hearing of confessions in churches and public oratories for any and all penitents, women and men alike, though the option of hearing the confessions of men in private homes which is granted in virtue of canon 910, § 2, remains intact.

the veiling placed over the grilles, the presence of stole and surplice,[148] the fixing of a crucifix or devout image in a prominent spot on the wall of the confessional, and the proper listing of the reserved sins in the diocese, whenever these items are prescribed by particular law. Then he should inquire whether women's confessions are ever heard outside the confessional, and, if they are, he should ask where they are heard and what precautions are taken.[149] Besides, he may ask what arrangements are made for hearing the confessions of the deaf. Finally, if there be a confessional in the sacristy, he should in this case also examine whether it is provided with the required screen.

Relics

Concerning relics exposed for public veneration, the bishop will investigate whether they are attested by a document of authenticity;[150] whether the approval or approbation of the local ordinary was also obtained,[151] and whether they are enclosed in a sealed reliquary.[152] Moreover he should remember that the relics of the Most Holy Cross are not to be exposed for veneration in a reliquary containing the relics of saints; that the relics of the blessed may not be carried in procession without a special indult, or exposed in churches which lack the faculty to celebrate their office and mass;[153] and that relics must be removed from the altar during the exposition of the Blessed Sacrament.[154]

The relics are placed between the candlesticks on the altar where the Blessed Sacrament is reserved[155] and two candles are kept lighted

148. Augustine, *A commentary on the new code of canon law,* II, 372.

149. C. 910, § 1.

150. C. 1283, § 1.

151. Dooley, *Church law on sacred relics* (Catholic University of America, Canon Law Studies, n. 70, Washington, D. C., 1931), p. 78.

152. C. 1287, § 1.

153. C. 1287, §§ 2, 3.

154. S. R. C., *Aquen.*, 2 sept. 1741, ad 1 — *Decr. Auth.*, n. 2365; *Lauden.*, 17 iun. 1900, ad 2 — *Decr. Auth.*, n. 4059.

155. S. R. C., *Ariminen.*, 7 apr. 1832, ad 3 — *Decr. Auth.*, n. 2689; *Fontes*, n. 5860; *Briocen.*, 12 aug. 1854, ad 13 — *Decr. Auth.*, n. 3029.

while they are exposed for veneration.[156] When they are not exposed for public veneration the relics should be kept in an ambry or in a safe place under lock and key. Furthermore, no important relics may ever be alienated or permanently transferred without permission from the Holy See,[157] nor may any relics be sold, exposed in any way to the danger of profanation or destruction, or kept in an unbecoming manner.[158]

Altars

The inspection of altars presents the ordinary with an occasion to find out whether at least one altar in a consecrated church is immovable;[159] and whether the stone covering the sepulchre for the relics is a single slab of natural stone.[160] In connection with the loss of the consecration of altars, he will investigate whether the table of an immovable altar was or is separated from its support;[161] whether there is an "enormous fracture" in either the immovable or also the portable

156. S. R. C., *Congregationis Montis Coronae,* 22 ian. 1701, ad 9 — *Decr. Auth.,* n. 2067; *Briocen.,* 12 aug. 1854, ad 13 — *Decr. Auth.,* n. 3029; *Sancti Miniati,* 20 mart. 1869 — *Decr. Auth.,* n. 3204. No kind of relic is to be placed on top of the tabernacle or before the door of the tabernacle. — S. R. C., *Decretum Generale,* 3 apr. 1821, ad 6 — *Decr. Auth.,* n. 2613; *Fontes,* n. 5841; *Tridentina,* 12 mart. 1836, ad 1 — *Decr. Auth.,* n. 2740; *Fontes,* n. 5880; *Sancti Angeli in Vado,* 6 sept. 1845 — *Decr. Auth.,* n. 2906.

157. C. 1281, § 1. It is forbidden to keep important relics in private houses or oratories (c. 1282).

158. C. 1289, §§ 1, 2.

159. C. 1197, §§ 1, 2. An altar can be consecrated without the church being consecrated, but together with the church at least the main altar, if it has not been consecrated, or some other altar must be consecrated. (C. 1165, § 5.)

160. C. 1198, § 4. The relics should be those of martyrs according to the words of the Apocalypse: "Vidi sub altare Dei animas interfectorum." S. R. C., *Rhedonen.,* Instructio, 6 oct. 1837 — *Decr. Auth.,* n. 2777; *Fontes,* n. 2777. Nevertheless, the Sacred Congregation of Rites decided that the relics of one martyr alone, or the relics of a martyr and of confessors or virgins sufficed for the valid consecration of either a fixed or a portable altar. — S. R. C., *Vilnen.,* 16 febr. 1906, ad 3 — *Decr. Auth.,* n. 4180; *Fontes,* n. 6348.

161. C. 1200, § 1. If the table of an immovable altar rests upon four columns and is momentarily dislodged from one or two of them, the consecration is not lost. — Bliley, *Altars according to the code of canon law* (Catholic University of America, Canon Law Studies, n. 38, Washington, D. C., 1927), p. 91.

altar stone; whether there is a fracture at a spot which was anointed;[162] whether the relics were removed; whether there is a large break in the stone cover of the sepulchre,[163] and whether this stone cover was removed.[164]

Then he may inquire whether every immovable altar has its proper title;[165] whether the title of a movable altar was changed without his permission,[166] whether the altars are exposed to uses other than that of divine service; whether at any time a body was buried under the altar,[167] and, finally, whether any masses have been said or are being said on a nonconsecrated altar.[168]

Statues

In connection with the inspection of statues and images the ordinary should be aware that his approval is required for the placing of any unusual image in any church whatsoever;[169] that he should not give his approval to the public exposition of images for the veneration of the faithful if these representations or images are not in harmony with the approved usage of the Church;[170] and that he is never to allow

162. C. 1200, § 2, n. 1. If the break extends to the relics, then the consecration is lost. S. R. C., *Policastren.*, 23 iun. 1879, ad 1 — *Decr. Auth.*, n. 3497; *Fontes,* n. 6119.

163. A slight fracture of the stone cover of the sepulchre does not cause a loss of consecration. C. 1200, § 3.

164. C. 1200, § 2, n. 2. The removal does not entail the loss of consecration whenever the bishop or his delegate removes the cover for the purpose of fastening, repairing, or replacing it, or for the inspection of the relics themselves.

165. C. 1201. The primary title of the main altar must be the same as that of the church (c. 1201, § 2).

166. C. 1201, § 3. For an altar to be dedicated to a beatified person an indult of the Holy See must be obtained (c. 1201, § 4).

167. C. 1202, §§ 1, 2.

168. C. 1199, § 1.

169. An image depicting the Sorrowful Mother dressed in black and holding a crucifix in the left hand would be considered unusual. S. R. C., *Triventina,* 23 febr. 1894, ad 2 — *Decr. Auth.*, n. 3818; *Fontes,* n. 6231.

170. The emblem of the Sacred Heart in the Most Holy Eucharist is not to be tolerated. (S. C. S. Off., decr., 30 maii 1891 — *Fontes,* n. 1136). To represent the Holy Ghost in human form is forbidden. (S. C. S. Off., 16 mar. 1928 — *AAS,* XXX [1928], 103). Pictures of the Sacred Heart alone are

the exhibition, in churches or other sacred places, of images which are dogmatically incorrect, which lack decency and propriety, and which are likely to furnish the ill-instructed an occasion for error.[171] Furthermore, repairs on images that are of great value by reason of their antiquity, their art, or the veneration given them, require his written consent. Before giving it he should seek prudent and expert advice on the matter.[172]

Other Church Appointments

With respect to the other furnishings of the altar, of the sanctuary, and of the other parts of the church,[173] such as crucifixes, candlesticks, candles, the chrismale, altar cloths, flowers, altar cards, sanctus bell, sacred vessels, sacred linens, sacred vestments, etc., the ordinary is to see that their material, form and arrangement correspond to liturgical requirements.[174] He is also to investigate their use, care, maintenance, custody, and condition.[175] Moreover, he may require an accurate up-to-date inventory of all sacred furnishings.[176] It is to be noted that the sacred furnishings which have been blessed or consecrated lose their blessing or consecration if they are so badly damaged, or have undergone such a change that they have lost their original form and are unfit for their proper purpose; or if they have been used for unbecoming purposes, or exhibited for public sale.[177] Contrary to the pre-Code doctrine and regulations of the Sacred Congregation of Rites,[178] chalices and patens do not lose their consecration when the gilding wears off or when they are regilded.[179]

prohibited for public exhibition. (S. C. S. Off., 26 aug. 1891 — *Coll. P. F.*, n. 1767). Representations of the Blessed Virgin garbed in priestly vestments are condemned. — S. C. S. Off., apr. 1916 — *AAS*, VIII (1916), 146.

171. C. 1279, §§ 1, 2, 3.

172. C. 1280.

173. It is beyond the scope of this treatise to treat these articles individually, or in any detail whatsoever.

174. C. 1296, § 3.

175. Cc. 1296, § 1; 1302.

176. C. 1296, § 2.

177. C. 1305, § 1.

178. S. R. C., *Leodien.*, 14 iun. 1845 — *Decr. Auth.*, n. 2889; *Strigonien.*, 9 maii 1857, ad 1 — *Decr. Auth.*, n. 3042.

179. C. 1305, § 2.

Parochial Archives

The ordinary is directed by canon 470, § 4, to visit the parochial archives either personally or through a delegate, either in the course of the visitation or at some other opportune time. Hence the bishop is to inspect the Registers of Baptism, of Confirmation, and of Matrimony, the Record of the Dead and the Record of the spiritual status of the parishioners,[180] in order to note whether the required entries have been made, and whether the annotations in the Baptismal Register have been inserted in a neat, orderly, readable fashion.[181] Other books and documents, such as the First Communion Register, Sick Call Register, the Preliminary Marriage Register, the Cemetery Register, the History of the Parish, the Announcement Book, the Book of Minutes of the Trustees, the Inventory of all the Church Goods, the Book of Donations and Bequests, the Book of Accounts, the Daybook and Ledger, the Book which records the names of the visiting-priests,[182] the binder for insurance policies, deeds, mortgages, etc., and the binder for pastoral letters, dispensations, and other episcopal communications[183] also come under his scrutiny.

Temporalities

Mindful of the injunction of the Roman Pontifical to inquire diligently "qualiter . . . temporalia in ipsa Ecclesia ministrantur"[184] and of the prescription in canon 1519 which gives him the right of supervision over the administration of ecclesiastical goods in his territory, the bishop will make a careful examination of the material belongings of the parish. Furthermore, he will demand an account of the ad-

180. C. 470, § 1.

181. C. 470, §§ 1, 2.

182. C. 804, § 2.

183. C. 470, § 4. The Third Plenary Council of Baltimore prescribed the use of a safe (*arca ferrea*) which would be easy of access to the pastor. *Acta et decreta,* n. 278. A fireproof safe is usually required by particular law. Cf. e. g., *Statuta Synodi Philadelphiensis,* IX (1934), n. 22c.

184. Tit. *Ordo ad Visitandas parochias,* § XIV. The second reason advanced by the Pontifical for the bishop's arrival at a parish is "ut sciat et videat qualiter Ecclesia ipsa spiritualiter et *temporaliter* gubernetur." § IV.

ministration of all the temporalities. In this matter he is subject to no restriction in a secular parish. Likewise in parishes connected in any way with religious of exclusively diocesan approval, whether the parochial church is secular or religious in character, the ordinary's right of inquiry is unrestricted.

With respect to parishes in the care of an exempt or nonexempt pontifical religious institute the local ordinary has the right to inquire about the property and funds for the building, maintaining, repairing and decorating of the parochial church,[185] if the church is a secular church. Similarly offerings for the benefit of the parishioners[186] come under his authority. Then, as regards funds and legacies[187] donated directly to the parish, or to the religious for the parish, the ordinary enjoys the right to demand an account of their administration.

According to canon 1515, § 1, the bishop is the executor of all charitable bequests made to beneficiaries under his jurisdiction. On that account he must exercise vigilance over them to the extent of making a visitation, so as to ensure their fulfillment.[188] As has been pointed out above, the bishop is expressly directed to visit all corporate ecclesiastical institutions, even though they be exempt,[189] and all non-corporate ecclesiastical institutions which are not under the care of religious of pontifical approval.[190] Moreover, he is to see that the pious wishes of the faithful expressed in the charters of these institutions be fully carried out.[191] Hence for this express purpose, in virtue of canon 1515, § 2, he may visit such institutions even if they are otherwise exempt from his visitation.[192]

Furthermore, whenever a cleric, secular or religious, is a trustee of property left in favor of any church of the place or of the diocese, or

185. C. 630, § 4.
186. C. 630, § 4. Reilly, *The visitation of religious,* pp. 141, 144.
187. Cc. 535, § 3, 2°; 533, § 1, 4°.
188. C. 1515, § 2.
189. C. 1491, § 1.
190. C. 1491, § 2.
191. C. 1493.
192. C. 1492, § 2. Vermeersch-Creusen, *Epitome,* II, 836; Vromant, *De bonis ecclesiae temporalibus,* n. 159; Hannan, *The canon law of wills* (The Catholic University of America, Canon Law Studies, n. 86, Washington, D. C., 1934), n. 774; Cocchi, *Commentarium,* VI, n. 194, p. 379.

in support of the residents or of pious works of the diocese, the bishop has the obligation to supervise the fulfillment of the trust even by means of a visitation.[193] However, property given a nonexempt religious of a pontifically approved religious institute for work entrusted to his community does not come under the bishop's supervision.[194] The same is true if it is given for pious causes in general without any determination of the place where these causes are to be promoted.[195] But if the pious cause is other than that of the community, and the place is specified, then the bishop will have power over the trust.[196] It is to be noted that lay persons are likewise bound to allow a visitation by the ordinary in this matter.[197]

The ordinary or bishop of the place where the bequest is to be fulfilled, and not the ordinary of the trustee, is the proper ordinary.[198] On the other hand, when the specification of a place for the fulfillment of the bequest is wanting, then the domicile of the trustee provides the norm for determining the properly competent ordinary for making the visitation.[199]

In relation to pious foundations[200] established in any church[201] or oratory,[202] the Code authorizes the ordinary to see that the intentions and stipulations of the donors are carried out in detail. This vigilance

193. Cc. 1516, §§ 2, 3; 1515, § 2.

194. Schaefer, *De religiosis*, p. 414; Vromant, *De bonis ecclesiae temporalibus*, n. 164, bis. In this case there is, strictly considered, no real trust. The pious cause is identified with the work of the community.

195. Schaefer, *De religiosis*, p. 414.

196. Vromant, *De bonis ecclesiae temporalibus*, n. 164, bis.

197. Cc. 1515, § 2; 1521, § 2; Vromant, *De bonis ecclesiae temporalibus*, nn. 161, 163; Vermeersch-Creusen, Epitome, II, 836; Hannan, *The canon law of wills*, n. 782.

198. Nebreda, "Studia canonica"—*CpR*, VII (1926), 328; Vromant, *De bonis ecclesiae temporalibus*, n. 163; Hannan, *The canon law of wills*, n. 787.

199. Vromant, *De bonis temporalibus*, n. 163, bis; Hannan, *The canon law of wills*, n. 787.

200. C. 1544.

201. According to Vermeersch-Creusen (*Epitome*, II, 868) and Vromant (*De bonis ecclesiae temporalibus*, n. 351) the word "church" has reference to any ecclesiastical moral person.

202. C. 1191, § 1.

includes a right of visitation to that end.[203] Hence the bishop suffers no curtailment of his right in a secular parish or in a religious parish in the care of a nonexempt institute.[204] He may inspect the list of obligations resulting from a pious foundation, as well as the book wherein are entered all the perpetual and temporary obligations arising from such a pious foundation, the fulfillment of these obligations and the stipends paid.[205] In religious churches of an exempt institute the major superior has the right of supervision and visitation,[206] but the ordinary may demand an account of the administration of foundations whose object is the promotion of ecclesiastical functions or the exercise of works of charity in the place in question.[207]

The bishop will also have authority over a foundation if it is not given to an individual religious house but to the religious community or institute, even though this religious community be an exempt clerical institute, if the foundation is destined for works of charity or religion in a determined parish or diocese.[208] The same power is given the bishop with respect to trusts or foundations given to a nonexempt institute with a view to aiding a particular pious establishment or determinate diocese.[209] On the other hand, if the foundation connotes a general grant to a nonexempt community of pontifical approval without any specification as to the place in which or the purpose for which the foundation is to be utilized other than the advantage or interest of the community itself, then even such a nonexempt religious com-

203. C. 1549, § 1, (c. 1515, § 2).

204. Vromant, *De bonis ecclesiae temporalibus*, nn. 355, 356; Reilly, *The visitation of religious*, p. 145.

205. C. 1549, § 2.

206. C. 1550.

207. Cc. 533, § 1, n. 3; 535, § 3, n. 2. Cf. Pont. Comm. Intr., 25 iul. 1926, ad IV—*AAS*, XVII (1926), 393; Vromant, *De bonis ecclesiae temporalibus*, n. 355; Schaefer, *De religiosis*, p. 440. Larraona ("Commentarium codicis"—*CpR*, XIII [1932], 27-31) admirably answers the objections of those who claim that canon 533, § 1, n. 3, excludes clerical exempt religious from giving an account to the local ordinary.

208. Nebreda, "Studia canonica"—*CpR*, VIII (1926), 266; Vromant, *De bonis ecclesiae temporalibus*, n. 164; Hannan, *The canon law of wills*, n. 770.

209. Vromant, *De bonis ecclesiae temporalibus*, nn. 164, 356; Hannan, *The canon law of wills*, n. 770.

munity is not under any subjection to the local ordinary in this matter in the course of his canonical visitation.[210]

Since religious institutes of diocesan approval are of their very nature under the immediate authority of the bishop, the foundations established in these communities, or in their individual houses, come under his plenary powers. The bishop enjoys the same right with respect to juridical lay associations,[211] even though they be established in churches of exempt religious,[212] or also when they are constituted as independent charitable noncollegiate institutions.[213]

Registers of Mass Obligations

Finally, ordinaries have the obligation to inspect, at least once a year, either personally or through another, the registers of manual mass obligations wherein rectors[214] of churches and pious places are obliged to enter the number, the intention, the amount of the stipend and the date of fulfillment.[215] It is to be noted that the canon does not speak of personal stipends, but rather of stipends offered in view of, or out of consideration for, a certain church or pious place.[216] Hence a bishop will exercise this right in secular churches which are placed in the charge of diocesan priests and also in secular or religious churches which are in the care of a religious institute of diocesan approval or of a nonexempt religious congregation. As is evident, this applies in a similar manner to corporate charitable ecclesiastical institutions[217] and to noncorporate institutions[218] subject to the episcopal visitation. Reilly claims that in a secular church which is placed under the care of exempt clerical religious the latter's ordinary and not the

210. Vromant, *De bonis ecclesiae temporalibus,* nn. 164, 356; Hannan, *The canon law of wills,* n. 771.

211. C. 690, § 1.

212. C. 690, § 2; Vromant, *De fidelium associationibus* (Louvain, Museum Lessianum, 1932), nn. 19, 20.

213. C. 1491, § § 1, 2; Hannan, *The canon law of wills,* n. 772.

214. The term includes pastors, chaplains and every priest having charge of a church, public oratory or chapel. — Keller, *Mass stipends* (Catholic University of America, Canon Law Studies, n. 27; Washington, D. C., 1925), p. 152.

215. C. 843, §§ 1, 2.

216. Vromant, *De bonis ecclesiae temporalibus,* n. 235.

217. C. 1491, § 1.

218. C. 1491, § 2.

bishop is obligated to inspect the register in question.[219] On the other hand, Vromant[220] states that the bishop has the right of inspection even in churches of exempt religious.[221] However, it seems more proper in view of the fact that the Code merely uses the word *ordinarii* to confine the right of the bishop to *secular* churches under the care of exempt clerical religious. Futhermore, the right of demanding an account and the right of visitation or inspection are not identical.

In the writer's opinion the private or personal registers of manual stipends of diocesan clerics are not subject to the visitation or inspection of the bishop.[222] Nevertheless he may inquire into the fulfillment of these obligations, but since such registers constitute strictly personal and private items of property, and cannot be classified in the category of ecclesiastical goods, the bishop lacks the title of visitatorial competence.

ARTICLE 3. PERSONAL VISITATION

The personal visitation embraces physical and moral persons. It includes the clergy, the religious, and the laity.

219. *The visitation of religious,* pp. 111, 145. Cappello says: "Episcopus in canonica dioecesis visitatione nequit sibi vindicare ius inspiciendi libros Missarum manualium (aut fundatorum) in ecclesiis religiosorum exemptorum etsi paroeciales sint". — *De Sacramentis* (3. ed., Romae: Marietti, 1938), I, n. 714. They base their stand on a particular declaration of the Congregation of Bishops and Regulars of May 11, 1904, which had to do with a visitation of a parish of the Friars Minor. — *Fontes,* n. 2047.

220. *De bonis ecclesiae temporalibus,* nn. 233, 235, 355. Pejska seems to be of the same opinion, for he declares: "Episcopus et superior major tenentur obligatione libros intentionum *ecclesiarum sibi subditarum* singulis saltem annis sive per se sive per alios recognoscendi." — *Jus canonicum religiosum,* p. 272.

221. "Libros eleemosynarum pro missis manualibus, quae in beneficentiam non personalem sed potius *localem* sunt datae, apud religiosos *congregationis etiam exemptae* recognoscet Ordinarius loci." *Op. cit.,* n. 233; "Jus autem singulis annis libros eleemosynarum Missarum vi can. 843, § 2, recognoscendi, pro sodalibus *congregationis* religiosae, sive ecclesia vel locus pius sit saecularis sive religiosus, semper pertinet ad *Ordinarium loci.*" — *Op. cit.,* n. 235.

222. This is also the view of Cappello ("Huiusmodi libri mere privati non subsunt canonicae inspectioni Ordinarii. Optandum tamen, ut sacerdotes sponte eos subiiciant examini et inspectioni Ordinarii." — *loc. cit.*) whereas Cance says: "L'ordinaire n'a pas l'obligation, mais a le droit, s'il le juge nécessaire ou utile, de se faire présenter ce carnet de Messes". — *Droit canonique,* II (6. ed., Paris: Libraire Lecoffre, 1930), p. 176.

Clergy

As regards the clergy in general, the bishop will be concerned with their character, reputation, morals, conduct and obligations. Hence concerning the latter he will inquire whether they approach the Sacrament of Penance frequently, whether they meditate, visit the Blessed Sacrament, recite the rosary, and make an examination of conscience daily;[223] whether they make the retreat at the specified time;[224] whether the younger clergy have taken the annual junior clergy examination;[225] and whether any of the clergy attend secular universities or colleges without his permission.[226]

In addition to the foregoing points he will investigate whether those charged with the care of souls attend the clerical diocesan conferences;[227] whether any members of the clergy are under suspicion of familiarity with any person of the other sex;[228] whether they duly recite their divine office;[229] whether they conform to the accepted custom of the country or diocese as regards clerical dress;[230] whether they go bail for anyone;[231] whether they gamble in public; whether they indulge in hunting that is accompanied with great display and publicity, for instance, in a fox chase; whether they visit saloons, taverns, taprooms, or any similar places;[232] whether they are taken

223. C. 125, nn. 1, 2.

224. C. 126 obliges a priest to make a retreat every three years, but the III Plenary Council of Baltimore (1884) obliges the bishop to make a retreat with his priests annually, or at least every two years. — *Acta et decreta*, n. 75.

225. C. 130 sets the minimum requirement at three years, whereas the III Plenary Council of Baltimore determined it as a period of five years. — *Acta et decreta*, n. 187.

226. S. C. Consist., decr., 30 apr. 1918 — *AAS*, X (1918), 237.

227. C. 131 states that these conferences should be held frequently (*saepius*) during the year. The legislation of the II and III Plenary Councils of Baltimore calls for four sessions a year in the cities — nn. 68 (II), 192 (III). Religious assistants and chaplains who take the place of the pastor and aid him in the parochial ministry have an obligation to attend. — Pont. Comm. Intr., 12 feb. 1935 — *AAS*, XXVII (1935), 92,

228. C. 133.

229. C. 135.

230. C. 136. S. C. C., decr., 28 iul. 1931 — *AAS*, XXIII (1931), 336.

231. C. 137.

232. C. 138.

up with affairs that are foreign to the clerical state,[233] or which entail the rendering of an account to civil authorities.[234] The visitor is also to see that his clergy never attend theatres, shows, night clubs, ballrooms and races at which their presence is a source of scandal.[235] Besides, they are not to sponsor dances or picnics[236] or engage in business or trading.[237] Finally, he will discover whether his priests comply with the law on residence;[238] whether they manifest charity to priests of other rites;[239] whether they wear a cassock reaching to the ankles and put on the proper vestments while saying mass;[240] whether they write articles in newspapers, magazines, periodicals, or publish books on secular topics without his permission;[241] whether they read scandalous and unbecoming literature;[242] and whether the pastor and curates live a harmonious and peaceful community life.[243] Moreover, the bishop may take the opportunity of examining the clergy on their knowledge of the rubrics and the ceremonies.[244]

233. C. 139, § 1.

234. C. 139, § 3; Pont. Comm. Intr., 3 iun. 1918 — *AAS*, X (1918), 344.

235. C. 140; *Acta et decreta*, n. 79. Barrett claims it is no longer an open question whether or not horse races are included under the forbidden *spectacula* of the Code or whether or not custom may not have tempered the law of the III Plenary Council of Baltimore. For he says it is commonly known that the Holy See has urged our bishops to punish clerics who attend races. — *A comparative study of the councils of Baltimore and the code of canon law*, p. 53.

236. *Acta et decreta*, n. 290; S. C. Consist., decr., 31 mart. 1916; declar., 10 dec. 1917 — *AAS*, VIII (1916), 147; X (1918), 17; Vermeersch-Creusen, *Epitome*, I, 255.

237. C. 142. The III Plenary Council of Baltimore forbade *banking* to bishops, rectors and to all ecclesiastics secular or religious. — *Acta et decreta*, n. 274. As this prohibition in no way contravenes the law of the Code, it seems that this legislation is still in force.

238. C. 143.

239. S. C. Consist., *De relationibus dioecesanis, Formula*, 4 nov. 1918, n. 49 — *AAS*, X (1918), 496.

240. C. 811, § 1; S. C. C., decr., 28 iul. 1931 — *AAS*, XXIII (1931), 336.

241. C. 1386, § 1.

242. S. C. Consist., *De relationibus dioecesanis, Formula*, 4 nov. 1918, n. 52 — *AAS*, X (1918), 496.

243. Cc. 134; 476, § 5.

244. The early councils considered this the chief duty of the bishop during the visitation. Cf., for example, the II Council of Braga (572) — Bruns, II, 39; cf. *supra*, pp. 13, 14.

In the visitation of the vicar forane the bishop will inquire about the vigilance of the latter over the priests of his district as concerns the observance of liturgical laws, the administration of church goods, the execution of the decrees of the last episcopal visitation, the proper care of the parochial records and of the church furniture, the vicar's care of the sick priests in his district, his arrangements for their burial, his custody of church property in the parishes of deceased priests and his visitation of the district entrusted to his care.[245] The bishop's own visitation of the district will of necessity reveal to what extent the rural dean has really fulfilled his duty. Moreover, like any other pastor, the rural dean will himself be examined on the points that follow concerning pastors.

A pastor is to be examined especially with respect to his gratuitous ministration,[246] his residence,[247] his application of the *Missa pro populo,*[248] his administration of the sacraments and his zeal for souls as manifested by his intimate knowledge of his parishioners, his prudent correction of the errant, his paternal charity toward the poor and suffering, and his unfailing interest in the instruction of the children in the Catholic faith.[249] He is also to be questioned concerning the visitation and care of the sick, especially at the hour of death, through the ministration of the sacraments and the giving of the apostolic benediction,[250] the constant vigilance against the dissemination of errors concerning faith and morals, and the spreading of vices,[251] the fostering of works of charity, faith and piety within his parish,[252] the diligent and orderly care of the parochial archives and parochial registers,[253] the annual transfer of authentic copies of these parochial records to the diocesan curia,[254] and the custody of the holy oils.[255]

245. C. 447.
246. C. 463, § 4.
247. C. 465.
248. C. 466.
249. C. 467.
250. C. 468.
251. C. 469.
252. C. 469.
253. C. 470.
254. C. 470, § 3.
255. Cc. 735, 946.

Another matter for inquiry is whether or not he has frequently exhorted the faithful to receive the Holy Eucharist often or even daily,[256] to cultivate a devotion to the Most Blessed Sacrament, to assist at daily Mass, and to make daily visits to the Blessed Sacrament,[257] especially in the evenings.[258] Then there is the important matter of the ministration of Holy Viaticum and Extreme Unction to the sick while they are fully conscious.[259] The visitor is likewise to inquire about the exposition of the Blessed Sacrament on the days appointed,[260] and the annual celebration of the Forty Hours devotion;[261] the careful selection of children for their first Holy Communion at the proper age, and the avoidance of delays and abuses in this regard;[262] the diligent preparation of the children at stated times each year for their first Confession, their first Holy Communion and their reception of Confirmation;[263] the catechetical instruction of children and adults on Sundays and holydays of obligation;[264] the prenuptial investigations as to freedom of status; the publication of the banns; the certification about the existence or nonexistence of matrimonial impediments; the application for the proper dispensations in the event of their existence; the prudent inquiry into the prospective exchange of a free and unhindered matrimonial consent; the proper care in everything that concerns the form, the time and place of the celebration of Christian marriage; the careful notation of the contracted marriage in the parochial matrimonial register;[265] the preaching of a homily on Sundays and holydays

256. C. 863.

257. C. 1273.

258. S. C. Consist., *De relationibus dioecesanis, Formula*, 4 nov. 1918, n. 72 — *AAS*, X (1918), 498.

259. Cc. 865, 944.

260. C. 1274.

261. C. 1275.

262. C. 854.

263. C. 1330.

264. Cc. 1331, 1332. The III Plenary Council of Baltimore requires priests to visit every class (*unamquamque partem*) of their parochial school at least once a week and to impart religious instruction to the children therein — *Acta et decreta*, nn. 201, 217.

265. Cc. 1012-1109. If a bishop has prescribed a course of instructions in Catholic doctrine for the non-Catholic party before the celebration of a mixed marriage, he should inquire concerning the faithful observance of the regulation.

of obligation;[266] the giving of sermon courses during Advent and Lent,[267] and the conducting of missions at least every ten years.[268]

What has been said above likewise applies to the religious pastors or parochial vicars, for they too are subject to the jurisdiction, visitations, and correction of the local ordinary, just as are the diocesan pastors, even if it happen that their major religious superiors have their ordinary residence in the house or place where these pastors or vicars are exercising their ministry. However, the bishop has no right to inquire into the observance of their rule of life.[269]

Then the ordinary is also to investigate the fulfillment of the curates' obligations relative to the responsibilities entrusted to them in the care of the faithful.

Wherever a collegiate chapter exists the bishop makes a visitation of the entire group and of each individual member thereof in connection with their duties and obligations.[270] However, in this country no such visitation takes place, since no cathedral or collegiate chapters are here in existence.

266. C. 1344.

267. C. 1346.

268. C. 1349.

269. C. 631, § 1. Pope Benedict XIV in his constitution "*Firmandis*" stated that the local ordinary was to make an investigation into the life and morals of religious pastors. Then he noted that the ordinary had a right and duty to examine whether the pastor exercises the care of souls by a legitimate title, whether he has been and is observing the law of residence, whether he attends the clerical conferences whenever he has been notified, whether he says the *Missa pro populo* on Sundays and holydays of obligation, whether he preaches the word of God and instructs the children in Christian doctrine on these days as prescribed by the Council of Trent, whether on set days he hears the confessions of the faithful, whether he is zealous in assisting the sick and dying and administers the sacraments in due time, whether he gives the proper instruction to boys and girls before Confirmation and First Communion, whether before admitting the faithful to marry *in facie Ecclesiae* he made and is making the necessary investigations to verify their state of freedom to marry, and is providing for their instruction in Christian doctrine, especially in the principal mysteries of the faith; and whether he keeps in good order the Baptismal Register, the Register of Confirmation, the Marriage Record, and the Record of the Spiritual Status of the Parishioners. 6 nov. 1744, § 9 — *Fontes,* n. 349.

270. Cc. 395-422.

The officers of the diocesan curia, especially the vicar general, the judge of the diocesan tribunal, the promoter of justice, the defender of the sacred bond of Orders and Matrimony, the notary and the chancellor should likewise be investigated relative to the faithful and conscientious execution of their duties as required by law.

Teachers in the various schools should be questioned about the teaching matter, its doctrinal import, and their own theories. Catechists and those participating in the spread of Christian doctrine may also be examined on their knowledge of the Catholic faith.

Religious

According to canon 512 the bishop is obliged to make a quinquennial visitation of the different religious houses either personally or through someone else. He need not have a legitimate reason for the use of a substitute, for the canon does not include the clause, *si legitime fuerit impeditus*,[271] or any equivalently expressed condition. However, he cannot dispense himself from the obligation.[272] On the other hand there is nothing in the law prohibiting the bishop from performing the visitation more frequently whenever conditions would warrant such action. In case a bishop is guilty of serious neglect the metropolitan has the obligation to make the visitation,[273] for the visitation of religious is part of the visitation of the diocese. Moreover, if the right of the archbishop did not embrace the visitation of religious, there would be no one properly indicated to supply the neglect. However, the metropolitan must first inform the Holy See of the neglect and receive its approval.

Accordingly, the bishop must visit nuns subject to him or immediately subject to the Apostolic See.[274] Canon 512 makes no mention of restrictions. Hence he proceeds with plenary authority, and his visitatorial jurisdiction extends to all matters. Besides, he has the specific obligation to inquire into the administration of the dowry funds.[275]

271. Cf. c. 343, § 1.
272. Larraona, "Commentarium codicis" — *CpR,* VIII (1927), 441.
273. C. 274, n. 5.
274. C. 512, § 1, 1°.
275. C. 550, § 2.

In like manner he shall visit the diocesan congregations of men and women religious,[276] for he has complete jurisdiction over the houses of these religious.[277] With respect to women religious the bishop is to watch over the preservation of the dowries, and must investigate the administration of the funds accruing therefrom.[278] However, it is the local ordinary of the provincial or general house wherein the dowries are administered[279] who has this right to supervise the proper fulfillment of the law on dowries and to receive an accounting thereof during the visitation.[280] Although some authors[281] deny the local ordinary of the motherhouse the right to visit the general curia and to inquire into the administration of the general funds in the event that a diocesan congregation is established in several dioceses, the opposite opinion is more compelling.[282] For, if this were not so, the general curia would be exempt, which is contrary to the very nature of diocesan congregations, since they are to be completely subject to the local ordinaries.[283]

In the visitation of nuns subject to regulars and not to the bishop, the bishop's visitation is restricted to the matters which deal with the proper canonical establishment and observance of the enclosure.[284] Nevertheless, he may conduct a *personal* visitation to the extent of questioning the nuns at the grille on matters pertaining to the enclosure.[285] He is like-

276. C. 512, § 1, 2°.

277. Cc. 488, 3°; 492, § 2.

278. Cc. 550, § 2; 535, § 2.

279. C. 550, § 1.

280. Reilly, *The visitation of religious*, p. 93.

281. Bastien, *Directoire canonique à l'usage des congregations a voeux simples* (3. ed. Charles Beyaert, Bruges [Belgique] 1923, n. 305; Larraona, "De visitatorum potestate applicandi poenas in can. 2413 statutas" — *CpR*, X (1929), 373-376.

282. D'Ambrosio, "De domo generalitia instituti polydioecesani quoad canonicam visitationem can. 512, § 1, n. 2, praescriptam et quoad poenas can. 2413 sancitas," — *Apollinaris*, I (1928), 417-422; Reilly, *The visitation of religious*, pp. 93-97.

283. C. 492, § 2.

284. C. 512, § 2, 1°.

285. Pont. Comm. Intr., 24 nov. 1920 — *AAS*, XII (1920), 575. S. C. de Religiosis, Instructio, 1 febr. 1924, § III, n. 2, b. — *AAS*, XVI (1924), 96.

wise to make an inquiry concerning the dowry funds.[286] Finally the Code states that the bishop must perform a complete visitation if the regular superior has failed to do so.[287]

When visiting the clerical congregations of pontifical approval, the bishop's investigation is limited to the church, the sacristy, the public oratory, and the confessionals,[288] i. e., those used in hearing the confessions of the faithful,[289] even though they be not placed in the church or public oratory.[290] Hence, neither semipublic oratories nor the confessionals erected therein for the religious are subject to the episcopal visitation.[291]

The remarks just made are also relative to lay congregations of pontifical approval.[292] What is more, the bishop has the added obligation to investigate whether the prevailing discipline conforms to the constitutions; whether sound doctrine and good morals have suffered in any way; whether the law of the enclosure has been violated, and whether the reception of the sacraments is regular and frequent.[293] As a consequence he may conduct a personal visitation in regard to the above points. Finally, in congregations of women religious he has the duty of inquiring into the administration of the dowry funds.[294]

The provisions of canon 512 mentioned above with reference to diocesan congregations, exempt and nonexempt clerical congregations of pontifical approval and lay congregations of pontifical approval apply equally as well to societies without vows.[295] Due and proper correlation must be made for the nature of their subjection to the visitation of the bishop will depend on the status they enjoy in the eyes of the law.

286. C. 550, § 2.

287. C. 512, § 2, 1°.

288. C. 512, § 2, 2°.

289. C. 908.

290. Larraona, "Commentarium codicis" — *CpR,* VIII (1927), 447.

291. Larraona, *loc. cit.,* note 501; Schaefer, *De religiosis,* p. 310; Goyeneche, "Consultationes" — *CpR,* III (1922), 335, 336. Cf. *supra,* pp. 96, 97.

292. C. 512, § 2, 3°.

293. Cc. 512, § 2, 3°; 618.

294. Cc. 535, § 2; 550, § 2.

295. Cf. c. 674; Blat, *Commentarium, Ius de religiosis et laicis iuxta codicis ordinem,* p. 170, n. 159.

Laity

Lastly the laity are to be taken into consideration. The bishop is to take cognizance of their faith and morals. He is to discover whether the spirit of true Christian living is in evidence in both the private and public lives of the people, and whether the spirit of genuine piety exists. He may inquire in what regard the clergy, his own person, and that of the Pope are held.[296] Then he is to investigate concerning attendance at mass on Sundays and holydays of obligation, abstention from servile works,[297] the observance of fast and abstinence,[298] the extent of remissness in the fulfillment of the Easter duty,[299] the number of communions and their frequency,[300] the attitude of the faithful toward the last sacraments,[301] the prevalence of cremation[302] and the frequency of denial of Christian burial,[303] the number of nonreligious or civil funerals, and whether they are due to exorbitant stole fees;[304] the prevalence of civil marriages, public concubinage, mixed marriages and evils against the sanctity of marriage.[305]

In addition to the foregoing an inquiry may be made concerning the negligence of parents and guardians in the Christian education of children;[306] the failure to send children to Catholic schools;[307] the possible membership of lay Catholics in non-Catholic or sectarian organizations, in masonic lodges, in other forbidden societies, even in socialistic or communistic parties, and the extent of the diffusion of salacious, pornographic, irreligious, atheistic, liberal and modernistic

296. C. 119; S. C. Consist., *De relationibus dioecesanis, Formula,* 4 nov. 1918, n. 85—*AAS,* X (1918), 501.

297. Cc. 1247, 1248.

298. Cc. 1252, 1254.

299. C. 859.

300. C. 863.

301. Cc. 865, 944.

302. C. 1203.

303. Cc. 1239, 1240.

304. Cf. cc. 1234, 1235.

305. S. C. Consist., *De relationibus dioecesanis, Formula,* 4 nov. 1918, nn. 87, 88—*AAS,* X (1918), 501.

306. C. 1113, 1372.

307. C. 1374.

literature in the form of books, magazines, pamphlets, and newspapers among the Catholic laity.[308]

Finally canon 690, which declares that, unless a special privilege exists to the contrary, all associations of the faithful, even those which are established by the Holy See, are under the jurisdiction and vigilance of the local ordinary, also gives him the right and duty to visit them in accord with the rules of the sacred canons. Thus the bishop may inquire into their internal discipline or spiritual direction, their care and decoration of the altar and chapel, their conduct of divine services, their adherence to the ceremonies required in the celebration of sacred functions, and, if the associations have been established into juridical entities, their administration and use of ecclesiastical property.[309]

However, the bishop's visitatorial rights suffer a partial restriction in relation to associations erected by exempt religious in their own churches in virtue of an apostolic privilege.[310] In such cases the bishop cannot interfere in the internal discipline or spiritual direction of the association.[311]

308. S. C. Consist., *De relationibus dioecesanis, Formula,* 4 nov. 1918, nn. 96, 97, 98.—*AAS,* X (1918), 502.

309. Vromant, *De fidelium associationibus,* n. 19.

310. It is to be noted that this exemption also extends to the parochial churches of exempt religious.—Vromant, *op. cit.,* n. 20.

311. C. 690, § 2.

CHAPTER VIII

THE PROCEDURE IN VISITATION

Canon 345: Visitator, in iis quae obiectum et finem visitationis respiciunt, debet paterna forma procedere, et ab eius praeceptis ac decretis datur recursus in devolutivo tantum; in aliis vero causis, etiam tempore visitationis, Episcopus ad normam iuris procedat necesse est.

Canon 345 treats of the procedure to be followed in the course of the visitation. The information it offers is very general. Its parallel, namely, canon 513 on the procedure during the visitation of religious, adds little else. Both specify the outstanding elements in the visitation without descending into particulars and without mentioning other related points. Thus canon 345 states the general characteristic of the investigation proper and the force of precepts and decrees in matters having a bearing on the material object and purpose of the visitation. It also mentions when the prescriptions of law are to be followed. Canon 513 adds the right of the bishop to inspect and question together with the corresponding obligation of the religious to answer truthfully. Then it subjoins a cautionary reminder to superiors against interference. This is the sum total of the law on procedure during the visitation. Before any comments are made, it may not prove useless to make some pertinent remarks.[1]

Prior to the actual visitation it is advisable to notify the pastor or rector of the forthcoming visitation.[2] This announcement will contain instructions to the pastor and people which will be largely dependent on the nature of the practice in vogue in the particular diocese. It will state the actual date and hour of the visitation. This will enable the pastor to have everything in readiness on the bishop's arrival. However, the bishop is not strictly obliged to make known his coming.[3] Circumstances and conditions may be such as to preclude the

1. The procedure for the visitation of religious is outlined by Reilly, *Tbo visitation of religious*, pp. 146-165.

2. Some bishops, e. g., the present incumbents of the dioceses of Sioux Falls and Camden, before making their initial canonical visitation issued an instruction concerned mainly with the liturgical requirements with respect to the church and its furnishings.

3. Evidently the practice of making a previous announcement is taken for granted, as canon 2413 includes the phrase *post indictam visitationem.*

advisability of making an announcement lest the visitation lose its efficacy.

The announcement may contain an exhortation to the people to be present for the occasion. In passing, it may be recalled that in the early days the people were subject to an excommunication if they failed to be present.[4] This practice was also in effect even after the Council of Trent.[5] It may likewise include an exhortation to reveal in secret any crime that may have been committed. But a bishop is not permitted to command his subjects to do so in virtue of holy obedience or under pain of an excommunication.[6] Furthermore the bishop may ask the people to pray that the visitation produce salutary effects and he may counsel them to approach the sacraments in preparation for the occasion. For this purpose he may even send secular or religious missionaries ahead of him to preach and to administer the Sacraments of Penance and the Eucharist.[7]

Since no special method is prescribed by the Code for the canonical visitation of the bishop he may proceed to perform it with or without the use of forms, that is, questionnaires or visitation articles. The use of these forms is backed by experience throughout the years. It proves very helpful, makes for exactness, does away with useless delays, and constitutes a permanent record of the visitation of each parish.[8] In adopting this method the bishop may have the pastor or rector answer the questions in the course of the visitation itself. Or he may forward a copy of the visitation articles with the announcement of the oncoming visitation. A better policy would be to send two copies to each parish. One would be returned to the curia for a permanent record some time before the actual visitation of the parish in question takes place, while the other would be kept on record in a folder or binder in the parochial archives under the title of Book of Visitations. In this manner the bishop will have a chance to detect

4. Council of Rouen (650), c. 16—Mansi, X, 1203; Bruns, II, 271.

5. Barbosa, *De officio et potestate episcopi*, alleg. 73, n. 57.

6. Barbosa, *De officio et potestate episcopi*, alleg. 73, n. 29; Piasecius, *Praxis episcopalis*, pars 2, c. 3, art. 8, n. 3. Both of these authors claim that this was the view taken by the Sacred Congregation of the Council.

7. Benedictus XIV, const. "*Firmandis*," 6 nov. 1744, § 5—*Fontes*, n. 349.

8. To the writer's knowledge such forms are in use in this country in the dioceses of Detroit, Marquette, Saginaw and San Francisco.

beforehand the salient points of inquiry. Moreover, this arrangement will afford the bishop the opportunity to inspect the pastor's copy. Thus the pastor in question will stand acquitted or convicted by the evidence on hand according as the copies do or do not agree and harmonize in their content.

It would be helpful and appropriate to arrange the structure of the questionnaire in accordance with the order which is followed in the Formula for the quinquennial report. In the drawing up of this form due consideration could simultaneously be given to the additional questions called for by the legislation of plenary and provincial councils or by the exigencies occasioned in view of the locally obtaining conditions. A very useful guide for composing a questionnaire which would entail a thorough investigation will be found in the Norms published by the Sacred Congregation of the Apostolic Visitation for the visitation of the city of Rome.[9]

If articles and records of past visitations are available it would prove profitable to some extent to examine them.[10] Their content may help to evaluate the progress or deterioration that has been effected in the various places and may present the visitor with a basis for his approach in making corrections.

Without a doubt, in order to facilitate matters, the bishop will have a complete list in geographical sequence of all churches, oratories, schools, hospitals, etc., which he is to visit. Appended to this will be an itinerary indicating the order and the approximate time for each visitation.

9. Decr. 8 mart. 1904—*ASS,* XXXVII (1904-1905), 202, 275, 403; cf. also, "La visite pastorale d'après la methode, les conciles, les synodes et les ordinnances diocésaines du cardinal Orsini, archevêque de Bénévent (Benoit XIII),"—*Analecta juris pontificii,* (*AJP*), XV (1876), 49, 257, 401, 1094; Monacellus, *Formularium legale practicum fori ecclesiastici,* tom. I, 505-520 Ferraris, *Bibliotheca,* ad v. "visitare," n. 121; Gavantus, *Praxis compendaria visitationis episcopalis* (Romae, 1628), pp. 16-27; Martinucci, *Manuale sacrarum caeremoniarium* (3. ed., Romae: Pustet, 1915), pars II, vol. 2, 371-385; d'Angelo, *La curia dioecesana* (Giarre [Sicilia]: casa Editrice di Pietro Lisi, 1928) II, 172-191; Mothon, *Institutions canoniques* (3 vols., Desclée, Brouwer et Cié., 1922), III, 246.

10. Barbosa, *De officio et potestate episcopi,* alleg. 73, n. 57; De Pavinis, *Baculus pastoralis,* pars I, cap. 5, n. 32, in *Praxi criminali regularium saeculariumque omnium absolutissima nuncupata, quaestionum regularium,* tomus quartus (Antverpiae, 1624), tit. 4, p. 46.

The bishop will also avail himself of the services of a notary.[11] The latter's duty is to make out the decrees and to take down the observations for the accurate report of each visitation. According to the III Plenary Council of Batlimore this report is to be kept in the diocesan archives.[12]

No particular time of the year is specified by the law for the inception of the visitation. Hence it rests with the prudent judgment of the ordinary to determine this time. Neither is the order of the visitation determined. However, it is generally agreed that unless local conditions or particular circumstances point to the contrary it is expedient and proper for the bishop to begin the visitation with the cathedral church.[13] After the visitation of the cathedral church the other churches of the episcopal city ought to be visited prior to the visitation of outlying districts.

The III Plenary Council of Baltimore obliges the bishops of this country to administer the Sacrament of Confirmation on the occasion of the visitation.[14] Therefore this fact should be made known to the pastor in the notification of the visitation.

If the bishop has a legitimate excuse for not making the visitation in person[15] he should make known the name of his substitute in the announcement. Moreover, he should give a written authorization to his delegate wherein he declares that he grants the said person all the requisite faculties. This document or these credentials must be presented and then read at each place before the visitation begins.

11. "Visitanti enim soli non creditur" — Salodius, *Praxis compendiosa de visitatione*, pars 2, cap. 1, p. 19.

12. *Acta et decreta*, n. 14.

13. "Annotazioni" — *Il monitore ecclesiastico*, 5 Serie, II (1931), 182; Monacellus, *Formularium*, pars I, tit. 5, form. 2, n. 27; Melchers, *De canonica visitatione*, p. 18.

14. "... Unusquisque igitur Episcopus saltem unoquoque triennio totam dioecesim perlustrari teneatur, non solum ut gregem suum cognoscat ... sed etiam ut fideles tot amittendae fidei in hac regione periculis expositos Sacramento Confirmationis munire possit." — *Acta et decreta*, n. 14. The prescription of the II Plenary Council that each candidate for Confirmation produce a card with his or her name on it is still in effect as it is *praeter codicem*. However, this is required only when a large number is to be confirmed. — *Acta et decreta*, n. 252.

15. C. 343, § 1.

The Code in accord with canon 2 makes no reference to the concomitant ceremonies of the visitation. The Roman Pontifical outlines the ceremonies for the visitation of parishes by the local ordinary.[16] However, the III Plenary Council of Baltimore prescribes the use of the Baltimore Ceremonial.[17] The II Plenary Council directs the bishops to make an inquiry concerning all those things which are prescribed in the Roman Pontifical. Moreover, it charges the bishops not to perform this most important function very hastily or perfunctorily, but with all due diligence and zeal for souls.[18]

The Investigation or Visitation Proper

The diocesan visitation is an act of jurisdiction,[19] an exercise of the bishop's governing powers. Like every ruler he has the right to investigate conditions within his territory for the purpose of setting them aright. Hence the Council of Trent declared that the bishops had the right and power in all those things which pertain to visitation and to the correction of morals, namely, to ordain, regulate, correct and execute in accord with the law those things which, in their prudence, they consider necessary for the amendment of their subjects and for the good of their respective dioceses.[20] The same Council warned the bish-

16. Tit. *Ordo ad visitandas parochias.*

17. "In visitatione peragenda, *praeter caeremonias praescriptas,* serventur quae in jure praecipiuntur. (Vide *Caeremoniale Baltimorae* anno 1883 editum)." *Acta et decreta,* n. 14; cf. also *concilii plenarii Baltimorensis II, acta et decreta,* n. 217.

18. *Acta et decreta,* n. 86.

19. Barbosa, *De officio et potestate episcopi,* alleg. 73, n. 2.

20. "Episcopi, in omnibus iis, quae ad visitationem ac morum correctionem subditorum suorum spectant, jus et potestatem habeant, ea ordinandi, moderandi, puniendi et exequendi juxta canonum sanctiones, quae illi ex prudentia sua pro subditorum emendatione ac dioecesis suae utilitate necessaria videbuntur." Sessio XXIV, *de ref.,* c. 10. The Code in canon 274, n. 5, sets forth the extent of the jurisdiction enjoyed by the metropolitan whenever he supplies the neglect of the bishop in the matter of visitation. He may preach without obtaining permission (c. 1337), hear confessions and absolve from reserved sins, make a general inquiry into the life, regularity and conduct of the clergy in the fulfillment of their obligations, denounce those clerics who labor under infamy, be it of law or of fact (cc. 2320, 2328, 2343, 2314, 2359, § 2), to the suffragan or to the religious ordinary to enable him to punish them. Moreover, he may exercise his coercive power against those who are guilty of crimes that are notorious

ops to treat all persons with fatherly love and Christian zeal.[21] Today the Code reiterates the obligation to proceed in a paternal manner (*paterna forma*) in all those things which pertain to the material object and purpose of the visitation. Thus this paternal procedure is to be manifest as regards persons, places and things under the visitor's authority whenever the preservation of sound orthodox doctrine, the maintenance of good morals, the correction of such as are evil, the promotion of peace, innocence, piety, discipline, and the good of religion are concerned. Therefore every act in the course of the visitation having a direct bearing on its object and purpose is not to be of a judicial character, but paternal in the manner of its performance.

Thus the investigation will be paternal and all semblance of a judicial act must be eliminated. The investigation is paternal when it seeks the correction and reformation of the individual.[22] It is judicial if it is intended as a public vindication against crime. Moreover, the investigation should ordinarily be of a general nature.[23] However,

in fact (c. 2197, n. 3), because if they are notorious *notorietate iuris* the ordinary or competent judge passes sentence (c. 2197, n. 2). Finally, the metropolitan may punish with just and proportionate penalties all affronts and insults which are notorious in fact and manifest in culpability, whether they were effected in word, writing or deed, in the course of the visitation against his own person or against that of any one in his entourage. Censures, which are not excluded, may be inflicted *per modum praecepti* outside a judicial process. — Blat, *Commentarium*, II, 292; Augustine, *A commentary on the new code of canon law*, II, 290, 291; cf. c. 1, *de censibus, exactionibus et procurationibus*, III, 20, in VI°, § Sane.

21. "... Monentur praedicti omnes et singuli patriarchae, primates, metropolitani et episcopi ad quos visitatio spectat, ut paterna charitate christianoque zelo omnes amplectantur. ..." — Sess. XXIV, *de ref.*, c. 4.

22. This paternal investigation may be general, special or of the nature of both (*mixta*). It is general if an inquiry is made into the life and morals of subjects without any particular reference to individuals or any suspicion of wrongdoing. The special investigation is an inquiry concerning a specific misdeed or concerning a particular person. The partly general, partly special investigation is an inquiry made about a specific crime which is certain but not in regard to a particular individual, or vice versa. Bouix, *Tractatus de judiciis ecclesiasticis* (3. ed., Parisiis, 1884), II, 60, 61; Reiffenstuel, lib. V, tit. 1, nn. 150-152; Wernz-Vidal, *Ius canonicum*, VI (Romae, 1927), n. 718.

23. Monacellus, *Formularium*, pars I, tit. 5, form. 2, n. 57; Cocchi, *Commentarium*, II, 217; Goyeneche, *Iuris canonici summa principia* (Tip. Pol. Cuore di Maria, Romae —), I, 301; Chelodi, *Ius de personis*, p. 318.

when persons in public office, such as pastors, curates and superiors, are concerned, the visitor is obliged to make an inquiry concerning the fulfillment of their office and their conduct.[24] A reasonable suspicion would be required to make an inquiry concerning a particular crime or misdeed. Wherefore the bishop may question certain upright laymen in private concerning the life and deportment of the clerics and laity.[25] In keeping with the paternal character of his visitatorial office the bishop will make inquiries in private from the pastor and curates with respect to their corresponding obligations, conduct and communal life. He may question the pastor concerning the curates, and the curates concerning each other as well as concerning the pastor.[26] During these personal interviews the notary or co-visitors are not to be in attendance. The bishop, if he has reasonable grounds for doing so, may even inquire about the faults and crimes of a particular cleric. But personal questions involving a partial or complete manifestation of conscience must be avoided. The visitor's prudence will determine the quality of the questions and the duration of the interview, especially if a questionnaire has been used or if the visitor has a personal knowledge of the persons involved.

The Application of Corrective Measures

In applying corrective remedies the paternal character of the procedure ought to be especially taken into consideration.[27] When anyone is found deficient or negligent in anything that pertains to his office

24. "Traité de la visite pastorale", *AJP*, I (1855), 512.

25. Barbosa, *De officio et potestate episcopi*, alleg. 73, n. 57; Salodius, pars 3, c. 1, p. 48; Maupied, *Juris canonici universi compendium*, I, 541.

26. "... quoad mores inquirere et interrogare debent sigillatim singulos clericos ut quisque deponet circa vitam alterius." — Zerola, *Praxis episcopalis* (Coloniae Agrippinae, 1680), ad v. "visitatio," p. 448. "Sane hujusmodi [i. e. visitationis] impensurus officium ... quaerat de vita et conversatione ministrantium in ecclesiis et locis aliis divino cultui deputatis, ac ceteris quae ad officium ipsum spectant. ..." — C. 1, *de censibus, exactionibus et procurationibus*, III, 20, in VI°.

27. The idea behind paternal correction is well expressed by the glossa:

"Qui nimis emungit, solet extorquere cruorem
Et violenta facit correctio deteriorem
Sed moderata satis correctio gignit amorem,"

referred to in "La visite pastorale" — *AJP*, XV (1876), 52.

the bishop should ordinarily give a paternal admonition in private, exhorting the party to amend the situation. In reference to accusations of misdeeds, the bishop will use his prudent judgment. He will consider the information as to its source, its nature, its object, the motivating reason and the manner in which it is offered. The words of the Provincial Council of Aquilea (1596) are pertinent:

> Episcopi omnia exquirant, caute audiant, non facile admittant aut probent, ita tamen quae afferuntur recipiant, ut nec fidem habeant, nec fidem denegent; duce vero Christiana prudentia probent, quae vera quae recta ac sincera sunt: quae commentitia calumniisque infecta aut dolo despiciant. . . .[28]

Hence, if it is probable that a person is in the proximate occasion of committing some offense, or if an investigation gives reasonable grounds for a suspicion that the person did commit the offense, then a secret admonition is in order.[29] If the party persists in his way, but the negligence, deficiency or offense is not grave and public, then another secret admonition or a rebuke may be given.[30]

However, as the paternal procedure of necessity rests on equity, on charity and on the prudent judgment of the bishop, he is to suit the remedy to the situation. Thus, if a cleric manifests ignorance or laziness in the performance of his official duties the bishop may give a secret rebuke,[31] or if circumstances warrant it then a precept can be administered with the threat of a penalty for the failure to comply with it.[32] Then, too, he may prescribe penances, such as a retreat or the recitation of certain prayers.[33] In short, it may be safely stated that the use of penal remedies and of penances does not transgress the limits of paternal procedure.

The Sacred Congregation of the Council stated repeatedly that bishops were not to inflict ordinary but rather extraordinary penalties, which were more in keeping with the emendation and correction of

28. Rubrica XIII, *De visitatione* — Hardouin, X, 1909.

29. Cc. 2307, 2309.

30. C. 2309, § 6.

31. C. 2308. A record of the secret admonitions and rebukes should be made and placed in the secret diocesan archives. — c. 2309, § 5; Noval, "De ratione corrigendi," *JP*, III (1923), 206.

32. C. 2310.

33. C. 2313.

morals than with the infliction of punishment.[34] Moreover, the bishop may not impose a penalty on those who have received a punishment for a misdeed at the hands of an inferior prelate.[35] The infliction of an ecclesiastical censure would not be in keeping with the paternal procedure.[36] Some authors[37] consider a suspension for a brief and determinate period of time a minor or a light penalty. Hence it would not be repugnant for the bishop in his rôle as a visitor to use this means as an *extreme* measure in his effort to bring about the correction of an individual.[38]

Thus it seems that the phrase "*paterna forma*" is to be interpreted broadly as giving the bishop the use of remedies beyond the paternal admonition or rebuke. Moreover, the paternal aspect ought to be characteristic of the bishop's general demeanor. He is expected to act within his diocese as a father would act within his household. He will manifest a zeal and interest toward all concerned. His approach will be kind and friendly, sympathetic and considerate. And, finally, his priests and people to a certain extent should feel free to approach him.

The Effect of Precepts and Decrees

When a visitor has made the investigation and has obtained the necessary information he may issue precepts and decrees. Obviously the precept referred to is not to receive the restricted interpretation of canon 2310 as a penal remedy. It is an order or a command given to an individual or a community in a particular case. Under the term decree may be classified any regulation, decision or correction made by the visitor in his administrative capacity. Hence, it must be observed

34. S. C. C., *Calaguritana,* 23 sept. 1591 — *Fontes,* n. 2237; *Nullius,* 24 apr. 1597 — *Fontes,* n. 2309; *Derthusen.,* 11 aug. 1605 — *Fontes,* n. 2357.

35. Barbosa, *De officio et potestate episcopi,* alleg. 73, n. 31; cf. c. 2223, § 3, n. 2.

36. S. C. C., *Recimeten.,* 12 apr. 1710, ad 1 — *Fontes,* n. 3088; Augustine, *A commentary on the new code of canon law,* II, 373.

37. Claeys Bouuaert-Simenon, *Manuale iuris canonici,* I, p. 274, n. 485; Beste, *Introductio in codicem,* p. 271; Melchers, *De canonica visitatione,* p. 28.

38. "Quod si ob . . . pertinacem reorum contumaciam poena aliqua inferenda sit, lenitate est attemperanda." — Sebastianelli, *Praelectiones juris canonici* (*De personis*), p. 219.

that a distinction between the two terms cannot be made with mathematical precision.[39]

Although the Code does not oblige the bishop to put his decrees in writing, nevertheless it is advisable for him to do so, since in that manner matters will be facilitated for the rural dean who has the duty in the parishes within his district to see that all the decrees issued by the bishop during the visitation are put into effect.[40] In fact, a record of all pertinent points effected during the visitation should be kept for future reference. Still the visitor is not to put the correction of personal misdeeds or the application of penalties in the form of decrees. Such matters are to be placed on record in the secret archives of the curia.

Since the required paternal procedure implies a restatement of the old law, the Code repeats the principle that recourse from the paternal administrative decrees of the visitor cannot be lodged with the effect of suspending the binding force of these decrees.[41] The precepts and decrees bind and are to be obeyed until upon recourse the proper authority modifies or abrogates them. Furthermore, these decrees may not be rejected on the plea that the visitor is considered suspect.[42] However, if the bishop exceeded his powers, for example, by inflicting a censure or a grave vindictive penalty instead of a corrective measure, there would be room for an appeal.[43]

Augustine[44] states that metropolitans should not accept any recourse against the visitor's paternal decrees provided the latter has confined his acts within the limits set by law. As a matter of fact the metropolitan is not competent in such an instance. For the law makes no provision for recourse to the metropolitan against the decree of an ordinary in matters administrative. Then, too, the Pontifical Commis-

39. Lardone, "I decreti della visita pastorale" — *Perfice Munus*, XI (1936), 669.

40. C. 447, § 1, n. 2.

41. "Pareant et deinde recurrant." — Piatus, *Praelectiones juris regularis* (3. ed., Tornaci, 1906), II, q. 615.

42. Barbosa, *De officio et potestate episcopi*, alleg. 73, n. 38; Wernz-Vidal, *Ius canonicum*, II, 608.

43. Chelodi, *Ius de personis*, p. 318; Coronata, *Institutiones iuris canonici*, I, 466.

44. *A commentary on the new code of canon law*, II, 373.

sion for the Interpretation of the Code has declared that the Sacred Congregations have exclusive competence in actions against the decrees of ordinaries pertaining to the administration of their dioceses.[45]

The *"aliae causae"* mentioned in canon 345 are those which are outside the scope of the visitation, that is, those which do not fall directly under the object and purpose of the visitation. The purpose of the visitation is to effect the removal of abuses and to bring about the better observance of ecclesiastical law. Hence, if any matter undertaken in the course of the visitation cannot be considered an object of the visitation or is not primarily concerned with its purpose, then the bishop must comply with the rules of law prescribed by the canons. In other words, in such instances he may not proceed in a paternal manner. Thus not only would criminal cases or cases requiring a judicial process be included, but also such as call for a special administrative process. Therefore the process for the removal of pastors or also the procedure against clerics violating the law of residence could not be carried out in a paternal manner.

Although the bishop is to follow the rules of law in these cases, there is no implication that an appeal is permitted in all cases outside of the paternal procedure. Nor is it lawful to assume that an appeal is allowed only when the visitor engages in a judicial process.[46] For, whenever the Code allows an appeal against a decree or penalty, the appeal suspends the decree or penalty despite the fact that the decree was issued or the penalty was inflicted in the course of the visitation. A case in point is the extrajudicial infliction of a vindictive penalty.[47]

45. Pont. Comm. Intr., 22 maii 1923 — *AAS,* XVI (1924), 251. Under the old law the recourse was lodged with the metropolitan — Zerola, *Praxis episcopalis,* pars II, ad v. visitatio, p. 156; Barbosa, *De officio et potestate episcopi,* alleg. 73, n. 35; S. C. C., *Hydruntina,* 14 iun. 1594 — *Fontes,* n. 2269.

46. Cf. c. 513, § 2.

47. C. 2287.

CHAPTER IX

PROCURATION

Canon 346. — Studeant Episcopi debita cum diligentia, sine inutilibus tamen moris, pastoralem visitationem absolvere: caveant, ne superfluis sumptibus cuiquam graves onerosive sint, neve ratione visitationis ipsi aut quisquam suorum pro se suisve dona quodvis genus petant aut accipiant, reprobata quavis contraria consuetudine; circa vero victualia sibi suisque ministranda vel procurationes et expensas itineris, servetur legitima locorum consuetudo.

Canon 346 is practically a succint restatement of the Tridentine law on the questions connected with the material cost of the visitation. It mentions its main features dealing with delays, expenses, and gifts and then sanctions the remuneration to which every visitor is entitled by law. The compensation for the visitation is to be regulated by legitimate local custom. This consideration on the occasion of the canonical visitation is better known under the name of procuration.

When procuration is considered objectively it is the contribution or presentation of suitable food and lodging, or the equivalent in money, by those visited to the visitor and his entourage on the occasion of the canonical visitation.[1] Subjectively procuration is the right of the visitor to this maintenance in virtue of the visitation.[2] Originally the procuration was supplied only in consumable goods so that *procuratio* and *victualia*[3] were practically synonymous. However, Pope Boniface VIII left it to the discretion of the parties visited to decide

1. Cf. Schmalzgrueber, lib. III, tit. 39, n. 100; Reiffenstuel, lib. III, tit. 39, n. 49; Ferraris, *Bibliotheca,* ad v. "procuratio," nn. 1, 2.

2. Fagnanus, lib. I, tit. 31, cap. 16, n. 37; Couly, "Droit de visite ou procuration" — *Le canoniste contemporain,* XLIV (1921), 208.

3. "Victualium igitur appelatione . . . veniunt tantum illa quae consistunt in victu, non tamen ea quae concernunt alia necessaria personae." — Barbosa, *Tractatus de appellatione verborum utriusque iuris significatione* (Lugduni, 1660), appell. CCLXX (victualia), n. 3. "Sub procuratione comprehenduntur omnia quae sunt necessaria pro victu, nempe cibus, potus et habitatio ipsius visitatoris et honesti comitatus ejusdem." — Ferraris, *Bibliotheca,* ad v. "procuratio," n. 2.

whether they were to supply the food and lodging or to make a payment in money.[4]

The basis for this right of a bishop on the occasion of the visitation is either custom,[5] some privilege or special law,[6] some lawful agreement or pact entered into at the time of a foundation by the visitor and those to be visited,[7] or, finally, the visitation itself. For as the decretals put it: "Procuratio est visitationi annexa".[8] Although the first three mentioned causes are acknowledged by the common law of the Church, nevertheless the first and primary basis is the visitation itself. It is a standing principle and as such it basically affects all the persons and places visited by the bishop provided they fall under his jurisdiction.

A variety of reasons have been adduced why the visitation should give rise to the existence of this hospitality. It is supposed to vindicate the visitor's jurisdiction as it were, since it is an indication or sign of subjection.[9] Then it is offered as an inducement for prelates to make the visitation.[10] A parallel is cited in the case of canons who receive remuneration for fulfilling an obligation which arises from their status as clerics.

Fagnanus, while discussing the prescription of procuration, ridicules the idea that if the visitor were obliged to perform the visitation gratis there would be danger of neglect on the part of the prelates with its resultant spiritual harm. He claims the visitation is for the public good and therefore negligence in this regard is not to be tolerated.[11] In

4. C. 3, *de censibus, exactionibus et procurationibus,* III, 20, in VI°.

5. Barbosa, *De officio et potestate episcopi,* alleg. 73, n. 43; Monacellus, *Formularium,* pars III, tit. I, form 4, n. 12.

6. Barbosa, *De officio et potestate episcopi,* alleg. 73, n. 43; Monacellus, *op. cit.,* pars III, tit. I, form 4, n. 12.

7. C. 23, X, *de iure patronatus,* I, 38; c. 16, X, *de censibus, exactionibus et procurationibus,* III, 39; Barbosa, *De officio et potestate episcopi,* alleg. 73, n. 43.

8. C. 2, X, *de censibus, exactionibus et procurationibus,* III, 39.

9. "Quare autem episcopus potest exigere procurationem ratione visitationis cum propter haec onera habeat redditus episcopatus? Dicit Innoc. in d. c. I, quod habet *in signum subiectionis*". — Panormitanus, lib. III, tit. 39, c. 24, n. 5.

10. Panormitanus, *loc. cit.*

11. Lib. III, tit. 39, c. 24, n. 23. "Hoc autem constat esse absurdum, quia jus iterandi visitationem est publicum utilitate, et auctoritate . . . et consuetudo in talibus non est toleranda."

fact the Council of Trent[12] clearly stated that wherever such customs against the payment of procuration existed they were to continue in force, and the Code also plainly implies the prevalence of legitimate customs.[13] Another reason, which Barbosa[14] claims is proximate and immediate, is based on the words of St. Paul[15]: "What soldier ever serves at his own expense? . . . If we have sown for you spiritual things, is it a great matter if we reap from you carnal things?"[16] Thus it is a stipend, a consideration, for labor expended by the visitor.

It has been seen above that procuration is the food and lodging or its monetary equivalent offered the visitor and his entourage.[17] In the past it included the fodder and stabling of horses.[18] Undoubtedly today with changed conditions the oil, gasoline and garage for the automobile would be included. Under the old law the visitor could not seek compensation for accidents occurring in the course of his travels, v. g., if he lost a horse. Nor could he demand that transportation be furnished him from place to place or that the cost for the same be supplied him.[19]

Under the present law the payment of traveling expenses is determined according to legitimate local custom.[20] Thus wherever a custom

12. Sess. XXIV, *de ref.*, c. 3.

13. C. 346. ". . . servetur legitima locorum consuetudo".

14. *De officio et potestate episcopi,* alleg. 73, n. 43.

15. I Cor., IX: 7, 11.

16. Cf. also, C. 21, X, *de censibus, exactionibus et procurationibus,* III, 39; c. 16, X, *de praescriptione,* II, 26; c. 6, *de officio iudicis ordinarii,* I, 16, in VI°; S. Thomas, 2a 2ae, q. 100, a. 3, ad 3; Pirhing, lib. III, tit. 39, n. 59; De Pavinis, *Baculus pastoralis,* pars I, cap. 9, n. 1.

17. In the resumé of one of the cases of the Sacred Congregation of the Council procuration was defined thus: "cuius nomine veniunt omnia, dum qui visitat in loco est, quae sub victus verbo continentur, nempe quae esui potui, quoque ad vivendum homini sunt necessaria, ut Ulpianus dixit" (D. 50, [16, 43]). Cf. S. C. C., *in Senogallien. Procurationis,* 14 dec. 1765, § Quod—*Thesaurus,* XXXIV, 199.

18. Fagnanus, lib. III, tit. 39, c. 23, n. 16.

19. S. C. C., in *Tarentina Procurationis,* 25 feb. 1826, ad 4—*Thesaurus,* LXXXVI, 74; Pallottini, IX, p. 522; De Pavinis, *Baculus pastoralis,* pars I, q. 9, nn. 8 and 9; Barbosa, *De officio et potestate episcopi,* alleg. 73, n. 57; Fagnanus, lib. III, tit. 39, c. 23, n. 16; Panormitanus, lib. III, tit. 39, c. 23, n. 4. Cf. also S. C. C., *Resolutio, Melivetana,* 23 apr. 1917, *AAS,* X (1918), 239.

20. C. 346.

arose in contravention of the decrees of the Sacred Congregation and the teaching of the authors, today it enjoys the privilege of law. Therefore the interpretation given this term in the different localities is to prevail. Furthermore, since the Code allows the payment of traveling expenses where it is the custom to do so, the bishop has the right to demand this additional contribution wherever no definite custom as regards procuration and traveling expenses obtains. Nevertheless where a contrary custom is in effect he may not require a remuneration for traveling expenses. However, the meaning of the term *expensae itineris*, traveling expenses, is not unmistakably clear. What is its comprehension? Is it all-inclusive or are there any restrictions? In the old law no transportation charges were allowed the ordinary visitor except the apostolic visitor.[21] Does it include the salary of the chauffeur, of the co-visitors,[22] the expense for new tires, repairs, or the costs of damages?[23] Or does the term merely refer to the oil, gasoline and garage for the automobile — a counterpart to the fodder and stabling given the animals in the past, all of which was included under the term *procuratio* or *victualia?* It certainly includes the toll for bridges, tunnels, ferries and highways. Since the term is used without any attached qualifications to restrict its naturally comprehensive significance, it seems that all expenses in any reasonable way whatsoever occasioned by the very making of the visitation trips come under the term *expensae itineris*.[24] However, as stated above, local customs are the norms to be followed with respect to the payment of the traveling expenses.

21. Barbosa, *De officio et potestate episcopi*, alleg. 73, n. 57.

22. Under the old law the canons of the cathedral who accompanied the visitor did not forfeit their share in the daily distributions and allotments accruing from choir service. They did not however partake in the apportionment which yielded to only such canons as were actually present for the choir service (*distributiones inter praesentes*). The same holds true today (c. 420, no. 1, n. 12; § 2).

23. The apostolic visitor had the right to demand a new team of horses or a carriage if a mishap overtook him on the way. — Azorius, *Institutiones morales*, pars II, lib. III, cap. 42, q. 8; Schmalzgrueber, lib. III, tit. 39, n. 100.

24. It would not seem that the places visited would be bound to pay the full price of an aeroplane trip expressly made by a visitor. They are not bound to such extraordinary expenses which certainly could not be classified as moderate.

Although in the past the word *procuratio* has been taken to mean the pecuniary equivalent for the food and lodging, or the *victualia*,[25] nevertheless it has not been the dominant interpretation. Ever since the time of Pope Boniface VIII the term has always conveyed the generic idea of maintenance to be supplied in the form of food and lodging or by its equivalent in money.[26]

Authors have given various interpretations to the word *procurationes* in the canon. Blat[27] thinks it refers, for example, to money, carriages and horses. Cance,[28] Claeys Bouuaert-Simenon[29] and Beste[30] are for all practical purposes of the same opinion. Cance says it signifies pecuniary and above all nonpecuniary payments, Claeys Bouuaert-Simenon think it includes especially nonpecuniary payments such as carriages, horses and work in services (*labores*). Beste maintains that it means nonpecuniary contributions. D'Angelo, however, claims that it means the money equivalent of the *victualia*.[31]

It is not evident upon what basis the interpretation rests when it identifies the procuration with nonpecuniary contributions in the form of the means of transportation. Certainly, the history of the right of the bishops shows that the term *procuratio* did not comprise

25. "Victualia enim non potest Ep̃us exigere, exacta *procuratione* in visitatione . . .": S. C. C., *in Troiana Assertorum Gravaminum,* 20 dec. 1664 — Pallottini, IX, p. 524, n. 223; "Munera nulla posse Episcopum accipere, sed victualia tantum, vel eorum loco procurationem." — S. C. C., *in Marsicana,* quoted by Lucidi, *De visitatione,* I, 166, n. 53.

26. "Haec procuratio est solvenda juxta arbitrium visitatorum vel in pecunia certa vel moderata taxata quantitate vel in victualibus" — Dubium, 13 aug. 1581. — Pallottini, IX, p. 524, n. 233; "An sit in facultate Capituli Cleri Aviliani subministrare Episcopo in visitatione procurationem in victualibus seu in pecunia?" Sacra Congregatio respondit: — "Ad primum, Affirmative" — *in Potentina Procurationis* 10, 24 ian. 1705 — Pallottini, IX, p. 523, n. 220.

27. *Commentarium,* II (*De personis*), n. 371.

28. *Commentaire succinct et pratique,* I (6. ed., Paris: Libraire Le Coffre, 1930), p. 334, note 6.

29. *Manuale iuris canonici,* I, p. 274, n. 486.

30. *Introductio in codicem,* p. 271.

31. *Tasse e pensioni nel codice di diritto canonico* (2. ed., Torino: Lega Italiana Cattolica, 1927), pp. 45, 46; Lardone, "Le procurazioni nella visita pastorale" — *Perfice Munus,* V (1930), 440.

traveling expenses, nor did it include means of transportation, except in the case of delegates of the Holy See.[32] Hence, there seems to be little if any reason for suggesting any interpretation which is at variance with the former accepted meaning of the word *procuratio* relative to the bishop's right in this matter. Besides, the expression *expensae itineris* seems well to cover those specific needs. On the other hand, D'Angelo's view is in keeping with the historical use of the term. Nevertheless it is more acceptable to interpret the word *procurationes* as referring both to a contribution in food and lodging,[33] and its equivalent in money. Thus *victualia* and *procurationes* are practically one and the same in meaning.

As is evident, the Code does not determine anything in particular concerning food and lodging or its monetary equivalent. It designates legitimate local custom as the determinant. However, as under the former law, the bishop cannot receive both the hospitality and the money for the same.

Hence the visitor will have a right to the *victualia,* that is, the hospitality in food and lodging, or, at times, he may have a right to the *victualia* plus the traveling expenses. When the *victualia* as such are not provided he will have the right to the monetary equivalent of the *victualia.* Sipos[34] thinks that the payment of a net sum (*solutio certae pecuniae taxatae*) instead of the food and lodging is prohibited. But this is not so, for wherever such a custom exists it has legal force. And certainly where no definite custom exists it may be introduced. Notwithstanding such a standing custom the writer thinks that the option offered the places visited, namely, to pay in either form, still stands.[35] The bishop may correspondingly have the right to receive not only the payment of money in place of the procuration provided in food and lodging, but also the defrayal of his traveling expenses.

32. S. C. C., *in Senogallien. Procurationis,* 14 dec. 1765, § Non.—*Thesaurus,* XXXIV, 199; Reiffenstuel, lib. III, tit. 39, n. 56; Schmalzgrueber, lib. III, tit. 39, n. 100.

33. Augustine, *A commentary on the new code of canon law,* II, 374; Coronata, *Institutiones iuris canonici,* I, 466.

34. *Enchiridion juris canonici,* p. 263.

35. Conc. Trid., sess. XXIV, *de ref.,* c. 3; S. C. C., *in Potentina,* 24 ian. 1705 —Pallottini, IX, p. 523, n. 220; *In S. Marci,* 16 ian. 1723, ad 3—*Thesaurus,* II, 262.

Again, he may have but a right to the traveling expenses without the *victualia* or their equivalent. Or he may be obliged to make the visitation at his own expense, if such be the custom,[36] or if the place visited is exempted from supplying any form of procuration.

The procuration is to be provided the visitor and his entourage, which may include besides the two co-visitors[37] others whom the bishop deems necessary for the fulfillment of the visitation.[38] The right given the bishop[39] to select two co-visitors is not to be interpreted as if the bishop were forbidden to have more than two companions on the visitation. This restricted number may perhaps be regarded as exclusive of others who could be called on to assist the bishop in the actual visitation or investigation proper, but it does not exclude the presence of others for his entire company. The Code fails to give the general admonition of the Council of Trent: to use a modest retinue (*modesto contenti equitatu famulatuque*). This is unquestionably due to changed conditions. In the past the Sacred Congregation of the Council evaded any direct answer in this regard. It claimed that no one was to determine the number but the bishop and he was to be guided by his discretion and conscience.[40] Hence nothing definite can be stated except that the bishop is the sole judge as to the number of attendants he requires.

As has been stated above, the entire entourage shared in the procuration, for the right of the bishop to the *procuratio* or *victualia* extended to his entire company, including the teams of horses or mules.[41] On the other hand, the other expenses of carriage and repair, such as the shoeing of horses, etc., and the transportation charges, were not in-

36. Conc. Trid. sess. XXIV, *de ref.*, c. 3; S. C. C., *in Nullius Orbetelli*, 1624 — Pallottini, IX, p. 532.

37. C. 343, § 2.

38. The councils subsequent to the Council of Trent made certain limitations with respect to the number of persons in the retinue. Cf. *supra*. p. 69, note 68.

39. C. 343, § 2.

40. Pallottini, IX, p. 523, n. 220; p. 530, n. 256; S. C. C., *in S. Marci*, 16 ian. 1723, ad 6 — *Thesaurus*, II, 262, *Fontes*, n. 3251.

41. Fodder and stabling were supplied the animals.

cluded.[42] Hence the modern vehicle of travel, the automobile, is also to receive consideration. Therefore in those places where the hospitality is given in kind this matter must also be given attention.[43] The right of procuration is not extinguished by the mere fact that the visitor is not the bishop himself, for the right is that of the visitor (*ratione visitationis*) who acts in the name of the bishop.[44]

The Code exhorts the bishop to see to it that he fulfill the pastoral visitation with due diligence and care but without useless delays. Therefore, the bishop is not to give himself over to recreations which would extend his stay at any given parish. It also warns the bishop against becoming burdensome to anyone by superfluous expenses. This would occur, for example, if the visitor were to demand extraordinary facilities and comforts, entertainment, luxuries in food or drink, or if he were to have a large retinue. On the other hand it must be observed that particular circumstances may allow a bishop to increase his retinue. Thus an aged or infirm bishop can augment his entourage according to his discretion and conscience.[45]

The old injunction against the acceptance of gifts of any kind is renewed.[46] Its obvious purpose is to avoid any uneasy situations due to unjust exactions and to act as a safeguard against the possibility of having undone the good effected through the visitation. Thus the visitation is not to be an occasion for deriving any revenue. The words of the canon are comprehensive. Neither the bishop nor any member of his entourage may *demand* or *accept* any kind of gift whatsoever in virtue of the visitation. This is true even though the gift is of-

42. Panormitanus, lib. III, c. 23, n. 14; Barbosa, *De officio et potestate episcopi,* alleg. 73, n. 57; Fagnanus, lib. III, c. 23, n. 16; Zerola, *Praxis episcopalis,* v. "visitatio," p. 451; Pallottini, IX, n. 206; Piasecius, pars 2, cap. 3, art. 8, n. 14.

43. C. 15, X, *de officio iudicis ordinarii,* I, 31; glossa to c. 3, *de censibus, exactionibus et procurationibus,* III, 20, in VI°; c. 6, *de officio iudicis ordinarii,* I, 16, in VI°; Fagnanus, lib. III, tit. 30, cap. 23, n. 12; Zerola, *Praxis episcopalis,* v. "visitatio," p. 451; Monacellus, *Formularium,* pars III, tit. I, form. 4, n. 3; Panormitanus, lib. III, tit. 39, c. 23, n. 5.

44. Panormitanus, lib. III, tit. 39, c. 23, n. 5; "qui facit per alium est perinde ac si faciat per seipsum." — Reg. 72, R. J., in VI°.

45. *Potentina* proc., 10 and 24 ian. 1705 — Pallottini, IX, 523.

46. Cc. 1, 2, *de censibus, exactionibus et procurationibus,* III, 20, in VI°; Conc. Trid. sess. XXIV, *de ref.,* c. 3.

fered spontaneously.[47] Hence, a visitor cannot even receive a gift at his departure after the visitation is completed.[48] In fact, this prohibition would hold even after he has left the premises. Moreover, all customs to the contrary are reprobated. Therefore, no custom in contravention to this canon can be lawfully revived,[49] inasmuch as a custom expressly reprobated by the Code is considered unreasonable,[50] and a custom to gain the force of law must be reasonable.[51] The phrase "by reason of the visitation" (*ratione visitationis*) is not to be construed in a restricted sense so as to open the way for the acceptance of gifts under any other pretext.[52] Piasecius[53] and Barbosa[54] admit that

47. Cc. 1, 2, *de censibus, exactionibus et procurationibus,* III, 20, in VI°; Piasecius, *Praxis episcopalis,* pars 2, cap. 3, art. 8, n. 14; Fagnanus, lib. III, tit. 39, cap. 23, n. 24; Pallottini, IX, p. 524.

48. Barbosa, *De officio et potestate episcopi,* alleg. 73, n. 55.

49. C. 5.

50. C. 27, § 2.

51. C. 27, § 1.

52. Conc. Trid.: "Caveant... neve ipsi aut quisquam, suorum quidquam procurationis causa pro visitatione... aut *alio quovis nomine* nec pecuniam, nec munus quodcumque sit, *etiam qualitercumque offeratur,* accipiant". — Sess. XXIV, *de ref.,* c. 3. It is interesting to note in this connection that when the procuration is supplied in kind, authors (Piasecius [pars 2, cap. 3, art. 8, n. 14]; Pirhing [lib. III, tit. 39, n. 63]; Monacellus [pars III, tit. I, form. 4, n. 9]; Barbosa [*Collectanea doctorum tam veterum quam recentiorum in ius pontificium universum,* Lugduni, 1656, tom. III, in c. 1, *de censibus, exactionibus et procurationibus,* III, 20, in VI°, n. 23]) allow eatables or drink to be accepted in small quantities provided they are consumed on the premises, but when money is offered not even this is allowed. Monacellus (*loc. cit.*), who advocates accepting nothing at any time because of what he calls the absolute exclusion of any gift by the words of the Council of Trent, misquotes Pirhing. He states that Pirhing in following Joannes Andreae claims such gifts cannot be received (*recipi*) without sinning. In reality Pirhing says that they cannot be exacted or demanded without sinning, although they can be accepted as stated above. ("Esculenta vero, quae ibi absumuntur, possunt *recipi,* Jo. Andr.... ubi tamen addit, non posse *exigi* sine peccato") *loc. cit.* Thus a bishop cannot demand a certain sum of money sufficient for a larger retinue, when he actually has but one, two or three attendants, under the plea that he is entitled to a greater entourage. The procuration is for the actual number present.

53. "Neque cancellarius, auditor vel notarius Episcopi recipere quicquam potest a visitatis *pro scriptura processus visitationis,* pro *copia* tamen *actorum* seu *decretorum* visitationis ab eis qui ea petunt, licite posset petere mercedem competentem." — *Praxis episcopalis,* pars 2, cap. 3, art. 8, n. 14.

54. *De officio et potestate episcopi,* alleg. 73, n. 41.

a notary cannot accept anything for a record of the visitation from those who are visited, although they permit him to ask for a commensurate consideration from those who seek a copy of the acts or decrees of the visitation. Zerola,[55] however, claims a notary cannot even receive anything for his work in writing, in transcribing, or in making out a copy of the visitation itself.[56] Today, however, on account of changed conditions this seems to have little practical significance or value.

The old law ordered that frugal and moderate *victualia* be provided on the occasion of the visitation.[57] Reiffenstuel aptly observes that only a moderate procuration must be asked for and given.[58] Thus the obligation rests on both the visitor and visited. The present law not only fails to define specifically the monetary equivalent of the hospitality, but likewise refrains from repeating the injunction of the old law. It leaves everything to lawfully existing local customs.[59] Nevertheless, a variable norm which rests on the disparate resources of the places visited is available.[60] Furthermore, in the event that several churches, chapels, benefices, confraternities or other pious places are visited on the same day they are to contribute to the procuration of the day on the basis of the amount of work and time expended at a particular place together with a consideration of the means of each.[61]

55. *Praxis episcopalis*, v. "visitatio," p. 451.

56. Glossa in cap. 23, lib. III, *de censibus, exactionibus et procurationibus;* "Quartum dubium, an secretarius, vel scriba possit aliquid recipere pro suis laboribus scribendo, et transcribendo, vel dando copiam ipsius visitationis, gloss. in dict. § procurationes, in ver. officio, dicit negative". Zerola, *loc cit.*

57. C. 23, X, *de censibus, exactionibus et procurationibus*, III, 39; cc. 1, 3, *de censibus, exactionibus et procurationibus*, III, 20, in VI°; Conc. Trid. sess. XXIV, *de ref.*, c. 3.

58. Lib. III, tit. 39, n. 57: "Debet tantum moderata [procuratio] peti et dari."

59. C. 346.

60. Cc. 6, 14, 17, X, *de censibus, exactionibus et procurationibus*, III, 39; c. un., *de censibus, exactionibus, et procurationibus* III, 10, in Extravag. com.; S. C. C., *in Vasionen. Procurationis*, 9 aug. 1766 — "illud semper est observandum ut secundum facultates ecclesiarum procuratio exhibetur" — *Thesaurus*, XXXV, 191; Schmalzgrueber, lib. III, tit. XXXIX, n. 104.

61. S. C. C., *in Fanen. Procurationis*, 24 aug. 1743 — *Thesaurus*, XII, 155; Pallottini, IX, p. 484, n. 33; p. 493, n. 72; p. 506, n. 127; p. 532, n. 265.

The number of procurations is commensurate to the number of days taken up for the visitation.[62] Besides, the visitor is not allowed more than one full procuration a day regardless of whether he visits one or more churches or institutions.[63] And this is so even though each place visited is in a position to supply an entire procuration.[64] If one place alone cannot supply the necessary procuration, two or three or even more are to join together.[65] In spite of the fact that a bishop, if necessity demands it, may make more than one visitation a year at a particular parish, he is nevertheless entitled to but one procuration a year.[66]

If a custom exists whereby nothing is offered to the visitor, then such custom is to hold sway.[67] Likewise, if the visit is not personally performed by the bishop and there exists in a place an established custom which does not call for the payment of the procuration, such a custom also remains in effect. Nevertheless, if there is an agreement which stipulates that the bishop will be the recipient of the entire procuration even though he fulfills the visitation through his vicar general, then the procuration is to be paid him.[68] The same practice may likewise obtain when a bishop has an apostolic privilege which entitles him to a procuration despite his failure to make the visitation.[69]

62. C. 23, X, *de censibus, exactionibus et procurationibus,* III, 39.

63. C. 3, *de censibus, exactionibus et procurationibus,* III, 20, in VI°; Zerola, *Praxis episcopalis,* v. "visitatio," p. 542; Reiffenstuel, lib. III, tit. 39, n. 60.

64. C. 3, *de censibus, exactionibus et procurationibus,* III, 20, in VI°; S. C. C., *in Perusina Visitationis,* 16 junii 1770, § Cautum—*Thesaurus,* XXXIX, 170; Pallottini, IX, p. 532, n. 267.

65. C. 23, X, *de censibus, exactionibus et procurationibus,* III, 39; Piasecius, *Praxis episcopalis,* pars 2, cap. 3, art. 8, n. 14.

66. S. C. C., *in S. Marci plurium,* 16 ian. 1723, ad 1—*Thesaurus,* II, 262; *in Policastren.,* 1 iun. 1737—*Thesaurus,* VIII, 87; Pallottini, IX, p. 532, n. 269; p. 533, n. 270; Fagnanus, lib. III, tit. 39, cap. 21, n. 3. In relation to this practical norm determined by the Sacred Congregation of the Council it ought to be pointed out that according to the old decretal law (c. 23, X, *de censibus, exactionibus et procurationibus,* III, 39) the bishop was allowed two procurations a year.

67. Conc. Trid. sess. XXIV, *de ref.,* c. 3. Pallottini, IX, p. 532, n. 264.

68. S. C. C., *in Cassanen. Visitationis,* 14 iun. 1749, ad 1—*Thesaurus* XVIII, 47; Pallottini, IX, p. 534, n. 282.

69. Fagnanus, lib. III, tit. 39, c. 23, n. 6; Pirhing, lib. III, tit. 39, nn. 68, 69; Schmalzgrueber, lib. III, tit. 39, n. 103.

The condition or status of the visitor is also to be taken into account together with the custom of the place.[70] Thus, when a vicar general, a vicar forane or any other substitute of the bishop makes the visitation, he is to receive but one-half the procuration that would be offered the bishop were he to make the visit personally.[71] This is also true of the vicar capitular or, in this country, of the administrator of a vacant diocese.[72] The writer is inclined to believe that in dioceses where the auxiliary bishop is also the vicar general of the diocese he should be accorded practically the same treatment as his superior, the archbishop. The basis for this contention is the dignity of his office as bishop. The distinction should by no means be as great as between an archbishop and a simple vicar general. Moreover, if such a custom exists it has legal force,[73] since it has not been reprobated by the Code and is not contrary to any of its laws.[74]

The bishop has a right to demand the procuration only when he makes the visit personally, for it is his due only in virtue of the visitation.[75] Therefore there is the corresponding obligation on the places

70. "Et quamvis etiam attendi posset et debet consuetudo loci, et conditio visitatoris." — Reiffenstuel, lib. III, tit. 39, n. 57; cfr. c. un., *de censibus, exactionibus et procurationibus,* III, 10, in Extravag. com.

71. S. C. C., *in S. Marci Visitationis,* 18 iulii, 1733, § Pluries — *Thesaurus,* VI, 143.

72. Monacellus, *Formularium,* pars III, tit. I, form. 4, n. 3; Pallottini, IX, p. 534, n. 283.

73. C. 346.

74. Cc. 27 and 5. Pallottini presents a case involving the vicar general of an archbishop who was allowed by the Sacred Congregation of the Council to receive but one-half the share of the archbishop. However, he does not state whether he was of episcopal rank or not. — IX, p. 533, n. 278. Nevertheless, cf. the III General Lateran Council, c. 4 (Hardouin, VII, 1675; Mansi, XXII, 219; c. 6, X, *de censibus, exactionibus et procurationibus,* III, 39), where an archbishop was allowed 40 to 50 horses on his visitation while a bishop was allowed but 20 to 30; also the constitution *"Vas Electionis,"* whose terms were not put into effect in many places and which consequently fell into desuetude — (c. un., *de censibus, exactionibus et procurationibus,* III, 10, in Extravag. com.) — where the proportion of the sums of money allowed as procurations from the various classes of places visited was about two to three. On the other hand it is to be noted that today the prerogatives of the archbishop are not as extensive as those he enjoyed under decretal law.

75. C. 23, X, *de censibus, exactionibus et procurationibus,* III, 39; "Procurationis non debet recipere beneficium qui non facit visitationis officium" —

visited to supply it unless they can prove some form of exemption. And this right prevails even though the bishop has ample income otherwise.[76] Since the procuration is to be paid only when a personal visit is made, therefore under no pretext may a bishop *demand* a sum of money from any parish or institution if he actually fails to make a visitation that year.[77] This holds true even if the bishop were to begin the visitation and be forced to desist on account of sickness.[78] Likewise the bishop cannot demand anything from his delegate, because the procuration is due to the visitor.

Fagnanus is of the opinion that a bishop cannot receive anything if he does not make the visitation personally unless he enjoys an apostolic privilege.[79] He bases his argument on the text of the constitution "*Vas Electionis*,"[80] which, he claims, supposes that this is allowed the bishops only because of a privilege from the Holy See. The text and gloss to the text of cap. *Felicis* (c. 3, *de censibus*, etc. III, 20, in VI°) seem to support his contention. He also adduces two cases. One without any details of date, etc., concerns an agreement entered into by the bishop and his clergy and by its terms a certain sum of money was to be paid him despite his failure to make the visitation. This, according to Fagnanus, received the confirmation of Pope Paul IV.[81] The other had to do with a bishop who was taken ill in the course of the visitation and who besought the Sacred Congregation of

Hostiensis, *Commentaria in quinque decretalium libros* (Venetiis, 1581), lib. III, tit. 39, cap. 23, n. 2; Panormitanus, lib. III, tit. 23, n. 4; Fagnanus, lib. III, tit. 39, c. 23, n. 6; Pirhing, lib. III, tit. 23, n. 68; Schmalzgrueber, lib. III, tit. 39, n. 102.

76. Panormitanus, lib. II, tit. 26, cap. 16, n. 9; lib. III, tit. 39, cap. 23, n. 5; Reiffenstuel, lib. III, tit. 39, n. 50; Schmalzgrueber, lib. III, tit. 39, n. 101; Hieronymus Venero et Leyva, *Examen episcoporum* (Venetiis, 1645), cap. 26, n. 58.

77. Pallottini, IX, p. 532, n. 268.

78. Fagnanus, lib. III, tit. 39, c. 23, n. 14; Pallottini, IX, p. 533, n. 272; S. C. C., *in Perusina Procurationis*, 16 iun. 1770, § Hanc—*Thesaurus*, XXXIX, 169.

79. Lib. III, tit. 39, c. 23, n. 6.

80. C. un. *de censibus, exactionibus et procurationibus*, III, 10, in Extravag. com. "Si vero praefata Archiepiscopi Praelati et aliae personae ecclesiasticae ex privilegio Apostolico per alios visitare et procurationes recipere valeant."

81. Lib. III, tit. 39, c. 23, n. 6.

the Council for the faculty to delegate someone to complete the visitation of the diocese, but to reserve the right of procuration to himself, as if he were personally performing the visitation. Needless to say the Sacred Congregation (23 nov. 1613,) refused the bishop his petition.[82] Moreover, he adds that the Council of Trent[83] uses the words "pro temporis tantum necessitate et non ultra erunt ministranda".[84]

Outside of the constitution *"Vas Electionis,"* the law of the decretals[85] and the Council of Trent place their emphasis on the right of the bishop to ask or demand the procuration. The text in the *Liber Sextus*[86] which forbids the acceptance of anything obviously refers to the case in which no one fulfills the obligation of making the visitation. The constitution *"Vas Electionis"*, with its elaborate scale of procurations classified and graded according to the dignity of the visitor and the capacity and size of the place visited, as Pirhing testifies,[87] was not put into practice in many places. As a consequence it fell into disuse. Therefore, as he expresses it, "circa illam non est immorandam".[88] Then, too, the force of the word *exigere* and of the future periphrastic *ministranda,* which the Code uses as a modifier of *victualia,* is that the bishop has a right to demand the procuration and the places visited have the obligation to supply it only when the visitation is carried out personally and only for the duration of the visitation.

Fagnanus (†1678), however, bears witness that Joannes Andreae (†1348) seemed to be of the opinion that a bishop could receive money from anyone who was willing to give it even when the visitation had been conducted by a substitute.[89] Furthermore, the Sacred Congregation allowed the bishop of the diocese of Cassano to require the entire procuration, even though he had a substitute perform the visita-

82. *Ibid.,* n. 14.

83. Sess. XXIV, *de ref.,* c. 3.

84. *Ibid.,* n. 13.

85. V. g., c. 23, X, *de censibus, exactionibus et procurationibus,* III, 39.

86. "... recipiendo munera sive visitationis officio non impenso procurationem in victualibus aut aliquid aliud procurationis occasione violare praesumpserint." — c. 2, *de censibus, exactionibus et procurationibus,* III, 20, in VI°.

87. Lib. III, tit. 39, n. 69.

88. *Loc. cit.*

89. Lib. III, tit. 39, cap. 23, n. 13: "Joannes Andreae in caput *Felicis* (c. 3, *de censibus, exactionibus et procurationibus,* III, 20, in VI°) — videatur tenere Episcopum visitantem per alium posse recipere pecuniam a volente."

tion, in view of an agreement entered into by a Cardinal Cajetan, then bishop of Cassano, and the clergy of the town of Castelluca, in the year 1604.[90] No mention is made that this agreement was confirmed by the Holy See. Therefore, if the clergy are free to enter into an agreement to hand over the procuration to a bishop and the bishop is free to accept it whether or not he himself performs the visitation, they are certainly free to supply it when he fails to make a personal appearance without entering into any agreement. Thus the bishop may receive a procuration but he may not demand it, just as those who are visited may supply it if they wish but cannot be forced to do so.

Under the strict letter of the law of the decretals, the churches and institutions of the episcopal city were bound to supply the bishop with a procuration.[91] Practically all authors were in agreement that no exemption was extended to these churches. However, since the time of the Council of Trent, which in acknowledging the right of the visitor to a procuration either in money or in *victualia* used the limiting clause in its legislation "*pro tempore necessitatis et non ultra erunt ministranda*", the general opinion has been and is that they are exempt from the obligation. The reason why there is no cause for a procuration when a visitation has been completed in the city and the visitor can return home, is that no *necessitas temporis* exists, or rather because the *necessitas temporis* ceases.[92] In other words, the procuration is conditioned by a time element qualified by necessity. Moreover, the Sacred Congregation of the Council has repeatedly favored this view.[93] A dissenting voice from this doctrine was that of Salodius, who insisted

90. S. C. C., *Cassanen. Visitationis,* 17 maii, 14 iunii 1749 — *Thesaurus,* XVIII, 40, 47.

91. C. 24, X, *de censibus, exactionibus et procurationibus,* III, 39.

92. Barbosa, *de officio et potestate episcopi,* alleg. 73, n. 46; Piasecius, *Praxis episcopalis,* pars 2, cap. 3, a. 8, n. 15; Fagnanus, lib. III, tit. 39, cap. 24, n. 15; Monacellus, *Formularium,* pars III, tit. 2, form. 4, n. 2; Reiffenstuel, lib. III, tit. 39, n. 54; Schmalzgrueber, lib. III, tit. 39, n. 104; Bouix, *De episcopo,* II, 45; Wernz, *Ius decretalium,* III, 225; Chelodi, *Ius de personis,* p. 319, nota 1; Coronata, *Institutiones iuris canonici,* I, 466; Cappello, *Summa iuris canonici,* I, 471.

93. S. C. C., *in Tarentina,* anno 1573; *in Castren. Procurationis,* 17 nov. 1685; *in Aliphana Procurationis,* 18 iulii 1705 — Pallottini, IX, 495; *in Civitatis Plebis Procurationis,* 19 aprilis 1823, § Profecto — *Thesaurus,* LXXXIII, 82.

that the bishop had a right to the procuration when he visited the churches of the episcopal city, because the procuration was given in token of an obediential subjection to the bishop.[94]

A newly erected church which bears the status of a cathedral, if it be united *aeque principaliter* to the old one, is also exempt from the procuration, despite the fact that the bishop does not live in the same town, provided, however, he does not live far from it.[95] Therefore a bishop cannot exact a procuration from the cathedral even though he were to live elsewhere than in the city where it is situated.[96] The present law obliges the bishop to reside within his diocese, but it does not specify the cathedral city as his necessary residence.[97] Furthermore, if a bishop spends a certain part of the year (*aliqua parte*) in a particular place he cannot require a procuration from the churches or institutions while making a visitation there.[98] The Sacred Congregation of the Council, however, refused to accept as an excuse from furnishing the procuration the plea which was made by a pastor

94. "Expedita visitatione Civitatis, in qua Episcopus procurationem, etiam si Ecclesia Episcopatui contigua sit, et etiam si domum suam ad prandium revertatur recipere potest; cum procuratio in signum subiectionis detur." — *Praxis compendiosa de visitatione,* pars II, cap. 1, p. 19.

95. S. C. C., *in Aquinaten. et Pontiscurvi Procurationis,* 18 iunii 1808 — Pallottini, IX, pp. 498, 499, nn. 93-95.

96. S. C. C., *in Aquinaten. et Pontiscurvi Procurationis,* 19 iunii 1808, § Contra — Pallottini, IX, p. 500, n. 97; Monacellus, tom. 4, n. 78; *Supplementum* ad pars (tom.) III, tit. 2, form. 4, n. 2; Ferraris, *Bibliotheca,* v. "procuratio," n. 13.

97. C. 338, § 1. A view on the law of residence is expressed in the case S. C. C., *in Aquinaten. et Pontiscurvi Procurationis,* 19 iunii 1808, § Postremo, in the words. "Nam residentia juris satis est, ut Ecclesia cathedralis ad procurationem praestandam non teneatur; quandoquidem residentia juris ea est, quam Epus in cathedrali ex jure habere tenetur, licet revera non resideat, ac propterea Cathedralis immunis est a procuratione, licet Epus alibi moretur." — Pallottini, IX, 500. The Congregation also declared that a bishop satisfies his obligation with respect to residence provided he resides at the cathedral during the time specified by the Council of Trent (sess. XXIII, *de ref.,* cap. 1). His absence due to the fact that pontifical functions are required elsewhere does not militate against his compliance with this provision. Cf. S. C. C., *in Dubium,* 24 sept. 1622, et *in Calceatin.,* 4 ian. 1639 — Pallottini, IX, 539; cf. *supra,* p. 84.

98. S. C. C., *in Policastren. Procurationis,* 18 maii, 1 iunii 1737; 10 martii 1742, ad I — *Thesaurus,* VIII, 82, 83, 86, 87; XI, 32; Pallottini, IX, 500.

on the score that his parish was but *three miles* distant from the cathedral city.[99]

The question now arises: Who is responsible for the defrayal of the expenses of the hospitality offered to the bishop? The present law does not make mention of who is subject to or who is exempted from the obligation. In the first place the pastors and beneficed clerics are bound to furnish the procuration.[100] The Sacred Congregation was asked:

"V. An clerici et presbyteri ecclesiasticis redditibus carentes teneantur ad solutionem procurationis in casu? and answered: ad V, negative."[101] Therefore, if such clerics were accustomed to make a contribution they are not bound to continue doing so. Furthermore, no personal tax can be imposed on them.[102] Likewise the incumbents or possessors of simple benefices or chaplaincies conferred in title have the obligation to supply hospitality to the bishop and his entourage.[103]

However, strictly considered it is from the revenues, resources or funded incomes of the churches and benefices that the procuration is

99. S. C. C., *in Civitatis Plebis Procurationis,* 19 aprilis 1823 — *Thesaurus,* LXXXIII, 80-87.

100. "... episcopi et alii, quibus ex officio competit visitare *a volentibus* ecclesiarum et locorum visitatorum *rectoribus* seu *personis* pecuniam licite recipere valeant pro sumptibus moderatis faciendis in victualibus. ..." c. 3, *de censibus exactionibus et procurationibus,* III, 20, in VI°; S. C. C., *in Auximana Procurationis,* 15 martii 1727 — *Thesaurus,* IV (1727), 25; *in Civitatis Plebis Procurationis,* 17 aprilis 1823 — *Thesaurus,* LXXXIII (1823) 87; Schmalzgrueber, lib. III, tit. 39, n. 105; Zitelli, *Apparatus juris ecclesiasti* (2. ed., Romae, 1888), p. 96; Lucidi, *De visitatione,* I, p. 164, n. 46; Pallottini, IX, p. 491, n. 58 and note 1; also p. 494; D'Angelo, *Tasse e pensioni nel codice diritto canonico,* p. 43.

101. S. C. C., *in Tarentina Procurationis,* 18 martii 1826 — *Thesaurus,* LXXXVI, 75; Pallottini, IX, 494.

102. S. C. C., *in Tarentina Procurationis,* 18 martii 1826 — *Thesaurus,* LXXXVI, 49.

103. S. C. C., *in Triventina,* mense februarii 1599 — Pallottini, IX, p. 491, n. 58 and note 1. Cf. also S. C. C., *Narnien.,* 12 sept. 1654 — *Fontes,* n. 2739; *Boianen.,* 14 nov. 1654 — *Fontes,* n. 2740; *in Signina,* 2 aug. 1670 (quoted in *Sancti Marci Visitationis,* 18 iulii 1733) — *Thesaurus,* VI (1733), 143; Pallottini, IX, 492; *in Sabinen., Procurationis,* 26 martii, 4 iunii, 1707; 23 iunii 1708 — Pallottini, IX, 492; *in Amerina Visitationis,* 20 dec. 1755 — *Thesaurus,* XXIV, 113.

to be paid, since it is the latter which are subject to the visitation.[104] The obligation or duty rests with the clergy only indirectly. It is only as directors of the churches and as possessors or incumbents of the benefices that the obligation descends upon them.[105] The benefice of a cardinal is also subject to a *pro rata* procuration.[106] It is to be noted that churches in the hands of religious and charged with the care of souls[107] as also public oratories[108] are responsible in the same manner. The churches of nuns on the other hand are not under any obligation if an ecclesiastical benefice is not connected with them.[109]

The convents of nuns immediately subject to the ordinary or to the Holy See, the houses of diocesan congregations of men or women re-

104. "... parochias visitantes pro diversitate provinciarum et *facultatibus ecclesiarum.*" — c. 6, X, *de censibus, exactionibus et procurationibus,* III, 39; "non amplius e procurationis nomine requires ab eis nisi quantum *pensatis facultatibus* earumdem [i. e. ecclesiarum seu capellarum]" — c. 16, *de officio iudicis ordinarii,* I, 31; idem episcopus quum *ad ipsam ecclesiam* causa correctionis accesserit moderatam *ab ea* procurationem recipiat. — c. 21, X, *de censibus, exactionibus et procurationibus,* III, 39; procurationes recipiant moderatas *ab aliis ecclesiis vel personis.* — c. 23, X, *de censibus, exactionibus et procurationibus,* III, 39; cupientes pro diversitate conditionum *visitantium ac ecclesiasticarum facultatum.* — c. un., *de censibus, exactionibus et procurationibus,* III, 10, in Extravag. com.

105. "Itaque pro certo habendum est, ad procurationem solvendam, nempe ad conferendam symbolam pro frugali sustentatione Episcopi, ejusque sociorum in Sacra Visitatione *omnia* teneri *beneficia* et loca pia eidem visitationi obnoxia — *Onus* proinde *personis ecclesiasticis non inhaeret, sed ad ipsas pertinet propter Ecclesias, quas regunt, et beneficia, quae possident;* ideoque taxa personalis imponi ecclesiasticis non debet qui beneficiis et Ecclesiae redditibus careant." — S. C. C., in *Tarentina Procurationis,* 18 martii 1826 — *Thesaurus,* LXXXVI (1826), 49; — Verum enim vero ex regula *procurationem* dare *ad ecclesiam* spectat. — S. C. C., *in Vasconen. Procurationis,* 9 aug. 1766 — *Thesaurus,* XXXV, 191; Barbosa (pars III, alleg. 73, n. 43); Pirhing (lib. III, tit. 39, n. 71), Reiffenstuel (lib. III, tit. 39, n. 50) and Schmalzgrueber (lib. III, tit. 39, n. 105) all refer to the churches as subjects of the obligation.

106. S. C. C., *Nullius seu Neritonen.,* 13 sept. 1631 — Pallottini, IX, p. 492, n. 65.

107. C. 631, § 1.

108. C. 1191, § 1.

109. "Episcopo visitanti *ecclesiam monialium,* si *in ea non adsit beneficium,* non deberi procurationem, seu expensas victualium." — S. C. C., *in Volaterrana,* 13 nov. 1638 — Lucidi, *De visitatione,* I, p. 167, n. 56; Pallottini, IX, p. 481, n. 24. Cf. also c. 609, § 2.

ligious, the convents of nuns subject to a regular superior, the houses of clerical and lay congregations of papal approval,[110] the houses of clerical and lay communities or societies[111] are also bound to furnish the procuration in virtue of the visitation unless they have a privilege to the contrary. Lay confraternities and associations,[112] seminaries,[113] schools,[114] as well as pious institutions[115] are inherently liable for the procuration. As a general rule it can be said that whosoever is subject to the jurisdiction or visitation of the bishop is also subject to the obligation of offering the visitor a procuration.[116]

On the basis of equity and custom there are a few exceptions. First of all the lay people are excused from the obligation.[117] The exemption is due to custom.[118] However, if the visitor receives his hospitality from the laity — a custom which the authors tolerated but which the S. Congregation refused to enforce if the laity declined to comply with it — he cannot tax the place visited unless the party concerned refused to supply the procuration.[119] Private oratories are not subject to the law on procuration,[120] because they have no benefice attached to them nor do they have any resources, revenue or income whereby the procuration can be paid.[121] Hence it

110. C. 512.

111. Cc. 673, 675.

112. C. 690.

113. C. 1357, § 2.

114. C. 1382.

115. Cc. 1489, 1491.

116. Schmalzgrueber, lib. III, tit. 39, n. 108; Bouix, *De episcopo,* II, 45.

117. For a discussion *pro* and *con* concerning the obligation of the laity confer Barbosa, *De officio et potestate episcopi,* pars III, alleg. 73, n. 43.

118. Barbosa, *loc. cit.;* Schmalzgrueber, lib. III, tit. 39, n. 106; Pirhing, lib. III, tit. 39, n. 78; Monacellus, *Formularium,* pars III, tit. 1, form 4, n. 4; Zitelli, *Apparatus,* p. 96; S. C. C., *in Spoletana Procurationis super contributione,* 26 martii 1746, § Ceterum. — *Thesaurus,* XV, 32; *in Vasconen. Procurationis,* 9 aug. 1766, § Quemadmodum — *Thesaurus,* XXV, 191, 192.

119. Barbosa, *De officio et potestate episcopi,* pars III, alleg. 73, n. 45; Monacellus, *op. cit.,* pars III, tit. 1, form. 4, n. 6.

120. C. 27, X, *de censibus, exactionibus et procurationibus,* III, 39.

121. S. C. C., *in Senogallien. Procurationis,* 14 dec. 1765, § Exemptionem — *Thesaurus,* XXXIV, 200; Fagnanus, lib. III, tit. 39, cap. 27, n. 1; Pirhing, lib. III, tit. 39, n. 80; Reiffenstuel, lib. III, tit. 39, n. 51; Zitelli, *Apparatus,* p. 96.

cannot be insisted that the chapels of lay persons pay the procuration.[122] Similarly the clergy, churches, benefices and ecclesiastical persons whose poverty is well beyond dispute enjoy the exemption. This poverty[123] must be such that a procuration would really be a burden on their resources which are barely sufficient for the necessities of life and the divine worship. Thus charity demands that no procuration be exacted from them.[124] Fagnanus states that it is not to be accepted even if it is offered spontaneously.[125] The old authors claimed that if it were well known that the church visited could sustain the costs of a visitation, then the bishop could compel the rector to supply the procuration. In a case of doubt the visitor was to demand an oath in attestation of the church's inability to meet that cost before he definitely declared the church to be excused from making payment. If there remained any uncertainty concerning the church's obligation to pay the costs of the visitation, he could at most inflict an excommunication upon the rector of the church in a conditional manner, that is, the excommunication would become effective only when the rector had neglected to furnish the procuration which the church's means made available in the case.[126] A church of nuns which has no benefice connected with it is also exempt.[127] Moreover pious places and ecclesiastical persons possessing an apostolic privilege are relieved of the

122. S. C. C., *in Spoletana Procurationes super contributione*, 26 mart. 1746, § Ceterum — *Thesaurus*, XV, 32.

123. According to Salodius a church is said to be poor "quando non potest aliquem honeste et sufficienter alere, hospitesque supervenientes recipere; et quando sibi et suis non sufficit." — *Praxis compendiosa*, pars II, cap. 1, p. 21.

124. S. C. C., *in Senogallien.*, 14 dec. 1765, § Exemptione; *in Vasionen Procurationis*, 9 aug. 1766, § Ecclesiae — *Thesaurus*, XXXIV, 200; XXXV, 191; Panormitanus, lib. III, tit. 39, cap. 17, n. 7; Pirhing, lib. III, tit. 39, n. 82; Fagnanus, lib. III, tit. 39, cap. 24, n. 33; Barbosa, *De officio et potestate episcopi*, pars III, alleg. 73, nn. 50, 51, 52; Zerola, v. "visitatio," p. 452; Reiffenstuel, lib. III, tit. 39, n. 53; Schmalzgrueber, lib. III, tit. 39, n. 107; Zitelli, *Apparatus*, p. 96. The authors draw a parallel with a judge who does not charge a poor person (*quia nec judex exigit sportulas a pauperibus*).

125. Lib. III, tit. 39, cap. 23, n. 20.

126. Panormitanus, lib. III, tit. 39, cap. 23, n. 7; Pirhing, lib. III, tit. 39, n. 92; Reiffenstuel, lib. III, tit. 39, n. 53; Schmalzgrueber, lib. III, tit. 39, n. 107.

127. S. C. C., *in Volaterrana*, 13 nov. 1638 — Pallottini, IX, p. 481, n. 24; Lucidi, *De visitatione*, I, p. 167, n. 56.

burden.[128] However, this privilege must be expressed explicitly; it does not suffice that it be couched in general terms. It must specify whether the exemption is from the procuration of the bishop or from that of the apostolic visitor.[129] Finally, it is the common teaching of the authors[130] that hospitals, homes for the poor, the infirm, the aged, the suffering and any other institutions which are devoted to charity are not obligated in any way provided that they have been erected by episcopal authority and have no benefice attached to them. The reason for their existence is to use whatever resources are on hand for the alleviation of the needs of the indigent,[131] and for the support or sustenance of the directors and attendants. Hence, any support offered to the bishop would be a deflection from that purpose when in fact it is to be anticipated that the visitor will furnish aid to such an institution rather than derive aid from it.[132] It makes no difference according to Pirhing and Reiffenstuel whether the institutions under consideration have a small or a very large income.[133] In one instance it seems a hospital was not allowed an exemption because it had a church annexed to it,[134] although it must be admitted that the Sacred Congregation failed to advance any reason for its decision.

128. C. 17, X, *de censibus, exactionibus et procurationibus,* III, 39; Piasecius, *Praxis episcopalis,* pars 2, c. 3, a. 8, n. 16; Barbosa, *De officio et potestate episcopi,* pars III, alleg. 73, n. 47; *Ius eccl. univ.,* lib. 3, c. 22, n. 27; Pirhing, lib. III, tit. 39, n. 79; Reiffenstuel, lib. III, tit. 39, n. 52; Schmalzgrueber, lib. III, tit. 39, n. 108; Zitelli, *Apparatus,* n. 96.

129. Schmalzgrueber, *loc. cit.;* Zitelli, *loc. cit.;* cf. canons 49 and 67.

130. Schmalzgrueber, lib. III, tit. 39, n. 106; Zitelli, *Apparatus,* p. 96; Zerola, *Praxis episcopalis,* v. "visitatio," p. 452; Fagnanus, lib. III, tit. 39, cap. 24, nn. 34-42; Piasecius, Praxis episcopalis, pars II, cap. 3, a. 8, n. 16; Reiffenstuel, lib. III, tit. 39, n. 55; Barbosa, *De officio et potestate episcopi,* pars III, alleg. 73, n. 50; Pirhing, lib. III, tit. 39, n. 79; Bouix, *De episcopo,* II, 45; Coronata, *Institutiones iuris canonici,* I, 467, n. 2; Chelodi, *Ius de personis,* p. 319, n. 1.

131. C. 2, *de religiosis domibus ut episcopo sint subiectae,* III, 11, in Clem.

132. Fagnanus gives the arguments *pro* and *con* offered in this matter by the members of the Sacred Congregation of the Council at its session of Nov. 19, 1623—lib. III, tit. 39, cap. 24, nn. 34-42. The majority favored exemption, although no decision was given, since it was decided to review the case again and to examine the claims on which the common opinion rested.

133. *Loc. cit.*

134. S. C. C., *in Nullius Foripompilii Sacrae Visitationis,* 14 maii 1825—*Thesaurus,* LXXXV, 91, 100.

Uniformity of practice was evidently lacking for the defender of the Vatican Chapter (*Capituli Vaticani*), which enjoyed the right of visitation in the case in question, made a claim that the view of canonists was by no means certain.[135] The guiding principle and determining factor for the Sacred Congregation apparently was custom. In a certain case[136] it approved the provisions of a bishop's decree, made in 1660, which excluded the hospitals from the obligation. In another instance[137] a bishop claimed no pious institution or hospital was free from the obligation and the Congregation upheld the right of the bishop to receive a procuration from the particular hospital which appealed to it. Therefore, as then so now, custom should be our guide with respect to these institutions.

Prescription with Respect to Procuration

The question may be asked whether a bishop may forego the procuration due him by reason of the visitation. He may and can do so expressly or tacitly by not asking for it, inasmuch as he can allow the discontinuance of other services due him by any church subject to him.[138] But this holds good only in particular instances, for he cannot expressly or through an agreement remit the right of procuration altogether and perpetually so that a particular church would be completely excused in the future from furnishing any procuration whatsoever.[139] In the first case the bishop's action is not detrimental to a third party or to the public good but to himself. In the second case the nature of the right of procuration forbids such a procedure. The right of procuration pertains to public law, because it is annexed to the right of visitation which belongs to that category. Hence, since

135. "Nosocomium praeterea victualium praestationi jure subjectum fuisse suadere nititur. *Quidquid enim doceant canonistae de Hospitalium immunitate a procurando Episcopo, eorum sententia haud certa est.*" — S. C. C., *in Nullius Foripompilii Sacrae Visitationis,* 14 maii 1825 — *Thesaurus,* LXXXV, 97.

136. S. C. C., *in Aquipendien.,* 21 apr. 1787 — *Thesaurus,* LVI, 62-65.

137. S. C. C., *in Ariminen. Procurationis,* 27 maii 1837 — *Thesaurus,* XCVII, 167.

138. C. 7, X, *de donationibus,* III, 24; Panormitanus, lib. III, tit. 39, cap. 7, n. 4.

139. Panormitanus, lib. II, tit. 26, cap. 16, n. 14; Azorius, *Institutiones morales,* pars II, lib. 3, cap. 42, q. 11; Pirhing, lib. II, tit. 26, n. 24; lib. III, tit. 39, n. 83; Schmalzgrueber, lib. III, tit. 39, n. 109.

the right of procuration has its foundation in the public good (*quia procurationes sunt juris publici auctoritate et utilitate constitutae*) and since private agreements can in no way run counter to public law,[140] it follows that a bishop may neither expressly nor by a pact renounce entirely his right to the procuration.[141] However, a church or institute can enter into an agreement with a bishop with respect to the manner of furnishing the procuration, that is, either in money or in kind.[142] Moreover the procuration which is due not in virtue of the common law but in view of custom, prescription, a privilege or an agreement can be renounced by him who is not the proper prelate of the place since it is not a public law.[143]

The present legislation on procuration makes no mention of the force of prescription with respect to the right of procuration. According to the old law[144] this right could not be prescribed by any subject and the obligation remained on the part of the subject to supply it even though he had failed to do so in the past. This was also the common teaching of the authors.[145] The primary juridical reason advanced was this: Since the right of visitation itself could not be prescribed[146] and since the right to the procuration is joined to the right of visitation as an accessory to its principle, neither could the procuration be prescribed, for the same judgment should be made on

140. C. 12, X, *de foro competenti,* II, 2; "Ius publicum privatorum pactis mutari non potest" —*D.* (2.14) 38. cf. 152.

141. Panormitanus, *loc. cit.;* Pirhing, *loc. cit.;* Schmalzgrueber, lib. III, tit. 39, nn. 110, 111.

142. Glossa c. 2, *de censibus, exactionibus et procurationibus,* III, 13, in Clem., v. "compositiones"; Azorius, *Institutiones morales,* pars II, lib. III, cap. 42, q. 11; Barbosa, lib. II, tit. 26, c. 16, n. 11; Pirhing, lib. III, tit. 39, n. 83; Schmalzgrueber, lib. III, tit. 39, n. 110.

143. Azorius, *Institutiones morales,* pars II, lib. III, cap. 42, quaest. 11; Pirhing, *loc. cit.;* Schmalzgrueber, *ibid,* n. 111.

144. Cc. 11, 16, X, *de praescriptionibus,* II, 26; cc. 17, 24, X, *de censibus, exactionibus et procurationibus,* III, 39.

145. Panormitanus, lib. III, tit. 39, c. 17, n. 31; Pirhing, lib. III, tit. 39, n. 76; Reiffenstuel, lib. III, tit. 39, n. 63; Fagnanus, lib. III, tit. 39, cap. 24, nn. 23, 24; Monacellus, *Formularium,* pars III, tit. 2, form. 4, n. 12; Azorius, *Institutiones morales,* pars II, lib. III, cap. 42, q. 11, § Si roges; q. 14, § Constat; Zerola, v. "visitatio," Octavum dubium, p. 452.

146. C. 16, X, *de praescriptionibus,* II, 26.

connected or related matters.[147] And if the principle could not be prescribed, neither was its accessory subject to prescription.[148] It needs only to be recalled that a legal prescription against the right of visitation is still outlawed in the Code.[149] In view of the continued maintenance of this principle it follows naturally that the accessory item of the right to the procuration is likewise safeguarded against extinction by legal prescription.

Another but more profoundly moral reason was this: A prescription of this kind would be detrimental to the interests of the Church. For it was then as now believed that if such a situation were to exist the prelate would be deterred from making the visitation which in turn was so necessary for the public good of the Church.[150] The same may be said concerning legal prescription against the supplying of a notable part of the procuration,[151] for if an integral part is taken away the whole is no longer intact.[152]

Notwithstanding the fact that the right of procuration is not subject to legal prescription, there are certain instances wherein prescription may take its course. For example, it may enter into the manner of

147. "...de connexis idem debet esse judicium." — Panormitanus, *Consilia iuris,* pars II, 26, consilium n. 1; Pirhing, lib. II, tit. 26, n. 23; lib. III, tit. 39, n. 76; Barbosa, lib. II, tit. 26, cap. 16, n. 2; Fagnanus, lib. III, tit. 39, cap. 24, n. 23.

148. Panormitanus, lib. II, tit. 26, cap. 16, n. 5.

149. C. 1509, n. 7.

150. Panormitanus, lib. II, tit. 26, c. 16, n. 4; Barbosa, lib. II, tit. 26, c. 16, nn. 2, 4; Azorius, *Institutiones morales,* pars II, lib. III, cap. 42, q. 13; Pirhing, lib. II, tit. 26, n. 23; Schmalzgrueber, lib. III, tit. 39, n. 112. In this connection Fagnanus remarks, "Secunda ratio [cur adversus Episcopum huiusmodi praescriptio non currat, est...] quia si per consuetudinem, vel per praescriptionem Episcopi gratis deberent munus visitationis impendere, *verendum esset ne visitationem negligerent.... Hoc autem constat esse absurdum* quia jus iterandi visitationem est publicum utilitate et auctoritate et consuetudo in talibus non est toleranda." — lib. III, tit. 39, cap. 24, n. 23.

151. Azorius, *Institutiones morales,* pars 2, lib. III, cap. 42, q. 11; Barbosa, *Ius eccl. univ.,* lib. III, c. 22, n. 23; Schmalzgrueber, lib. III, tit. 39, n. 112. Some authors claim prescription cannot bring about even the slightest diminution of the procuration. Cf. Pirhing, lib. II, tit. 26, n. 24; Panormitanus, lib. II, tit. 26, cap. 16, n. 13; Azorius, *loc. cit.*

152. "Parte quacumque integrante sublata tollitur totum." Cf. *D.* (6, 1) 76.

furnishing the procuration.[153] It is to be reckoned with when the prelate and not the subject is the prescribing agent, so that the prelate obtains the exclusive right to the procuration. This *praescriptio translativa* is permitted inasmuch as the Code forbids only the *praescriptio extinctiva* with regard to the visitation.[154] Likewise legal prescription can effectively operate against the right of procuration which derives from custom, privilege or some other juridical agency.[155] Here the right of procuration is not founded on the common law, and hence does not enjoy its protection. Furthermore, procurations which are long overdue, even when the visitations have been personally conducted by the bishop, are also subject to prescription. The operation of prescription under such circumstances does not prove prejudicial either to the right of visitation or to the right of procuration as such, but simply redounds to a personal disadvantage of the bishop who performed the visitation.[156]

Finally, according to some authors prescription can take place in favor of one church to the detriment of the other. For example, when two or more churches are visited on the same day, the practice may be that the burden is shouldered entirely by one of the places visited.[157] However, the opposite is the more weighty opinion, for the texts[158] which forbid the prescription of the right of procuration seem to indicate that no one is excused and that the procuration is to be supplied

153. Barbosa, *Ius eccl. univ.*, lib. III, cap. 22, nn. 22, 24; Schmalzgrueber, lib. III, tit. 39, n. 113; Pirhing, lib. II, tit. 26, n. 24, not. 3.

154. C. 1509, n. 7; cf. c. 16, X, *de praescriptionibus*, II, 26, where it is clearly admitted that by legal prescription one prelate as against another can acquire the right of visitation and also its juridical sequel, namely, the right of procuration. "... etsi alius contra eum praescribere posset utramque ..." — Barbosa, *Ius eccl. univ.*, lib. III, c. 22, n. 3; Fagnanus, lib. III, tit. 39, cap. 24, n. 22.

155. Pirhing, lib. III, tit. 39, n. 76; Fagnanus, lib. III, tit. 39, cap. 24, n. 21; Schmalzgrueber, lib. III, tit. 39, n. 113.

156. Barbosa, *Ius eccl. univ.*, lib. III, cap. 22, n. 25; Schmalzgrueber, lib. III, tit. 39, n. 113.

157. Panormitanus, *Consilia iuris*, pars II, consilium 26, n. 5; Schmalzgrueber, lib. III, tit. 39, n. 113.

158. Cc. 11, 16, X, *de praescriptionibus*, II, 26; c. 17, X, *de censibus, exactionibus et procurationibus*, III, 39.

by all.[159] The Sacred Congregation of the Council undoubtedly supported this view when it required a (proportionate) contribution in cases wherein prescription was alleged as furnishing an excuse from supplying the procuration.[160]

The authors also take up the question whether an immemorial prescription has any force against the right of procuration. Azorius,[161] Pirhing[162] and Reiffenstuel[163] hold the negative opinion. They claim that every kind of prescription is forbidden by the texts in question. They do so despite the contention of other authors[164] that the Council of Trent opened the way for the more liberal opinion and even confirmed it inasmuch as it permitted the continuance of a custom whereby nothing was offered to the visitor.[165] Panormitanus and Schmalzgrueber even argue on the score that the texts of the decretals[166] do not exclude immemorial prescription as an agency for obviating and cancelling the right of procuration.[167] Moreover, Barbosa[168] and Schmalzgrueber[169] maintain that an immemorial prescription is equivalent to an apostolic privilege if the prescribing agent is in a position to

159. Barbosa, *Ius eccl. univ.*, pars III, cap. 22, n. 26; Fagnanus, lib. III, tit. 39, cap. 24, n. 28.

160. S. C. C., *in Fanen. Procurationis*, 24 aug. 1743, ad I; *in Pientina Procurationis*, 20 nov. 1756; *in Aquipendien.*, 21 aprilis 1787; *in Civitatis Plebis Procurationis*, 19 aprilis 1823.—*Thesaurus*, XII (1743), 155; XXV (1756); 95; LVI (1787), 65; LXXXIII (1823), 87. Cf. also S. C. C., *Signina*, 2 aug. 1670—*Fontes*, n. 2818.

161. *Institutiones morales*, pars II, cap. 42, q. 14.

162. Lib. II, tit. 26, n. 24.

163. Lib. III, tit. 39, n. 63.

164. Piasecius, *Praxis episcopalis*, pars II, cap. 3, a. 8, n. 17; Barbosa, alleg. 73, n. 48; Schmalzgrueber, lib. III, tit. 39, n. 116.

165. Sess. XXIV, *de ref.*, c. 3—"In iis vero *locis, seu provinciis, ubi consuetudo est*, ut nec victualia nec pecunia, nec quidquam aliud a visitatoribus accipiatur, sed omnia gratis fiant, ibi id observetur."

166. Cc. 11, 16, X, *de praescriptionibus*, II, 26.

167. "Nec obstante illa jura quae videntur reprobare praescriptionem longissimi temporis *quia non loquuntur de illa de cujus initio non est memoria.*"—Panormitanus, *Consilia iuris*, pars II, consilium 26, n. 4; Schmalzgrueber, lib. III, tit. 39, n. 116.

168. *Ius eccl. univ.*, pars II, lib. III, cap. 22, nn. 30, 31.

169. Lib. III, tit. 39, n. 115.

benefit by the prescription and if the common law does not militate against it.[170]

In answer to such a claim Pirhing says that because of the possible harm to the Church the Pope is not wont to dispense from the obligation of furnishing the procuration to the bishop. Hence it follows that not even such a period of time that its beginning reaches beyond the memory of man can give rise to the presumption of an antecedent title or a papal privilege in virtue of which the subject churches are exempted from supplying the procuration. For the Pope is not accustomed to grant such a privilege. Moreover, a bishop is incapable of renouncing his right to the procuration.[171]

With regard to the legislation of the Council of Trent, the authors who contend for the effectiveness of prescription seem to identify prescription with custom. In fact, Schmalzgrueber claims that the custom spoken of by the Council of Trent is properly prescription, because through it the right of a prelate is taken away.[172] The Council, however, appears to speak of custom, and not of prescription, for the words "*in iis locis seu provinciis*" do not seem suited for an interpretation according to which the word "custom" would refer to an observance of a particular church. For a custom to have value the practice must be as general as its equivalent, the written law. Fagnanus[173] and Reiffenstuel[174] understand the particle *seu* in a declarative and exposi-

170. "... quia immunitas haec acquiri potest privilegio apostolico ... sed praescriptio immemoralis, si praescribens sit capax possessionis, et jus commune ei non resistat, aequivalet privilegio; ergo. ..." — Schmalzgrueber, *loc. cit.;* cf. also c. 63, § 2.

171. Lib. II, tit. 26, n. 24. This becomes clearer in the case of legates of the Holy See who perform the visitation. For a privilege granted by the Holy See can be revoked, but thus a right is acquired by the prescribing agent against him in whose case the prescription connotes the loss of a right. Therefore prescription cannot run directly against the supreme power or the plenitude of power which the Pope has over ecclesiastical benefices. — Pirhing, *ibid.,* n. 26. Cf. also c. 1509, n. 2.

172. "... consuetudinem illam quae ibi permittitur proprie praescriptionem esse cum per eam jus praelati tollatur, et per quam possessionem tempore legibus definito continuatam, subditis acquiratur immunitas ab onere procurationes istas solvendi." — lib. III, tit. 39, n. 116.

173. Lib. III, tit. 39, c. 24, n. 27.

174. Lib. III, tit. 39, n. 63.

tive sense, rather than in a disjunctive or alternative sense, which, as Reiffenstuel claims, indicates that the words between which this particle stands are of the same meaning or signification. But it is difficult to see how Fagnanus can then claim that the word *locis* refers either to a diocese or to a town,[175] if the word *provincia* is to refer to a diocese or a province. The latter certainly cannot be called the equivalent of the word *oppidum*. The interpretation that is more in keeping with the accepted meaning of the words in the ecclesiastical parlance of the time is that *locis* refers to towns or cities and *provinciis* refers to dioceses. Thus the Sacred Congregation maintained that the standing custom in the *town* of Montefalco (*Terra Montes Falci*) in the archdiocese of Spoleto was to be observed. According to it the procuration to be paid was divided into thirteen parts. The archbishop wanted to introduce a change so that all the *loca pia* would be graded into four classes with respect to their income.[176]

Likewise, according to our present law it seems that the custom of a town or city affords an exemption if it be the existing practice not to offer a procuration, even though the other towns of the diocese furnish it. The Code avoids the use of the phrase of the Council of Trent, "*in locis seu provinciis,*" and offers in its stead "*legitima locorum consuetudo.*" Hence, though prescription by a particular church was not permitted in the light of the old law, yet inasmuch as the phrase "*seu provinciis*" is omitted from the text of the present law, the indications point to a town or a city within the diocese as being capable of establishing the custom which can serve as the guiding norm in determining the presence or the absence of an obligation in the matter of the bishop's procuration.

175. "Item illa dictio *seu* quae non est propria alternativa sed ponitur inter ea quae sunt ejusdem generis . . . ostendit Concilium accepisse locum non pro ecclesia particulari seu loco loci *sed pro dioecesi aut oppido,* alioquin si locum intellexisset pro ecclesia incongrue dixisset in loco, seu provincia. Item eo casu non possent verificari illa verba universalia Concilii ut gratis omnia fiant, si aliqua ecclesia loci procurationem solveret." — lib. III, tit. 39, cap. 24, n. 27.

176. S. C. C., *in Spoletana Procurationis,* 3 dec. 1842 — "An et quomodo confirmandum vel infirmandum sit Archiepiscopi Decretum in casu." — Resp.: "Servetur consuetudo." — Pallottini, IX, 480.

The III Plenary Council of Baltimore

The III Plenary Council of Baltimore declared that diocesan synods were to make provisions for the defrayal of the expenses connected with the visitation.[177] Therefore, if no such legislation has ever been passed in a diocesan synod, the customs prevalent in the towns or diocese are to be followed. However, it is needless to say, only legitimate customs are to be tolerated, namely, such as are in harmony with the old law, with the decisions of the Sacred Congregations, with the teachings of accepted authors, and such as have become entrenched against the law upon meeting the requirements of law concerning the effective and definitive establishment of them.

Barrett[178] is of the opinion that the common custom in this country for the bishops is to pay for the costs of the visitation from the cathedraticum. It is not evident on what he bases his claim, but it is obvious that the cathedraticum cannot be identified with procuration for they are two distinct rights. Moreover, it is certain that though such a custom be a laudable one the bishops are by no means bound to abide by it if it is not simultaneously the practice in their own dioceses. For they have a right to the procuration by reason of the visitation which is a *ius publicum*.[179] Then, too, the Code acknowledges the right to traveling expenses. Therefore the bishop may be refused the procuration only when it is the custom of the place not to make an offering.

177. *Acta et decreta*, n. 14.

178. *A comparative study of the councils of Baltimore and the code of canon law*, p. 67.

179. Bouix in his work "*De episcopo*" (Parisiis, 1859), II, 45, claimed that in all of France during his time the custom was to perform the visitation gratis. "Hodie in tota Gallia viget praefata consuetudo, inde in ea regione visitantibus episcopis nulla procuratio debetur."

PARTICULAR CONCLUSIONS

1. In small dioceses which can be visited completely within a year the bishop is obliged to make an annual visitation of the entire diocese.

2. The law requiring residence at the cathedral church during Advent and Lent does not prevent the bishop from making the visitation during these periods.

3. The bishop may not use a substitute visitor all the time, for the obligation of the visitation is a personal one.

4. The bishop has no right to inspect a priest's private register of mass stipends.

5. Private domestic oratories may be subject to visitation.

6. Since the visitation is not subject to extinctive prescription neither is procuration, for the accessory follows the principal.

7. The contention that in this country the procuration is paid from the cathedraticum is not substantiated by any proof. Wherever diocesan statutes have not been enacted in compliance with the request of the III Plenary Council of Baltimore local customs are still recognized. Where such customs are not in force, the visitor is still entitled to hospitality and traveling expenses.

BIBLIOGRAPHY

SOURCES

Acta Apostolicae Sedis, Commentarium Officiale, Romae, 1909 —
Acta Ecclesiae Mediolanensis, 2 vols., Mediolani, 1890.
Acta et Decreta Concilii Plenarii Australasiae, Sydney, 1887.
Acta et Decreta Concilii Plenarii Baltimorensis III (1884), Baltimorae, typis Joannis Murphy et Sociorum, 1886.
Acta et Decreta Concilii Plenarii Quebecensis Primi, Quebeci, 1912.
Acta et Decreta Conciliorum Recentiorum (Coll. Lacensis), 7 vols., Friburgi-Brisgoviae, 1870-1890.
Acta et Decreta Synodi Provincialis Ruthenorum Galiciae, Romae, Ex Typographia Polyglotta S. C. De Prop. Fide, 1896.
Acta Sanctae Sedis, 41 vols., Romae, 1865-1908.

Bruns, Herm. Theod., *Canones Apostolorum et Conciliorum Saeculorum IV-VII,* 2 vols., Berolini, 1839.

Canones et Decreta Sacrosancti Oecumenici Concilii Tridentini, Romae: Ex Typographia Polyglotta S. C. de Propaganda Fide, 1882.
Codex Iuris Canonici Pii X Pontificis Maximi iussu digestus Benedicti Papae XV auctoritate promulgatus, Romae: Typis Polyglottis Vaticanis, 1917.
Codicis Iuris Canonici Fontes cura Emi. Petri Card. Gasparri editi, 9 vols., Romae (Later Civitate Vaticana): Typis Polyglottis Vaticanis, 1923-1939 (Vols. VII, VIII, IX, ed. cura et studio Emi. Iustiniani Card. Serédi).
Concilii Plenarii Americae Latinae in Urbe Celebrati A. D. MDCCCXCIX, Acta et Decreta, Romae, 1902.
Concilii Plenarii Baltimorensis II (1866), Acta et Decreta, Baltimorae, typis Joannis Murphy et Sociorum, 1868.
Corpus Iuris Canonici, Editio Lipsiensis II (Richter-Friedberg), 2 vols., Lipsiae, 1922.
Corpus Iuris Civilis (Kreuger-Mommsen-Schoell-Kroll), 5. ed., 3 vols., Berolini, 1928-1929.

Decreta Authentica Congregationis Sacrorum Rituum, 5 vols., Romae, 1898; Appendix I, Romae, 1912; II, Romae, 1927.
Decretales D. Gregorii Papae IX, una cum Glossis Restitutae, Romae, 1582.

Haddan, A. W., and Stubbs, W., *Councils and Ecclesiastical Documents Relating to Great Britain and Ireland,* 3 vols., Oxford, 1869-1873.
Hardouin, Jean, *Acta Conciliorum et Epistolae Decretales ac Constitutiones Summorum Pontificum,* 12 vols., Parisiis, 1715.

Journel, M. J. Rouët de, *Enchiridion Patristicum,* 11. ed., Friburgi-Brisgoviae: Herder and Co., 1937.

Liber Sextus Decretalium, una cum Clementinis et Extravagantibus Earumque Glossis Restitutis, Romae, 1582.

Mansi, J. D., *Sacrorum Conciliorum Nova et Amplissima Collectio*, 58 vols., Paris, Arnhem, Leipzig, 1901-1927.

Migne, P. J., *Patrologiae Cursus Completus* — Series Latina, 221 vols., (*MPL*), Parisiis, 1844-1855; — Series Graeca, 161 vols., (*MPG*), Parisiis, 1857-1866.

Monumenta Germaniae Historica (*MGH*), *Leges*, 5 vols., I-IV, ed. Pertz; V. ed. Pertz-Waitz-Brunner, Hannoverae, 1835-1889.

Pallottini, Salvator, *Collectio Omnium Conclusionum et Resolutionum Congregationis Concilii ab anno 1564-1860*, 18 vols., Romae, 1868-1893.

Schroeder, H. J., *Disciplinary Decrees of the General Councils: Text, Translation, and Commentary*, St. Louis: B. Herder Book Co., 1937.

Statuta Synodi Dioecesanae Philadelphiensis IX (26 apr. 1934), Philadelphiae, 1934.

Thesaurus Resolutionum Sacrae Congregationis Concilii (*Thesaurus*), 167 vols., Romae, 1718-1908.

Wilkins, D., *Concilia Magnae Britannicae et Hiberniae*, 4 vols., Londini, 1737.

Reference Works

André, M. — Wagner, J., *Dictionnaire de Droit Canonique*, 3. ed., Paris, 1901.

Antoninus, B., *Summa Sacrae Theologiae, Iuris Pontificii, et Caesarei*, 4 vols., Venetiis, 1571.

Aquinas, Thomas, *Summa Theologica*, Vivès ed., Paris, 1895.

Auerbach, Josephus, *De Visitationum Ecclesiasticarum Progressu a primis temporibus usque ad Concil. Trid.*, Francofurti ad Moenum, 1862.

Ayrinhac, H. A., *Constitution of the Church in the New Code of Canon Law*, New York: Longmans, 1930.

Azorius, Joannes, *Institutiones morales in quibus universae quaestiones ad conscientiam recte, aut prave factorum pertinentes, breviter tractantur*, 3 vols., Brescia, 1617.

(Bachofen), Charles Augustine, *A Commentary on the New Code of Canon Law*, 8 vols. Vol. II, 5. ed., St. Louis: Herder, 1928.

Barbosa, Augustinus, *Iuris Ecclesiastici Universi Libri Tres*, Lugduni, 1634.

———, *Collectanea Doctorum tam Veterum quam Recentiorum in Ius Pontificium universum*, Lugduni, 1656.

———, *Tractatus de Appellatione Verborum Utriusque Iuris Significatione*, Lugduni, 1660.

———, *De Officio et Potestate Episcopi*, Lugduni, 1656.

Bargilliat, *Praelectiones Juris Canonici,* 24. ed., 2 vols., Parisiis, 1907; 37. ed., 1923-1924.

Baronius, *Annales Ecclesiastici,* 36 vols., Barri Ducis, 1864-1882.

Barrett, John D. M., *A Comparative Study of the Councils of Baltimore and the Code of Canon Law,* Catholic University of America Canon Law Studies: n. 83, Washington, D. C.: The Catholic University of America, 1930.

Bastien, Pierre, *Directoire Canonique à l'usage des Congregations à voeux simples,* 3. ed., Bruges: Beyaert, 1923.

Benedict XIV, *De Synodo Dioecesana,* 2 vols., Parmae, 1764.

———, *Institutiones Ecclesiasticae,* 3 vols., Louvain, 1762.

Beste, Udalricus, *Introductio in Codicem,* Collegeville, Minn., St. John's Abbey Press, 1938.

Bingham, Joseph, *Antiquities of the Christian Church,* 2 vols., London, 1865.

Blat, Albertus, *Commentarium Textus Codicis Iuris Canonici,* 6 vols., 1921-1927.

Bliley, Nicholas M., *Altars according to the Code of Canon Law,* The Catholic University of America, Canon Law Studies, n. 38, Washington, D. C.: The Catholic University of America, 1927.

Boffa, Conrad Humbert, *Canonical Provisions for Catholic Schools,* The Catholic University of America, Canon Law Studies, n. 117, Washington, D. C.: The Catholic University of America, 1939.

Bouix, D., *Tractatus de Episcopo ubi et de Synodo Dioecesana,* 2. ed., 2 vols., Parisiis, 1873.

———, *Tractatus de Judiciis Ecclesiasticis,* 3. ed., 2 vols., Parisiis, 1884.

Cance, Adrien, *Le Code de Droit Canonique,* 3 vols., Paris, 1930, Vols. I and II, 6. eds., Vol. III, 5. ed., 1930.

Cappello, Felix M., *De Visitatione Sacrorum Liminum et Dioeceseon,* 2 vols., Romae: Pustet, 1912.

———, *Summa Iuris Canonici,* 3 vols., Romae: Apud Aedes Universitatis Gregorianae, Vol. I, 2. ed., 1932; Vol. II, 3. ed., 1939; Vol. III, 1936.

———, *Tractatus canonico-moralis de sacramentis,* 3. ed., 3 vols. in 4, Taurinorum Augustae: Marietti, 1933-1935.

Catalanus, Josephus, *Pontificale Romanum,* 3 tomes, Parisiis, 1850.

Catholic Encyclopedia, The, 16 vols., and 2 suppls., New York, 1907-1922.

Cavanaugh, William T., *The Reservation of the Blessed Sacrament,* The Catholic University of America, Canon Law Studies, n. 40, Washington, D. C.: The Catholic University of America, 1927.

Chelodi, Ioannes, *Ius de Personis,* 2. ed., a Sac. Ernesto Bertagnolli recognita & aucta; Tridenti: Libr. Edit. Tridentinum, 1927.

Cicognani, Amleto, *Canon Law,* authorized English version by J. O'Hara and F. Brennan, 2. ed., Philadelphia: Dolphin Press, 1935.

Claeys-Bouuaert, F. et Simenon, G., *Manuale Iuris Canonici,* Vols. I and III, 4. ed., Vol. II, 2. ed., Ghent-Liège, 1934-1935.

Cocchi, Guidus, *Commentarium in Codicem Iuris Canonici ad Usum Scholarum,* 5 vols. in 8, Vols. III-VII, 3. ed., Vol. II et VIII, 4 ed., Vol. I, 5. ed., Taurinorum Augustae: Marietti, 1931-1938.

Collins, Harold E., *The Church Edifice and Its Appointments,* 2. ed., Philadelphia: Dolphin Press, 1940.

Coronata, Matthaeus Conte A., *Institutiones Iuris Canonici,* 5 vols., Taurini (Italia): Marietti, 1928-1936.

Cox, Joseph Godfrey, *The Administration of Seminaries,* The Catholic University of America Canon Law Studies, n. 67, Washington: The Catholic University of America.

Creusen, Joseph, *Religious Men and Women in the Code,* 5. ed., Milwaukee: Bruce, 1940.

Cutts, Edward L., *Parish Priests and their People in the Middle Ages in England,* London, 1898.

D'Angelo, Sosio, *Tasse e Pensioni nel Codice di Diritto Canonico,* 2. ed., Torino, 1927.

———, *La Curia Diocesana a norma del Codice di Diritto Canonico,* Vol. II, Funzionamento Giarre (Sicilia), 1928.

D'Aste, Francesco Maria, *Metodo della Santa Visita Apostolica,* Otranto, 1706.

De Meester, Alphonsus, *Juris Canonici et Juris Canonico-Civilis Compendium,* nova ed., 3 vols. in 4, Brugis, 1921-1928.

De Pavinis, *Baculus Pastoralis, in Praxi Criminali Regularium Saeculariumque omnium absolutissima nuncupata Quaestionum Regularium,* Tomus Quartus, Antverpiae, 1624.

De Rosa, Thomas, *De Vera Residentia Episcoporum,* Neapoli, 1679.

Dooley, Eugene A., *Church Law on Sacred Relics,* The Catholic University of America, Canon Law Studies, n. 38, Washington, D. C.: The Catholic University of America, 1927.

Encyclopédie Théologique, 52 vols., Vols. 13 and 14—*Dictionnaire des Conciles,* Migne, J. P., Paris, 1847.

Fagnanus, Prosper, *Ius Canonicum seu Commentaria Absolutissima in Decretalium Libros,* 3 vols., Venetiis, 1697.

Fanfani, L., *De Iure Religiosorum,* 2. ed., Taurini: Marietti, 1925.

Ferreres, Joannes B., *Institutiones Canonicae,* 2. ed., 2 vols., Barcinone, 1920.

Ferraris, F. Lucius, *Prompta Bibliotheca Canonica, Iuridica, Moralis, Theologica, nec non Ascetica, Polemica, Rubricistica, Historica,* 8 vols., Romae, 1885-1892; Bucceroni, Januarius, *Supplementum,* Romae, 1899.

Flanagan, Canon, *History of the Church in England,* 2 vols., London, 1857.

Fournier, Edouard, *Les Origines du Vicaire Général,* Paris, Auguste Picard, 1922.

Fournier, Paul et Le Bras, Gabriel, *Histoire des Collections Canoniques en Occident,* 2 vols., Paris: Recueil Sirey, 1931.

Gattico, Joannes B., *De Oratoriis Domesticis et de Usu Altaris Portatilis,* Romae, 1746.

Gavantus, Bartholomaeus, *Praxis Compendiaria Visitationis Episcopalis*, Romae, 1628.

Gillman, Franz, *Das Institut der Chorbischöfe im Orient*, München, 1903.

Gonzalez-Tellez, Emanuel, *Commentaria Perpetua in Singulos Textus Quinque Librorum Decretalium*, 5 vols., Venetiis, 1699.

Goyeneche, S., *Iuris Canonici Summa Principia*, Vol. I, Romae: Tip. Pol. "Cuore Di Maria".

Hannan, Jerome, *The Canon Law of Wills*, The Catholic University of America Canon Law Studies, n. 87, Washington, D. C.: The Catholic University of America, 1934.

Hefele, Carl et Leclercq, Henri, *Histoire des Conciles*, 10 tomes, Paris: Letouzey et Ané, 1907-1938.

Hostiensis, Cardinalis (Henricus de Segusio), *Commentaria in Quinque Decretalium Libros*, 5 vols. in 3, Venetiis, 1581.

Jansen, Raymond J., *Canonical Provisions for Catechetical Instruction*, The Catholic University of America Canon Law Studies, n. 107, Washington, D. C.: The Catholic University of America, 1937.

Kraus, F. X., *Real-Encyklopädie der Christlichen Alterthümer*, 2 vols., Freiburg im Breisgau, 1882-1886.

Leonis Papae XII, *Epistola Encyclica ad omnes Patriarchas, Primates, Archiepiscopos et Episcopos*, Romae, Ex Typographia Rev. Camarae Apostolicae, 1824.

Lucidi, Angelus, *De Visitatione Sacrorum Liminum*, 3. ed., 3 vols., Romae, 1883.

Maroto, Philippus, *Institutiones Iuris Canonici*, 2 vols., Matriti, 1919.

Martin, Conradus, *Omnium Concilii Vaticani Documentorum Collectio*, 2. ed., Paderbornae, 1873.

Martinucci, Pius, *Manuale Sacrarum Caeremoniarum*, 3. ed., 4 vols., Romae: Pustet, 1915.

Maupied, Franciscus, L. M., *Juris Canonici Universi Compendium*, 2 vols., Migne, J. P., Paris, 1863.

McManus, James E., *The Administration of Temporal Goods in Religious Institutes*, Catholic University of America, Canon Law Studies, n. 109, Washington, D. C.: The Catholic University of America, 1937.

Melchers, Paulus, Cardinal, *De Canonica Dioecesium Visitatione*, Coloniae ad Rhenum, 1893.

Monacellus, Franciscus, *Formularium Legale Practicum Fori Ecclesiastici*, 4 vols., Venetiis, 1706-1715.

Mothon, Joseph Pie, *Institutiones Canoniques*, 3 vols., Paris, 1922.

Najera, Francisco Blanco, *Derecho Docente de la Iglesia, la Familia y el Estado*, Linares: Impr. "El noticiero", 1934.

Panormitanus, Abbas (Nicholaus de Tudescis), *Commentaria in Quinque Libros Decretalium*, 8 vols., Venetiis, 1588.

Pejska, Josephus, *Ius Canonicum Religiosorum*, 3. ed., Friburgi Brisgoviae, Herder, 1927.

Piatus Montensis, F., *Praelectiones Iuris Regularis*, 3. ed., 2 vols., Tornaci, 1906.

Piasecius, Paulus, *Praxis Episcopalis*, Coloniae Agrippinae, 1620.

Pignatelli, Jacobus, *Consultationes Canonicae*, 12 vols. in 6, Coloniae Allobrogum, 1700.

Pirhing, Ernricus, *Ius Canonicum Novo Methodo Explicatum*, 5 vols. in 4, Dillingae, 1674-1678.

Prümmer, Dominicus M., *Manuale Iuris Canonici*, 4. et 5. eds., Friburgi Brisgoviae: Herder, 1927.

Reiffenstuel, Anacletus, *Ius Canonicum Universum*, 5 vols. in 7, Parisiis, 1864-1882.

Reilly, Thomas F., *The Visitation of Religious*, The Catholic University of American Canon Law Studies, n. 112, Washington, D. C.: The Catholic University of America, 1938.

Resta, Luca Ant., *Directorum Visitatorum ac Visitandorum*, Romae, 1593.

Rossi, Joseph, *De Paroecia*, Romae: Fredericus Pustet, 1923.

Salodius, Paulus, *Praxis Compendiosa de Visitatione*, Coloniae Agrippinae, 1620.

Sebastianelli, Gulielmus, *Praelectiones Iuris Canonici, De Personis*, 2. ed., Romae: Fredericus Pustet, 1905.

Schaefer, Timotheus, *De Religiosis ad Normam Codicis Iuris Canonici*, 3. ed., Romae, S. A. L. E. R., 1940.

Schmalzgrueber, Franciscus, *Ius Ecclesiasticum Universum*, 5 vols. in 12, Romae, 1843-1845.

Schröder, Alfred, *Entwicklung des Archidiakonats bis zum elften Jahrhundert*, Augsburg, 1890.

Schulte, A. J., *Benedicenda*, New York, 1907.

Sipos, Stephanus, *Enchiridion Juris Canonici*, 3. ed., Pecs (Hungary), 1936.

Stephens, W. R. W., and Hunt, William, *A History of the English Church*, 7 vols., London, 1900-1904; Vol. I — Hunt, William, *The English Church from Its Foundation to the Norman Conquest* (597-1066), London, 1901.

Taunton, Ethelred L., *The Law of the Church*, London, 1906.

Thomassin, L., *Ancienne et Nouvelle Discipline de l'Église*, 3 vols., Paris, 1725.

Toso, Albertus, *Ad Codicem Iuris Canonici Commentaria Minora*, 5 vols., Romae: Marietti, 1920-1934.

Van Espen, Zegerus Bernardus, *Ius Ecclesiasticum Universum*, 5 vols., Lovanii, 1753.

Van Hove, A., *Commentarium Lovaniense in Codicem Iuris Canonici*, Vol. I, *Prolegomena*, Mechliniae: H. Dessain, 1928.

Venero et Leyva, Hieronymus, *Examen Episcoporum*, Venetiis, 1645.
Vendeuvre, Jules, *L'Exemption de Visite Monastique*, Dijon, 1906.
Vermeersch, A., et Creusen, J., *Epitome Iuris Canonici*, 3 vols., Mechliniae et Romae: H. Dessain, Vol. I, 6. ed., 1937; Vol. II, 5. ed., 1934; Vol. III, 5. ed., 1936.
Vromant, G., *Ius Missionariorum*, Louvain Museum Lessianum, *De Personis*, 2. ed., 1935, *De Bonis Ecclesiae Temporalibus*, 2. ed., 1934, *De Fidelium Associationibus*, 1932.

Wernz, Franciscus, *Jus Decretalium*, 6 vols., Romae et Prati, 1898-1905.
Wernz-Vidal, *Ius Canonicum*, 7 vols. in 8, Romae: Apud Aedes Universitatis Gregorianae, 1925-1938; Vol. II, *De Personis*, 2. ed., 1928; Vol. VI, *De Processibus*, 1927.

Zaplotnik, Joannes Leo, *De Vicariis Foraneis*, Catholic University of America Canon Law Studies, n. 47, Catholica Universitas Americae, Washingtonii, D. C., 1927.
Zerola, Thomas D., *Praxis Episcopalis*, 2 vols., Coloniae Agrippinae, 1680.
Zitelli, Zephyrinus, *Apparatus Juris Ecclesiastici*, 2. ed., Romae, 1888.

Principal Articles

Amanieu, A., "Archidiacre" — *Dictionnaire de Droit Canonique*, I (1924-1935), 948-1004.

Barber DeMontault, X., "La visite pastorale" — *AJP*, XV (1876), 51-86, 257-323, 401-441.

Carrière, V., "Une visite synodale au moyen age" — *RQH*, XCII (1912), 117-141.
Couly, Aug., "Droit de visite ou Procuration" — *Le Canoniste Contemporain*, XLIV (1921), 208-210.
Creusen, Joseph, "L'école catholique" — *NRT*, LIII (1926), 184-200.

D'Ambrosio, Franciscus Xav., "De domo generalitia instituti polydioecesani quoad canonicam visitationem can. 512, § 1, n. 2, praescriptam et quoad poenas can. 2413 sancitas" — *Ap.* I (1928), 417-422.

Goyeneche, S., "Consultationes" — *CpR*, III (1922), 335-336.

Lardone, G., "Le procurazione nella visita pastorale" — *Perfice Munus*, V 1930), 437-440.
———, "I decreti della visita pastorale" — *Perfice Munus*, XI (1936), 668-670.
Larraona, A., "Commentarium Codicis" — *CpR*, VIII (1927), 440-448; IX (1928), 23-31, 100-102; XIII (1932), 24-35, 92-99.

Marcellus, "De exemptione ecclesiarum regularium a canonica episcopi visitatione" — *CpR,* IX (1928), 235-244.
Maroto, P., "Annotationes" — *CpR,* VII (1926), 438-442.

Nebreda, E., "Studia canonica" — *CpR,* VII (1926), 107-118, 191-198, 261-271, 317-332.
Noval, J., "De ratione corrigendi ac puniendi sive in judicio sive extra jure codicis juris canonici" — *JP,* III (1923), 204-210.

'Ο Θαρσεύς, "Canonical visitation of the diocese" — *American Ecclesiastical Review,* XVI (1897), 489-495.

Rampf, "Die bischöflichen visitationen" — *Archiv für katholisches Kirchenrecht,* XXXI (1874), 385-95.
(   ), "Traité de la visite pastorale" — *AJP,* I (1855), 511-543.

PERIODICALS

Analecta Juris Pontificii, Rome, 1855-1866; Paris, 1867-1888.
Apollinaris, Romae, 1928 —
Archiv für katholisches Kirchenrecht, Innsbruck, 1857-1861; Mainz, 1862 —

Canoniste Contemporain, Le, Paris, 1878 —
Commentarium pro Religiosis, Rome, 1920 —; ab anno 1935: *Commentarium pro Religiosis et Missionariis.*

Ecclesiastical Review, The (originally *The American Ecclesiastical Review*), Philadelphia, 1889 —

Homiletic and Pastoral Review, The, New York, 1900 —

Jus Pontificium, Romae, 1921 —

Monitore Ecclesiastico, Il, Romae, 1876 —

Nouvelle Revue Théologique, Paris, 1869 —

Perfice Munus, Turin, 1926 —
Periodica de re canonica et morali, Brugis, 1905 —; ab anno 1927: *Periodica de re canonica, morali, liturgica.*

Revue des Questions Historiques, Paris, 1866-1914; 1922 —

ABBREVIATIONS

AAS — *Acta Apostolicae Sedis*
AJP — *Analecta Juris Pontificii*
Ap — *Apollinaris*
ASS — *Acta Sanctae Sedis*
Bruns — *Canones Apostolorum*, etc.
c. — Canon
cc. — Canons
Coll. Lac. — *Acta et Decreta Conciliorum Recentiorum, Collectio Lacensis*
CpR — *Commentarium pro Religiosis et Missionariis*
D — *Digestum* (Justinianum)
Decr. Auth. — *Decreta Authentica Congregationis Sacrorum Ritum*
Fontes — *Codicis Iuris Canonici Fontes cura — Gasparri editi.*
Hardouin — *Acta Conciliorum*, etc.
Hefele-Leclercq — *Histoire des Conciles*
HPR — *Homiletic and Pastoral Review*
JP — *Jus Pontificium*
Mansi — *Sacrorum Conciliorum Nova et Amplissima Collectio*
MGH — *Monumenta Germaniae Historica*
MPG — Migne, *Patrologia, Series Graeca*
MPL — Migne, *Patrologia, Series Latina*
NRT — *Nouvelle Revue Théologique*
Pallottini — *Collectio Omnium Conclusionum et Resolutionum*, etc.
Periodica — *Periodica de Re Canonica et Morali Utili praesertim Religiosis et Missionariis*
Pont. Comm. Intr. — *Pontifical Commission for the Authentic Interpretation of the Canons of the Code*
RQH — *Revue des Questions Historiques*
Thesaurus — *Sacrae Congregationis Concilii Resolutiones* (1718-1908)

ALPHABETICAL INDEX

BIOGRAPHICAL NOTE

Andrew Leonard Slafkosky was born on November 18, 1913, at Bethlehem, Pennsylvania. He attended SS. Cyril and Methodius Parochial School, and Bethlehem Catholic High School, Bethlehem, Pennsylvania. In 1930 he entered St. Charles Seminary, Overbrook, Pennsylvania. After completing his course of studies he was ordained to the priesthood, May 26, 1938. In the fall of the same year he enrolled in the School of Canon Law at the Catholic University of America, where he received the degrees of J. C. B. and J. C. L. in the years 1939 and 1940 respectively.

CANON LAW STUDIES

1. Freriks, Rev. Celestine A., C.PP.S., J.C.D., Religious Congregations in Their External Relations, 121 pp., 1916.
2. Galliher, Rev. Daniel M., O.P., J.C.D., Canonical Elections, 117 pp., 1917.
3. Borkowski, Rev. Aurelius L., O.F.M., J.C.D., De Confraternitatibus Ecclesiasticis, 136 pp., 1918.
4. Castillo, Rev. Cayo, J.C.D., Disertación Historico-Canonica sobre la Potestad del Cabildo en Sede Vacante o Impedida del Vicario Capitular, 99 pp., 1919 (1918).
5. Kubelbeck, Rev. William J., S.T.B., J.C.D., The Sacred Penitentiaria and Its Relations to Faculties of Ordinaries and Priests, 129 pp., 1918.
6. Petrovits, Rev. Joseph, J.C., S.T.D., J.C.D., The New Church Law On Matrimony, X-461 pp., 1919.
7. Hickey, Rev. John J., S.T.B., J.C.D., Irregularities and Simple Impediments in the New Code of Canon Law, 100 pp., 1920.
8. Klekotka, Rev. Peter J., S.T.B., J.C.D., Diocesan Consultors, 179 pp., 1920.
9. Wanenmacher, Rev. Francis, J.C.D., The Evidence in Ecclesiastical Procedure Affecting the Marriage Bond, 1920 (Printed 1935).
10. Golden, Rev. Henry Francis, J.C.D., Parochial Benefices in the New Code, IV-119 pp., 1921 (Printed 1925).
11. Koudelka, Rev. Charles J., J.C.D., Pastors, Their Rights and Duties According to the New Code of Canon Law, 211 pp., 1921.
12. Melo, Rev. Antonius, O.F.M., J.C.D., De Exemptione Regularium, X-188 pp., 1921.
13. Schaaf, Rev. Valentine Theodore, O.F.M., S.T.B., J.C.D., The Cloister, X-180 pp., 1921.
14. Burke, Rev. Thomas Joseph, S.T.D., J.C.D., Competence in Ecclesiastical Tribunals, IV-117 pp., 1922.
15. Leech, Rev. George Leo, J.C.D., A Comparative Study of the Constitution, "Apostolicae Sedis" and the "Codex Juris Canonici," 179 pp., 1922.
16. Motry, Rev. Hubert Louis, S.T.D., J.C.D., Diocesan Faculties According to the Code of Canon Law, II-167 pp., 1922.
17. Murphy, Rev. George Lawrence, J.C.D., Delinquencies and Penalties in the Administration and Reception of the Sacraments, IV-121 pp., 1923.
18. O'Reilly, Rev. John Anthony, S.T.B., J.C.D., Ecclesiastical Sepulture in the New Code of Canon Law, II-129 pp., 1923.
19. Michalicka, Rev. Wenceslas Cyrill, O.S.B., J.C.D., Judicial Procedure in Dismissal of Clerical Exempt Religious, 107 pp., 1923.
20. Dargin, Rev. Edward Vincent, S.T.B., J.C.D., Reserved Cases According to the Code of Canon Law, IV-103, pp. 1924.
21. Godfrey, Rev. John A., S.T.B., J.C.D., The Right of Patronage According to the Code of Canon Law, 153 pp., 1924.
22. Hagedorn, Rev. Francis Edward, J.C.D., General Legislation on Indulgences, II-154 pp., 1924.

23. King, Rev. James Ignatius, J.C.D., The Administration of the Sacraments to Dying Non-Catholics, V-141 pp., 1924.
24. Winslow, Rev. Francis Joseph, O.F.M., J.C.D., Vicars and Prefects Apostolic, IV-149 pp., 1924.
25. Correa, Rev. Jose Servelion, S.T.L., J.C.D., La Potestad Legislativa de la Iglesia Catolica, IV-127 pp., 1925.
26. Dugan, Rev. Henry Francis, A.M., J.C.D., The Judiciary Department of the Diocesan Curia, 87 pp., 1925.
27. Keller, Rev. Charles Frederick, S.T.B., J.C.D., Mass Stipends, 167 pp., 1925.
28. Paschang, Rev. John Linus, J.C.D., The Sacramentals According to the Code of Canon Law, 129 pp., 1925.
29. Pointek, Rev. Cyrillus, O.F.M., S.T.B., J.C.D., De Indulto Exclaustrationis necnon Saecularizationis, XIII-289 pp., 1925.
30. Kearney, Rev. Richard Joseph, S.T.B., J.C.D., Sponsors at Baptism According to the Code of Canon Law, IV-127 pp., 1925.
31. Bartlett, Rev. Chester Joseph, A.M., LL.B., J.C.D., The Tenure of Parochial Property in the United States of America, V-108 pp., 1926.
32. Kilker, Rev. Adrian Jerome, J.C.D., Extreme Unction, V-425 pp., 1926.
33. McCormick, Rev. Robert Emmett, J.C.D., Confessors of Religious, VIII-266 pp., 1926.
34. Miller, Rev. Newton Thomas, J.C.D., Founded Masses According to the Code of Canon Law, VII-93 pp., 1926.
35. Roelker, Rev. Edward G., S.T.D., J.C.D., Principles of Privilege According to the Code of Canon Law, XI-166 pp., 1926.
36. Bakalarczyk, Rev. Richardus, M.I.C., J.U.D., De Novitiatu, VIII-208 pp., 1927.
37. Pizzuti, Rev. Lawrence, O.F.M., J.U.L., De Parochis Religiosis, 1927 (Not printed).
38. Bliley, Rev. Nicholas Martin, O.S.B., J.C.D., Altars According to the Code of Canon Law, XIX-132 pp., 1927.
39. Brown, Mr. Brendan Francis, A.B., LL.M., J.U.D., The Canonical Juristic Personality with Special Reference to Its Status in the United States of America, V-212 pp., 1927.
40. Cavanaugh, Rev. William Thomas, C.P., J.U.D., The Reservation of the Blessed Sacrament, VIII-101 pp., 1927.
41. Doheny, Rev. William J., C.S.C., A.B., J.U.D., Church Property: Modes of Acquisition, X-118 pp., 1927.
42. Feldhaus, Rev. Aloysius H., C.PP.S., J.C.D., Oratories, IX-141 pp., 1927.
43. Kelly, Rev. James Patrick, A.B., J.C.D., The Jurisdiction of the Simple Confessor, X-208 pp., 1927.
44. Neuberger, Rev. Nicholas J., J.C.D., Canon 6 or the Relation of the Codex Juris Canonici to the Preceding Legislation, V-95 pp., 1927.
45. O'Keefe, Rev. Gerald Michael, J.C.D., Matrimonial Dispensations, Powers of Bishops, Priests and Confessors, VIII-232 pp., 1927.

46. Quigley, Rev. Joseph, A. B., A. M., J. C. D., Condemned Societies, 139 pp., 1927.
47. Zaplotnik, Rev. Johannes Leo, J.C.D., De Vicariis Foraneis, X-142 pp., 1927.
48. Duskie, Rev. John Aloysius, A.B., J.C.D., The Canonical Status of the Orientals in the United States, VIII, 196 pp., 1928.
49. Hyland, Rev. Francis Edward, J.C.D., Excommunication, Its Nature, Historical Development and Effects, VIII-181 pp., 1928.
50. Reinmann, Rev. Gerald Joseph, O.M.C., J.C.D., The Third Order Secular of Saint Francis, 201 pp., 1928.
51. Schenk, Rev. Francis J., J.C.D., The Matrimonial Impediments of Mixed Religion and Disparity of Cult, XVI-318 pp., 1929.
52. Coady, Rev. John Joseph, S.T.D., J.U.D., A.M., The Appointment of Pastors, VIII-150 pp., 1929.
53. Kay, Thomas Henry, J.C.D., Competence in Matrimonial Procedure, VIII-164 pp., 1929.
54. Turner, Rev. Sidney Joseph, C.P., J.U.D., The Vow of Poverty, XLIX-217 pp., 1929.
55. Kearney, Rev. Raymond A., A.B., S.T.D., J.C.D., The Principles of Delegation, VII-149 pp., 1929.
56. Conran, Rev. Edward James, A.B., J.C.D., The Interdict, V-163 pp., 1930.
57. O'Neil, Rev. William H., J.C.D., Papal Rescripts of Favor, VII-218 pp., 1930.
58. Bastnagel, Rev. Clement Vincent, J.U.D., The Appointment of Parochial Adjutants and Assistants, XV-257 pp., 1930.
59. Ferry, Rev. William A., A.B., J.C.D., Stole Fees, V-135 pp., 1930.
60. Costello, Rev. John Michael, A.B., J.C.D., Domicile and Quasi-domicile, VII-201 pp., 1930.
61. Kremer, Rev. Michael Nicholas, A.B., S.T.B., J.C.D., Church Support in the United States, VI-1930.
62. Angulo, Rev. Luis, C.M., J.C.D., Legislación de la Iglesia sobre la intención en la aplicación de la Santa Misa, VII-104 pp., 1931.
63. Frey, Rev. Wolfgang Norbert, O.S.B., A.B., J.C.D., The Act of Religious Profession, VIII-174 pp., 1931.
64. Roberts, Rev. James Brendan, A.B., J.C.D., The Banns of Marriage, XIV-140 pp., 1931.
65. Ryder, Rev. Raymond Aloysius, A.B., J.C.D., Simony, IX-151 pp., 1931.
66. Campagna, Rev. Angelo, Ph.D., J.U.D., Il Vicario Generale del Vescovo, VII-205 pp., 1931.
67. Cox, Rev. Joseph Godfrey, A.B., J.C.D., The Administration of Seminaries, VI-124 pp., 1931.
68. Gregory, Rev. Donald J., J.U.D., The Pauline Privilege, XV-165 pp., 1931.
69. Donohue, Rev. John F., J.C.D., The Impediment of Crime, VII-110 pp., 1931.

70. Dooley, Rev. Eugene A., O.M.I., J.C.D., Church Law On Sacred Relics, IX-143 pp., 1931.
71. Orth, Rev. Raymond Clement, O.M.C., J.C.D., The Approbation of Religious Institutes, 171 pp., 1931.
72. Pernicone, Rev. Joseph M., A.B., J.C.D., The Ecclesiastical Prohibition of Books, XII-267 pp., 1932.
73. Clinton, Rev. Connell, A.B., J.C.D., The Paschal Precept, IX-108 pp., 1932.
74. Donnelly, Rev. Francis B., A.M., S.T.L., J.C.D., The Diocesan Synod, VIII-125 pp., 1932.
75. Torrente, Rev. Camilo, C.M.F., J.C.D., Las Processiones Sagradas, V-145 pp., 1932.
76. Murphy, Rev. Edwin J., C.PP.S., J.C.D., Suspension Ex Informata Conscientia, XI-122 pp., 1932.
77. Mackenzie, Rev. Eric F., A.M., S.T.L., J.C.D., The Delict of Heresy in its Commission, Penalization, Absolution, VII-124 pp., 1932.
78. Lyons, Rev. Avitus E., S.T.B., J.C.D., The Collegiate Tribunal of First Instance, XI-147 pp., 1932.
79. Connolly, Rev. Thomas A., J.C.D., Appeals, XI-195 pp., 1932.
80. Sangmeister, Rev. Joseph V., A.B., J.C.D., Force and Fear as Precluding Matrimonial Consent, V-211 pp., 1932.
81. Jaeger, Rev. Leo A., A.B., J.C.D., The Administration of Vacant and Quasi-vacant Episcopal Sees in the United States, IX-229 pp., 1932.
82. Rimlinger, Rev. Herbert T., J.C.D., Error Invalidating Matrimonial Consent, VII-79 pp., 1932.
83. Barrett, Rev. John D. M., S.S., J.C.D., A Comparative Study of the Third Plenary Council of Baltimore and the Code, IX-221 pp., 1932.
84. Carberry, Rev. John J., Ph.D., S.T.D., J.C.D., The Juridical Form of Marriage, X-177 pp., 1934.
85. Dolan, Rev. John L., A.B., J.C.D., The Defensor Vinculi, XII-157 pp., 1934.
86. Hannan, Rev. Jerome D., A.M., S.T.D., LL.B., J.C.D., The Canon Law of Wills, IX-517 pp., 1934.
87. Lemieux, Rev. Delisle A., A.M., J.C.D., The Sentence in Ecclesiastical Procedure, IX-131 pp., 1934.
88. O'Rourke, Rev. James J., A.B., J.C.D., Parish Registers, VII-109 pp., 1934.
89. Timlin, Rev. Bartholomew, O.F.M., A.M., J.C.D., Conditional Matrimonial Consent, X-381 pp., 1934.
90. Wahl, Rev. Francis X., A.B., J.C.D., The Matrimonial Impediments of Consanguinity and Affinity, VI-125 pp., 1934.
91. White, Rev. Robert J., A.B., LL.B., S.T.B., J.C.D., Canonical Ante-Nuptial Promises and the Civil Law, VI-152 pp., 1934.
92. Herrera, Rev. Antonio Parra, O.C.D., J.C.D., Legislación Eclesiástica sobre el Ayuno y la Abstinencia, XI-191 pp., 1935.

93. Kennedy, Rev. Edwin J., J.C.D., The Special Matrimonial Process in Cases of Evident Nullity, X-165 pp., 1935.
94. Manning, Rev. John J., A.B., J.C.D., Presumption of Law in Matrimonial Procedure, XI-111 pp., 1935.
95. Moeder, Rev. John M., J.C.D., The Proper Bishop for Ordination and Dimissorial Letters, VII-135 pp., 1935.
96. O'Mara, Rev. William A., A.B., J.C.D., Canonical Causes For Matrimonial Dispensations, IX-155 pp., 1935.
97. Reilly, Rev. Peter, J.C.D., Residence of Pastors, IX-81 pp., 1935.
98. Smith, Rev. Mariner T., O.P., S.T.L., J.C.D., The Penal Law For Religious, VII-169 pp., 1935.
99. Whalen, Rev. Donald W., A.M., J.C.D., The Value of Testimonial Evidence in Matrimonial Procedure, XIII-297 pp., 1935.
100. Cleary, Rev. Joseph F., J.C.D., Canonical Limitations on the Alienation of Church Property, VIII-141 pp., 1936.
101. Glynn, Rev. John C., J.C.D., The Promoter of Justice, XX-337 pp., 1936.
102. Brennan, Rev. James H., S.S., A.M., S.T.B., J.C.D., The Simple Convalidation of Marriage, VI-135 pp., 1937.
103. Brunini, Rev. Joseph Bernard, J.C.D., The Clerical Obligations of Canons 139 and 142, X-121 pp., 1937.
104. Connor, Rev. Maurice, A.B., J.C.D., The Administrative Removal of Pastors, VIII-159 pp., 1937.
105. Guilfoyle, Rev. Merlin Joseph, J.C.D., Custom, XI-144 pp., 1937.
106. Hughes, Rev. James Austin, A.B., A.M., J.C.D., Witnesses in Criminal Trials of Clerics, IX-140 pp., 1937.
107. Jansen, Rev. Raymond J., A.B., S.T.L., J.C.D., Canonical Provisions for Catechetical Instruction, VII-153 pp., 1937.
108. Kealy, Rev. John James, A.B., J.C.D., The Introductory Libellus in Church Court Procedure, XI-121 pp., 1937.
109. McManus, Rev. James Edward, C.SS.R., J.C.D., The Administration of Temporal Goods in Religious Institutes, XVI-196 pp., 1937.
110. Moriarity, Rev. Eugene James, J.C.D., Oaths in Ecclesiastical Courts, X-115 pp., 1937.
111. Rainer, Rev. Eligius George, C.SS.R., J.C.D., Suspension of Clerics, XVII-249 pp., 1937.
112. Reilly, Rev. Thomas F., C.SS.R., J.C.D., Visitation of Religious, VI-195 pp., 1938.
113. Moriarty, Rev. Francis E., C.SS.R., J.C.D., The Extraordinary Absolution from Censures, XV-334 pp., 1938.
114. Connolly, Rev. Nicholas P., J.C.D., The Canonical Erection of Parishes, X-132 pp., 1938.
115. Donovan, Rev. James Joseph, J.C.D., The Pastor's Obligation in Prenuptial Investigation, XII-322 pp., 1938.
116. Harrigan, Rev. Robert J., M.A., S.T.B., J.C.D., The Radical Sanation of Invalid Marriages, VIII-208 pp., 1938.

117. Boffa, Rev. Conrad Humbert, J.C.D., Canonical Provisions for Catholic Schools, X-211 pp., 1939.
118. Parsons, Rev. Anscar John, O.F.M. Cap., J.C.D., Canonical Elections, XII-236 pp., 1939.
119. Reilly, Rev. Edward Michael, A.B., J.C.D., The General Norms of Dispensation, X-156 pp., 1939.
120. Ryan, Rev. Gerald Aloysius, A.B., J.C.D., Principles of Episcopal Jurisdiction, XII-172 pp., 1939.
121. Burton, Rev. Francis James, C.S.C., A.B., J.C.D., A Commentary on Canon 1125, X-222 pp., 1940.
122. Miaskiewicz, Rev. Francis Sigismund, J.C.D., Supplied Jurisdiction According to Canon 209, XII-340 pp., 1940.
123. Rice, Rev. Patrick William, A.B., J.C.D., Proof of Death in Prenuptial Investigation, VIII-156 pp., 1940.
124. Anglin, Rev. Thomas Francis, M.S., J.C.L., The Eucharistic Fast.
125. Coleman, Rev. John Jerome, J.C.L., The Minister of Confirmation.
126. Downs, Rev. John Emmanuel, A.B., J.C.L., The Concept of Clerical Immunity.
127. Esswein, Rev. Anthony Albert, J.C.L., Extrajudicial Penal Powers of Ecclesiastical Superiors.
128. Farrell, Rev. Benjamin Francis, M.A., S.T.L., J.C.L., The Rights and Duties of the Local Ordinary Regarding Congregations of Women Religious of Pontifical Approval.
129. Feeney, Rev. Thomas John, A.B., S.T.L., J.C.L., Restitutio in Integrum.
130. Findlay, Rev. Stephen William, O.S.B., A.B., J.C.L., Canonical Norms Governing the Deposition and Degradation of Clerics.
131. Goodwine, Rev. John, A.B., S.T.L., J.C.L., The Right of the Church to Acquire Property.
132. Heston, Rev. Edward Louis, C.S.C., Ph.D., S.T.D., J.C.L., The Alienation of Church Property in the United States.
133. Hogan, Rev. James John, A.B., S.T.L., J.C.L., Judicial Advocates and Procurators.
134. Kealy, Rev. Thomas M., A.B., Litt. B., J.C.L., Dowry of Women Religious.
135. Keene, Rev. Michael James, O.S.B., J.C.L., Religious Ordinaries and Canon 198.
136. Kerin, Rev. Charles A., S.S., M.A., S.T.B., J.C.L., The Privation of Christian Burial.
137. Louis, Rev. William Francis, M.A., J.C.L., Diocesan Archives.
138. McDevitt, Rev. Gilbert Joseph, A.B., J.C.L., Legitimacy and Legitimation.
139. McDonough, Rev. Thomas Joseph, A.B., J.C.L., Apostolic Administrators.
140. Meier, Rev. Carl Anthony, A.B., J.C.L., Penal Administrative Procedure Against Negligent Pastors.
141. Schmidt, Rev. John Rogg, A.B., J.C.L., The Principles of Authentic Interpretation in Canon 17 of the Code of Canon Law.

142. Slafkosky, Rev. Andrew Leonard, A.B., J.C.L., The Canonical Episcopal Visitation of the Diocese.
143. Swoboda, Rev. Innocent Robert, O.F.M., J.C.L., Ignorance in Relation to the Imputability of Delicts.
144. Dubé, Rev. Arthur Joseph, A.B., J.C.L., The General Principles for the Reckoning of Time in Canon Law.
145. McBride, Rev. James T., A.B., J.C.L., Incardination and Excardination of Seculars.

www.ingramcontent.com/pod-product-compliance
Lightning Source LLC
LaVergne TN
LVHW050239080826
844660LV00012B/557

* 9 7 8 0 8 1 3 2 2 3 3 1 5 *